BLACK PERFORMANCE AND CULTURAL CRITICISM

Valerie Lee and E. Patrick Johnson, Series Editors

CONJURING FREEDOM

*Music and Masculinity in the
Civil War's "Gospel Army"*

∼

JOHARI JABIR

THE OHIO STATE UNIVERSITY PRESS

COLUMBUS

Library of Congress Cataloging-in-Publication Data
Names: Jabir, Johari, author.
Title: Conjuring freedom : music and masculinity in the Civil War's "Gospel Army" / Johari Jabir.
Other titles: Black performance and cultural criticism.
Description: Columbus : The Ohio State University Press, [2017] | Series: Black performance and cultural criticism | Includes bibliographical references and index.
Identifiers: LCCN 2016046333 | ISBN 9780814213308 (cloth ; alk. paper) | ISBN 0814213308 (cloth ; alk. paper)
Subjects: LCSH: African Americans—Music—History and criticism. | Spirituals (Songs)—History and criticism. | Ring shout (Dance) | Masculinity. | United States. Army. South Carolina Volunteers, 1st (1862–1864) | United States—History—Civil War, 1861–1865—African Americans. | United States. Army—African American troops. | Higginson, Thomas Wentworth, 1823–1911.
Classification: LCC ML3556 .J33 2017 | DDC 973.4/415—dc23
LC record available at https://lccn.loc.gov/2016046333

Cover design by Andrew Brozyna
Text design by Juliet Williams
Type set in Adobe Minion Pro

9 8 7 6 5 4 3 2 1

CONTENTS

PRELUDE

THE SANCTUARY of the historic Emmanuel AME Church in Charleston, SC, contains several images of African American figures ranging from Harriet Tubman and Frederick Douglass to one of the church's founders, Denmark Vesey. On December 31, 2013, as congregants slowly gathered for the yearly watch-night service, the sense of anticipation felt by enslaved Africans 150 years ago to that night made its way into the worship service that evening. During the watch-night service the phrase "henceforth now and forever free" was invoked several times as a way of "conjuring" the memory of those who witnessed the transition from slavery to legal freedom.

On January 1, 2013, a small group of people, mostly African Americans, gathered beneath "Emancipation Oak" tree in Beaufort, SC, to mark the 150th anniversary of the Emancipation Proclamation. "Emancipation Oak" stands on the Smith Plantation, which was converted to "Camp Saxton" after the Union Army's seizure of Port Royal. The historic Tabernacle Baptist Church in Beaufort hosted the ceremony. In the original ceremony a century and a half earlier, the nation's first black regiment to be mustered into the Union Army—the First South Carolina Volunteers regiment—was presented with a flag, and an elderly proud black man led the gatherers in "My Country, 'Tis of Thee." Such patriotic hope was notably absent from the 2013 commemoration. The pastor called for a deacon to lead us in one of the "old songs of *our* church." The deacon lifted his lyrical voice and sang:

All the way Lord,
All the way
All the way Lord

All the way
Jesus you brought us all the way

As we responded to the deacon's call I was made aware (again) of the journey that delivered me to the research of this book. As a son of a black Baptist working-class community and its traditions in St. Louis, MO, I was quite familiar with that "old song" led by the deacon. But also for me, as a researcher, the song had another layer: it resonated with a song from the regiment's repertoire. During the Civil War, black soldiers sang:

He had been with us, Jesus
He still with us, Jesus,
He will be with us, Jesus
Be with us to the end

Like the members of the First South Carolina Volunteers regiment, I had journeyed to a place on that day in 2013 that I had never been to with people I had never met before. Yet, it was collective singing that conjured a cosmic sense of the "we" who stood where "our" ancestors had to mark a seminal moment in African American and American history: the reading of the Emancipation Proclamation. Our ceremony concluded with the Chieftess of the Gullah/Geechie nation, who led us in a chant and a polyrhythmic signature Gullah clap.

My participation in the collective singing was indeed based upon a shared musical practice, but my knowledge of the regiment was also derived from that practice. As an undergraduate studying classical music I read about the regiment while researching "Negro Spirituals." The "both/and" meta-narrative of this book represents the genesis of my intellectual formation in the music of that black Baptist working-class church, which led me to engage in a formal study of classical music. "The collective will to conjure" that comprises a central theme in this book is an extension of the "Prince of Peace Choral Club," a premier gospel chorus of my childhood church. My theorization of "Black Communal Conservatories" is derived also from this early organic genesis of spiritual, moral, intellectual, and political formation that continued further at William Beaumont High School in St. Louis, Missouri. At Beaumont High School Larry Wade embodied the "both/and" aspects of Black Communal Conservatories with his emphasis on the history of black vocal production and his insistence on exposing us to the European choral canon. *Conjuring Freedom* is offered in textual form as a witness to the generative and organic possibilities of Black Communal Conservatories. The tireless efforts of Wade and countless other black music teachers who labored in public education deserves far more attention than is given here. As an undergraduate music major I learned from several teachers who were extensions of this teaching/ learning/performing tradition in black communities. I consider myself fortunate to encounter teachers who, while some did not share this formation first hand, were no less willing support my work as a scholar. At the Pacific School of Religion, Professors Randi Walker and Mary Ann Tolbert were exemplary scholars and teachers, along with Rev. Barbara Essex who provided a listening ear in difficult times. A special word of gratitude is offered in memory of the late scholar and activist Ibrahim Farajajè, who introduced me to the historical study of Islam in the African Diaspora. As a doctoral student at the University of California Santa Barbara Rudy Busto was a generous and patient advisor in the Department of Religious Studies. Also at UCSB, I received bountiful support from the Black Studies Department, specifically Professors Claudine Michel and George Lipsitz. Professor Maurice Wallace has been a supportive brother, comrade, and friend, for which I am deeply grateful.

An interdisciplinary work such as this one depends upon the generosity of individuals who work behind the scenes in archives and libraries across the country. I have been shown enormous patience and support from the Avery Research Center at the College of Charleston in Charleston, SC; the Houghton Library at Harvard; and the records on the United States Colored Troops at the National Archives in Washington, DC. Numerous colleagues at the University of Illinois at Chicago read drafts of chapters and offered constructive comments. Lastly, I am grateful to the many students whose questions and curiosity have been a source of drive and inspiration.

INTRODUCTION

Yet the captured came to this nation, surveyed this moral landscape, recognized the valleys as well as the hills, and deposited their dreams right here. Stepping off the ships to a language that demeaned them, to a topography totally unfamiliar, to a God they did not know, they nevertheless found a way to laugh, love and believe in tomorrow.

—NIKKI GIOVANNI[1]

"One More River"

O Jordan bank was a great old bank,
Dere ain't but one more river to cross.
We have some *valiant soldier* here.
Dere ain't but one more river to cross
O Jordan stream will never run dry
Dere ain't but one more river to cross

—1ST SOUTH CAROLINA VOLUNTEERS[2]

POET, ACTIVIST, and educator Nikki Giovanni argues that one secret to the survival of black people in America lies in the sacred songs that they first composed and sang collectively in slave quarters. People kidnapped from their African homes and brutally oppressed in the land of their captivity seemed to own nothing, not even the skin on their backs. They had no money, no

---

1. Giovanni, *On My Journey Now,* 2.
2. As recorded Higginson, *Army Life,* 155.

property, no weapons, no books, and no tools. Yet they possessed something else that proved to be extraordinarily valuable. Inside their heads, they possessed a blend of African retention and new world invention that enabled them to see that whatever they did not have, they could conjure. *Conjure* is the black cultural practice of summoning spiritual power as an intentional means of transforming reality and involves a belief in an invisible magical power that can be used for healing and/or harm.[3] Conjuring encompassed a wide range of practices. Denied access to trained physicians, slave communities produced their own conjure doctors, experts who followed a series of prescribed procedures using available materials to cure ailments and infirmities. The craft of conjuring extended beyond medicine to all realms of endeavor, including music. Enslaved Africans in America staved off hunger by turning the discarded intestines and fatty backs of pigs that their owners would not eat into cooked chitins and fatback. Remnants of cloth salvaged from garbage dumps became raw materials for quilts that kept people warm while depicting scenes and stories that preserved collective memories. Even the Bible passages that the slave owners ordered to be read to their bonds people to teach them humility and obedience would be channeled into inspiration for self-assertion and self-activity. Sermons about the need for slaves to respect their masters and to expect reward only in the next world became conjured into reassurances that the God of the oppressed had not forgotten them and that their prayers could summon him into their presence. In *Conjuring Freedom* conjure is part of a cultural labor of performed music in which "sound" enables a kind of "spirit work" aimed at black human dignity and freedom.[4] The performance of music as a means of conjure is a critical aspect for understanding black epistemologies—the unique ways of knowing forged collectively among African people in America. In this book, I explore how singing functions as a musical conjuration that aims to transform reality.

For soldiers in black regiments during the Civil War, freedom was not simply found, it had to be forged. They found themselves forced to conjure freedom out of the materials made available to them as soldiers who had been slaves but were not yet citizens. In much the same way that the coping religion of the slaveocracy became transformed into the enabling religion of the slaves, the forms of soldiering and citizenship made available to former slaves that were designed to assimilate them into a masculinist hierarchical, exploitative, and racist society became something else in practice. These tools of domination became conjured into new forms of masculinity, solidarity, and social

---

3. My discussion of conjure throughout the book is informed primarily by two religious studies scholars: Smith, *Conjuring Culture,* and Chireau, *Black Magic.*

4. Here, I draw from Murphy, *Working the Spirit,* 1–9.

membership that promoted democratic and egalitarian change in society at large. Just as conjurers healed the slave body with a mixture of efficacious materials, newly free Africans in America attempted to heal the body politic and cure society's ills through a tradition of organized protest with musical accompaniment that expressed alternate social visions of democracy.

The history of black soldiers proving their manhood and thereby rendering African Americans worthy of U.S. citizenship is a story that has been told often. But there is a story behind this story, a legacy of resistance and resilience beneath the master narrative of progress. *Conjuring Freedom* explains how sacred singing and soldiering enabled former slaves to conjure freedom for themselves and for others. The book's central thesis is that the 1st South Carolina Volunteers regiment creatively used music and religion to conjure a "cosmic vision of freedom," a vision of black freedom that was negotiated through *both* legal *and* cultural means. This cosmic vision of freedom was forged from the legal language of slavery and emancipation, from geography, from the experience of slavery, and from the American empire's proud proclamations of democracy. But this cosmic vision of freedom was also formed out of the West African cosmology of African people forcibly dispersed throughout the New World. The cosmic vision of freedom confronts—but also contradicts—the racialized logic of American freedom that has been so vexed by blackness and the racial paradox of America as a land of freedom premised on Indian removal and black slavery. Africans were forced to (re)make themselves as a "people" through the invention of black culture, while at the same time seizing and transforming knowledge of the laws that maintained them as property. Conjuring extraordinary power in ordinary circumstances meant that the definitions had to be changed—if only in private. On record they were the first black regiment in the Union Army, but they referred to themselves as "a gospel army," which is where this book draws its title (Higginson, 41). In the face of unremitting political evil and despite overwhelming odds, African people in America fought for freedom with the conviction that every problem has a solution, that willingness and work can change the world, that collective co-creation can make a way out of no way, and that disadvantage can be turned into advantage, poison into medicine, and humiliation into honor. They drew on a wisdom that told them that being in deep water was not the same as drowning: that the river could be *crossed*. The music that serves as the focal point of this book, the sacred singing of the 1st South Carolina Volunteers, the nation's first black regiment, expresses this wisdom in many different ways.

These soldiers viewed their service in combat during the Civil War as "one more river to cross" on the path to freedom. Crossing over to freedom was a collective and cosmic endeavor based on a communal epistemology of conjure, as performed in the counterclockwise song, story, drum, and dance known as the "ring shout." *Conjuring Freedom* is not a history of one military regiment, nor is it even the musical history of the regiment. My intention here is to reveal the interrelatedness between the regiment's creative uses of religion, their way of recombining soldiering and singing, and their cosmic view of the future in this world and in the world beyond. In order to accomplish this goal I do indeed honor the history of the regiment, but I present its history alongside its members' own unique narratives of religion, masculinity, and music, all of which form an integrative part of a history. *Conjuring Freedom* presents a story of the black Civil War soldier told through the songs that enabled them to seize their freedom. The counterclockwise effects of singing and soldiering, drumming and dancing, made musical sense and social solidarity out of what Du Bois called the "general strike" against the system of enslavement.[5] A common affinity for communal music making enabled a sense of "oneness" out of diversity. For while members of the regiment represented soldiers from throughout the Sea Islands and beyond, they participated in a common way of knowing that involved listening, learning, and singing. Sound, as a material "affect" of singing, played a crucial role here as a kind of aural epistemology. Music served as a performed mode of conjuring. The sounds produced from singing invoked flashes of terror and loss as well as the spirit of survival in their history. Collective singing enabled corporate *healing*; singing transformed *hope* from an emotional feeling and sentiment into a disciplinary practice. Enslaved Africans dreamed of freedom and reunion with lost friends and loved ones despite the conditions that dictated permanent separation and declared them unfree. They sang "no more auction block for me" and "we'll cross the mighty river" long before the war was officially ended. The power of collective singing by the oppressed imbues "hope" with the structural framework of a disciplined collective practice.

The sacred songs of the first black regiment to be mustered into the Union army during the Civil War authored and authorized new understandings of freedom, masculinity, citizenship, and social membership. Composing and singing songs together forged a new community among men with diverse experiences from different backgrounds. Their ancestors came from different parts of Africa. They came from different regions in the South. The regional religious affiliations of the soldiers were not simply an adoption of a colonizing "white Christianity." Theirs was a black religion that included influences of Protestantism, Catholicism, Islam, and the spirit-based worship traditions of the African diaspora. The 1st South Carolina Volunteers and other black

---

5. Du Bois, *Black Reconstruction in America*, 64.

regiments helped make history on the battlefield where their valor proved decisive in turning the tide of war. They shaped the victory that subdued the Confederacy and made it possible for Congress to pass the 13th Amendment to the constitution banning slavery. It was the effectiveness of black troops and the pressure put on the Union army and the U.S. government by newly freed slaves that transformed the Civil War from a conflict over secession into a conflict to end slavery.[6] Black people also helped make history once the war ended by helping craft the 1866 Civil Rights Act, the 13th, 14th, and 15th amendments to the constitution, and the democratic and egalitarian laws advanced by coalitions of poor whites and newly freed blacks to establish free public education, universal access to the franchise and jury service, state-supported health institutions, and internal improvements throughout the south. Between 1863 and 1877 they created what W. E. B. Du Bois described as Abolition Democracy, which he characterized as the first real democracy the nation had ever known.[7]

Yet the journey from slave to soldier to citizen was neither simple nor direct. Slaves had every reason to succumb to despair and resignation. Some did, but most did not. Their linked fate compelled them to turn the personal humiliations of slavery into strategies for collective resistance, to oppose a system of intended dehumanization with practices that promoted rehumanization. As they tried to counter the abstract logic of social death by which they were ruled by resorting to plural and diverse actions to make and savor a collective social life, they faced enormous opposition. For whites, slavery was not just an economic arrangement; it was a way of life, an ideological, cultural and political system that saturated every aspect of national life in both the North and the South. In a nation where white male propertied power pervaded all the main resources and institutions, black men and women found themselves forced to redefine citizenship and social membership. They could not simply assimilate into the social and cultural institutions and practices that previously existed; they had to change them and to create new ones grounded in a new definition of freedom.

The histories they made happen and the freedom dreams that propelled them and emerged from their struggles were riddled with contradictions. Black slaves, soldiers, citizens, servants, and sharecroppers did not have the luxury of determining the tools or terrains of struggle available to them. People can only fight with the tools they have in the arenas that are open to them. The very nature of conjuring depends on using the materials at hand and

---

6. Rawick, *From Sundown to Sunup*, 118.

7. Du Bois, *Black Reconstruction*, 184.

imagining alternative functions for familiar objects. Sometimes in attempting to fool their oppressors, however, members of aggrieved groups can fool themselves. Tools that seem like infinitely malleable and ideologically neutral technologies can instead be so structured in dominance that they reinforce rather than resist dominant ways of knowing and being. For the members of the 1st South Carolina Volunteers and other black regiments, the available tools included military masculinity, citizenship, and state recognition. Vital for the achievement of emancipation, these very tools intended to break the chains of slavery could become fetters themselves in the future by linking slave emancipation to heroic masculinity, patriarchy, state benevolence, and interest convergence with white elites.

Masculinity proved a particularly vexing vessel of identity. According to the dominant ideologies and their attendant economic and political structures, agency, citizenship, and freedom in the nineteenth-century U.S. were seen as innately masculine attributes. Women were considered unfit for self-activity, self-defense, or democratic participation. George Fitzhugh and other ideological defenders of the slave system grounded its legitimacy in this gendered hierarchy, effectively "feminizing" the entire black race as passive, dependent, and in need of guidance and supervision.[8] In this context, serving as combat soldiers in war provided an opportunity for blacks to demonstrate fitness as men, thereby opening the doors to claim full rights as citizens. Yet this point of entry into agency, social membership, and citizenship might have encouraged black men to make gains by separating their interests from those of black women. The measure of racial inclusion that it offered required a willingness to kill and die for the state and its interests. During the Civil War, when the self-activity of black soldiers and civilians connected state interests directly to the abolition of slavery, the choice was clear but fraught with unequal practices against black regiments. After emancipation, however, blacks were expected to prove their fitness for citizenship in a nation that continued to mistreat them by serving the state in combat actions against Native Americans in the conquest of the West, against Filipinos and Cubans in the 1898 war with Spain, against Mexicans in border skirmishes staged by U.S. troops in the wake of the Mexican Revolution, and in subsequent wars in Europe, Asia, Latin America, and the Middle East during the twentieth and twenty-first centuries.

It may appear that in embracing military masculinity, black troops simply emulated white men. The eloquent and oft-quoted words of Frederick Doug-

---

8. Horton, "Defending the Manhood of the Race, 8; Fitzhugh, *Cannibals All, passim* and 204–5; Roderick Ferguson notes the enduring legacy of this formulation in sociologist Robert Park's description in the 20th century of the Negro as the lady of the races. Ferguson, *Aberrations in Black,* 56–58.

lass loom large in this perception. As he advocated for the Abolitionist cause on the eve of the Civil War, Douglass predicted that once black men donned the uniform of the U.S. military, their right to full citizenship could not be questioned. "Once let the black man get upon his person the brass letters US, let him get an eagle on his button, a musket on his shoulder, and bullets in his pocket," Douglass exclaimed, "and there is no power on earth or under the earth which can deny that he has earned the right of citizenship in the United States."[9] This hopeful prediction did not come true, but as an argument it had enduring appeal. *Conjuring Freedom* expands on Douglass's eloquent formulation by demonstrating that it was not simply the symbolic eagle on the brass buttons or the pockets of bullets that could transform the slave into a soldier, but it was also the power of conjure embedded in the song, a power Douglass described interestingly in his autobiography as a "musical affliction."[10] After the war Corporal Thomas Long, who had been Chaplain of the 1st South Carolina Volunteers, argued that it was black service in the military that made the end of slavery irreversible. People could never say, he insisted, that Bbacks had been handed freedom by others because their service had made it clear that they won it for themselves with an irrefutable display of courage, energy, and manhood.[11] These predictions have never been fully realized and their betrayal is a legitimate and worthy focus of scholarly research.

Yet contemporary scholars have sharply and rightly critiqued this kind of desire for normative inclusion. Disturbed by the practices of conditional and subordinate inclusion in the present that enlist highly visible African American public figures such as Colin Powell and Condoleezza Rice to lend the moral legacy of the black freedom struggle and the civil rights movement to the administration of an undemocratic society at home and an empire overseas, Roderick Ferguson and Jodi Melamed (among others) have demonstrated the dangers of seeking inclusion under normative terms by members of aggrieved racial groups.[12] Other scholars argue that it is the very hope of eventual black inclusion in full citizenship and social membership that leaves the dominant epistemology and genocidal assumptions of white supremacy undisturbed.[13] The same state that can grant rights to people can also take them away. The Fifteenth Amendment to the constitution that gave blacks the

---

9. Douglass, "Men of Color, to Arms!," 319. This address was published in Douglass's own paper and reprinted widely in journals of the North.

10. Douglass, *The Autobiography of Frederick Douglass.*

11. Rawick, *From Sundown to Sunup,* 119.

12. Melamed, *Represent and Destroy*; Shah, *Contagious Divides*; Ferguson, *Aberrations in Black*; Reddy, *A Freedom With Violence.*

13. Wilderson III, *Red, White and Black*; Sexton, "The Social Life of Social Death; Cacho, *Social Death.*

right to vote specified that only black men qualified for this privilege. Thus the expansion of rights for black men came at the expense of express limits on the rights of black and white women. The hard-earned black military masculinity did not keep at bay the state's complicit role in allowing and enabling violent acts of terror that suppressed those same voting rights. The promise of full citizenship for blacks embodied in the 1866 Civil Rights Act and the 13th, 14th and 15th amendments was followed by the sharpening of the citizen-alien distinction through the Chinese Exclusion Act, Alien Land Laws, and the establishment of the Border Patrol. In placing black troops under the supervision of elite white men like Colonel Thomas Wentworth Higginson, who commanded the 1st South Carolina Volunteers, the model of white male masculine citizenship they were instructed to follow infused patriotism with the imperatives of patriarchy and paternalism. As we will see over and over again in this book, the publication and enduring popularity of Higginson's wartime memoir has rendered the story of the 1st South Carolina Volunteers as largely a tribute to white paternalism and benevolence rather than as a rendering of the self-activity of black people.

For political and economic reasons, the Union found itself compelled to terminate the direct rule of slave owners over slaves. It had no intention, however, of ending white supremacy. After a brief period of reform, elites in the North and South conspired in the suppression of Abolition Democracy, the mistranslation of anti-racial subordination laws into anti-racial recognition laws through the Supreme Court's Civil Rights Cases of the 1870s, the removal of federal troops from the South in 1877, the creation of Jim Crow segregation, and the deployment of mass incarceration, lynching, and voter suppression as forms of racial control. As radical Republican Albion Tourgee complained in the 1880s, "The South surrendered at Appomattox, the north has been surrendering ever since."[14] Moreover, the Union had no intention of challenging the rule of male over female, rich over poor, or citizen over alien. Recruiting black men to be soldiers entailed inviting them to adopt dominant notions of hierarchical manhood. They were offered a modicum of racial inclusion with the proviso that they help enforce the boundaries of gender exclusion. The masculinist definition of citizenship that emerged from the war helped lead to the creation of a postwar black culture of uplift, which, as Kevin Gaines and others have shown, functioned to create a stratified black community governed by concerns about propriety and protection of property. The black elite often policed the black working class, establishing an internal and internal-

---

14. Albion Tourgee, *Continent* 5 (April 2, 1884): 444, and *Continent* 6 (July 30, 1884): 156, quoted in Blight, "The Shaw Memorial," 81.

ized hierarchy of male over female, rich over poor, educated over uneducated, light skinned over dark skinned, sexual normativity over sexual diversity, and assimilation over collective struggle.

Yet the historical practices of conjuring had taught black men and women to see not only what things *are,* but would they *could be* as well. Conjuring freedom with the tools of sacred songs, military action, masculine identity, and state citizenship meant finding new possibilities in familiar objects. It required finding value in things and in people that seemed to have no value in the U.S. racial order. It also entailed practical work in the world to infuse the abstractions of religion, war, masculinity, and citizenship with unexpected new meanings. The U.S. military served as a primary vehicle for state-structured racial masculinity, but the regiment's use of music and religion allowed for and enabled what Ferguson describes (in another context) as "the disruption of normativity."[15] As black slaves inhabited new identities as men, soldiers, and citizens, they gave new meaning to manhood, service, and citizenship. The choices open to freed people in the wake of the Civil War did not allow them the luxury of either fully assimilating into U.S. society or of separating themselves completely from it. They could not fully embody normative white male military masculinity, but neither could they evade it. As they had learned through acts of conjuring over centuries, the urgent practical need to survive required them to think in terms of both/and rather than either/or, to embrace the complexity and possibility of contradictions rather than seeking to suppress them. As Toni Morrison frames it, the task facing black people in America is not whether the master's tools can dismantle the master's house, but instead how "to convert a racist house into a race-specific but non-racist home."[16]

The very same black community that seemed to capitulate readily to normative notions of citizenship and subjectivity also mobilized remnants of slave religion and politics to pose radical challenges to exploitation and hierarchy. At the Charleston Convention in 1865 newly freed people expressed their resolve to obtain neither revenge against their former masters nor personal property and power for themselves but rather "the right to develop our whole *being,* by all the appliances that belong to a civilized society."[17] In his keynote address at that meeting, Martin Delany proclaimed "our cause is not alone the cause of four millions of black men in this country, but we are intensely alive to the fact that it is also the cause of millions of oppressed men in other 'parts of God's beautiful earth,' who are now struggling to be free in the fullest sense

---

15. Ferguson, *Aberrations in Black.*

16. Morrison, "Home," 5.

17. Harding, *There Is a River,* 326.

of the word, and God and nature are pledged to their triumph."[18] After the war when the Fifteenth Amendment's language prevented black women from voting, black women and men found a way to subvert that prohibition. Black women played important roles in Republican Party organizations even though they could not vote. Moreover, the black community reconceived the franchise as the collective property of the whole family. Men cast the ballots, but only after deliberations that articulated the entire family's wishes. Men who failed to follow their family's instruction were disciplined and sometimes even ostracized from the community.[19] Inside communities whose recognized leaders identified with the hierarchical culture of uplift, secret societies, mutual aid organizations, and working-class church congregations generated alternatives to hierarchy and normativity that provided powerful resources to subsequent anti-capitalist race radicalisms over the next century.

How did people located farthest from democracy come to value it the most? How did a people who sought freedom but were handed only a limited form of subordinate inclusion become what historian Vincent Harding calls "the nation's foremost champions of human freedom and social justice, creators of many of its most native rhythms of life?"[20] One answer lies in the struggles with masculinity and manhood among the 1st South Carolina Volunteers. By addressing the contradictions of their condition as slaves becoming soldiers and then citizens, they envisioned and enacted new forms of identity. On paper they were soldiers in the U.S. Union Army, but through music they identified themselves as *one more valiant soldier.* Singing allowed for a disruptive and divergent masculinity. Just as they authored a new legal status for themselves and others through their victories in battle, they authorized new understandings of race and gender through the everyday practices and processes of conjuring freedom. The government needed their service in battle, and the economy needed their labor before and after the war. Yet they were not offered full inclusion because the nation's core institutions and beliefs had been founded on their suppression and inclusion. They could not escape from white supremacy either. As black abolitionist Henry Highland Garnet observed in the antebellum period, blacks in America were worse off than the Hebrew slaves in Egypt in the book of Exodus. With God's help, the Hebrews fled from bondage. In the United States, however, Garnet noted, "the Pharaohs are on both sides of the blood-red waters."[21] Unable to integrate

---

18. Ibid., 326.

19. See Robin Kelley's discussion of research by Elsa Barkley Brown in his splendid book *Race Rebels,* 36–37.

20. Harding, *There Is a River,* xii.

21. Ibid., 150.

seamlessly into a country that did not want them, yet unable to flee from a nation that profited too much from their bondage to let them go, people who had once been slaves had to create new ways of knowing and new ways of being to enable them to change the nation as they entered it. The singing and soldiering of the 1st South Carolina Volunteers was one of the crucibles of these new epistemologies and ontologies. It embodied the "both/and" plight of a predefined masculinity that was both vexed by enduring elements of racial patriarchy and ennobled by the social solidarity and musical creativity of black singing soldiers. This alternate musical masculinity was not simply recuperation of the normative state-sponsored notion of masculinity, but it was rather a generative form of engendering a community that continued to be reproduced in future expressions of black music and politics.

Entrapment in historical and social circumstances can impose fatal limits on oppositional movements. Dangers are always present inside the relations of power. Opposition can often replicate the oppressions that the oppressed seek to undermine. This has implications for the ongoing tradition of black freedom struggles. Ameliorative reform movements and pan-ethnic anti-racisms attempt to keep open possibilities for the future, but they always run the risk of accepting the lesser of two evils in the short run. They can underestimate the fundamental and foundational ways in which the human/slave binary at the core of Western epistemologies relegates whole populations to living as if they were socially dead.[22] Yet as Cedric Robinson argues, the aspiration to render blacks socially dead is not so easy to accomplish. Even seemingly conservative forms of culture and politics can do important work in undermining the logic of social death and creating a collective social life.[23]

There is a valuable core of truth in the critiques about the perils of linking the pursuit of freedom and justice to formal recognition by the state. Even resistance is always, at least partially, structured in dominance; it is always susceptible to cooptation. As Claire Jean Kim observes, when people speak truth to power, power can make sure the message comes out garbled.[24] Yet under conditions of asymmetrical power, it is often necessary for oppressed people to use covert tactics that fool the oppressor. The traditions of western radicalism have been replete with strategies designed to resolve this problem through activist expressive culture, general strikes, and armed struggle as mechanisms of revolutionary change. All of these forms of critique and struggle have value.

---

22. See for example, Tushnet, "An Essay on Rights," 1363; Reddy, "Time for Rights?," 2849; Fields and Fields, *Racecraft*; Melamed, *Represent and Destroy*; Wilderson III, *Red, White and Black*.

23. See for example, Robinson, *Forgeries of Memory and Meaning*.

24. Kim, *Bitter Fruit*, 11.

Yet none of them can escape the structuring in dominance that plagues the forms they challenge. We have something to learn, therefore, from the sacred singing of the 1st South Carolina Volunteers and the black radical tradition that shaped them and which they helped to shape. Their radicalism lies not in a univocal opposition to the state, the military, masculinity and religion, but rather in the practical work of repositioning and resignifying the meanings of those institutions to imbue them with a potential for envisioning and enacting new understandings of freedom. Like the "conjure doctors" in slavery and emancipation who healed the bodies of people without access to professional physicians through "prescribed operations involving a repertory of efficacious materials,"[25] the members of the 1st South Carolina Volunteers regiment sought to cure the ills of the body politic through practical activity designed to turn the toxic into the tonic. They could not embrace uncritically a legal system whose core institutions were constructed to guarantee their subordination, but they could not ignore that system either, given its power to set the rules by which society operates. They could not evade the law because the laws that dehumanized them had to be changed. They knew a great deal about the costs of brutality and violence, but in the midst of the Civil War they could not resist the logic and necessity of taking up arms to free themselves and to try to purge the nation of its allegiance to the slave system. They recognized that the termination of slavery did not guarantee them meaningful forms of freedom; that removing the negative obstacle of slavery would not magically produce new democratic practices and institutions. So they nurtured a capacity and desire for democracy among themselves and in others that eventually led to significant expansions of citizenship rights with the passing of the 1866 Civil Rights Act and 13th, 14th, and 15th amendments to the constitution.

Black people had survived slavery in the first place by turning hegemony on its head, by turning the world of the slave owners upside down. Rather than resting at night to prepare themselves for the next day's labors, they sneaked into the woods for "frolics" where the work body that produced wealth for the slave owner was reclaimed for individual and collective play and pleasure in dancing and singing. Slaves conjured the degrading images that white people had of them into tools of resistance. They got "lost" in the woods to live as outliers seizing a few days of leisure for themselves instead of submitting to forced labor. They "accidentally" broke tools to interrupt the demands of work and they set fires to destroy the master's property.[26] Some attempted to run away not by stealing the slave owner's horse, but taking the bridle and carrying

---

25. Smith, *Conjuring Culture*, 31.
26. Rawick, *From Sundown to Sunup*; Camp, *Closer to Freedom*.

it with them, so if caught they could claim they were simply looking for their master's runaway horse and seeking to take it back to the plantation.[27] These acts of covert resistance did not challenge the fundamental logic of the slave system, but they did serve as abeyance mechanisms preserving the tactics of resistance for a future time when they might have more effectiveness.[28]

The soldiers in the 1st South Carolina Volunteers regiment drew on these traditions to enhanced effect in a time of crisis. Their actions offer a valuable addition to the archive of anti-subordination struggles precisely because they depart from the sharp distinction between transcendent and immanent critique that plagues the critics of struggles grounded in rights, resources, and recognition. These struggles seem to some scholars to be categories that are structured in dominance and cannot be used for emancipatory ends. Yet As Kimberle Crenshaw notes, the abstract critique of rights rests on ideological presuppositions that occlude understanding how social change actually takes place. In her arguments responding to challenges to civil rights reforms by critical legal studies scholars, Crenshaw concedes that legal discourse serves hegemonic ends in this society. Yet the power of law would not simply disappear if people denied its legitimacy. Precisely because societies are structured in dominance, nearly all legible strategies for change will contain some measure of the prevailing ideologies and common sense. Rather than seeking a purely transcendent form of opposition, Crenshaw argues that "the possibility for ideological change is created through the very process of legitimation, which is triggered by crisis."[29] In a crisis, using the system's own logic against it offers an opportunity to turn hegemony on its head, to transform instruments of domination into tools for resistance. This way of thinking is deeply rooted in Afro-diasporic ways of knowing. As musicologist Christopher Small explains, ". . . while the European lives in a world of 'either/or,' the African's world is a world of 'both/and.'"[30] Theophus Smith expounds further,

> The wisdom tradition of black North American folk culture dissents from the predominant Western form of disjunctive thinking—that conventional "either/or." . . . Instead this tradition prefers the conjunctive "both/and" of archaic and oral cultures, in which ambiguity and multivocity are taken for granted (even promoted).[31]

---

27. Camp, *Closer to Freedom.*
28. Taylor, "Social Movement Continuity," 761–75.
29. Crenshaw, "Race, Reform and Retrenchment," 111.
30. Small, *Music of the Common Tongue,* 23.
31. Smith, *Conjuring Culture,* 143.

The conjunctive "both/and frame" is a leitmotif through this book that does not seek to bring neat resolution to the inherit contradictions of race, religion, nation, and culture. The master's version of religion, manhood, or even the attempt toward cultural legitimation is not what is at stake here. Instead, *Conjuring Freedom* presents the creative possibilities within these predefined categories in order to expose what is beyond them. New forms of freedom and humanity were articulated "beyond" the "either/or" binary of Western disjunction. For the 1st South Carolina Volunteers, categories that had long been structured in dominance—soldiering, citizenship, music, masculinity, and religion—could be repositioned and resignified in the midst of a national crisis. Their ability to blend singing with soldiering, to fuse combat with conjure and community making, and to author and implement new forms of social life under the threat of death emerged organically from the survival strategies (re)created by Africans in America during the long history of slavery and necessarily resonated with the contradictions of the slave system.

Slaves took the words of their masters' sacred book and inverted them so as to read light out of darkness. In the face of preachments that instructed them to obey their masters and to expect rewards in heaven but not on earth, they focused on imperfect biblical heroes like Moses, David, and Daniel whose propensity for action won victories in this world. Sacred music served as a site for biblical figuration. Slaves sang about the miracle that enabled Ezekiel to forge a unified body out of the scattered and shattered bones of a defeated people. They crossed the Red Sea with Moses and the River Jordan with Joshua. They affirmed their determination to survive by celebrating "this little light of mine," an *Africanism* that reveled in the "little man within," the spirit and purpose resident in all of humanity. Slaves "adopted" ancestors from the Old and New Testaments as surrogates for the African ancestors whose names they no longer knew. Though often unnamed, *their* ancestors constituted a "great cloud of witnesses" that soared in the sky but also marched alongside them on the ground. For them, the Bible was often seen not as a book of allegorical or metaphorical significance to black people, but rather the literal, ongoing, and contemporaneous story of black people.[32]

SLAVE SONGS EVIDENCED BOTH AFRICAN RETENTIONS AND NEW WORLD INVENTIONS[33]

Enslaved Africans in America came from different regions, spoke different languages, and worshipped different deities. Slave owners used force in an

---

32. Smith, *Conjuring Culture*; Levine, *Black Culture and Black Consciousness*.
33. Buff, *Immigration and the Political Economy of Home*, 31.

attempt to wipe out all manifestations of African identity. They banned African languages and customs, dispersed kinship groups, and denied Africans the right to use their own names. Yet suppression never succeeded completely. African culture did not die in America but was instead driven underground. The overt accommodation mandated by the totalitarian brutality of the slave system never completely eliminated practices of covert resistance. Art, music, dance, and religion served especially important functions as sources of moral and political instruction, repositories of collective memory, and mechanisms for calling communities into being through performance. In decorations on cabin walls, artifacts scattered on burial sites, quilts, pottery, and songs, slaves sent messages to each other about the importance of survival, subsistence, resistance, and affirmation. Dancing seized hold of the body that was thought to be mere "property" and transformed it from an instrument of labor into a public demonstration of black people's mastery, discipline, and imagination.[34] Slaves buried their dead in the African way, decorating gravesites with items that had been touched by the deceased. They kept African customs and folkways alive in the ways they wrapped their heads with cloth, conjured folk remedies for illnesses, and constructed and played musical instruments. They slipped away at night for midnight prayer services held in secret brush arbors where they gathered around overturned pots to chant and meet in clearings to dance the ring shout.[35] The counterclockwise motion of the song, dance, drum, and spoken narrative marked their own distinct temporality and kinship.

Sterling Stuckey identifies the ring shout as the core component of African American art-based community making, and it is the ring shout that holds the key to the sacred singing of Civil War black troops. In their collective counterclockwise movement around a circle, slaves expressed both individual difference and group allegiance. They turned physical segregation into congregation, dancing together to create identities resonant with their linked fate. "The ring in which the Africans danced and sang," Stuckey explains, "is the key to understanding the means by which they achieved oneness in America."[36] Following all-day training in military tactics, the soldiers in the 1st South Carolina Volunteers engaged nightly in the ring shout. In a regiment characterized by both regional and religious diversity, the ring shout enabled a "collective" sense of selfhood. It replicated and refined the techniques formerly forged in slavery to assert and embrace complex personhood in the midst of objectification and subordination. This cultural strategy of turning physi-

34. Rawick, *From Sundown to Sunup*; Camp, *Closer to Freedom*; Bernier, *African American Visual Arts*.

35. Rawick, *From Sundown to Sunup*.

36. Stuckey, *Slave Culture*, ix.

cal segregation into congregation is seen in the witness of Corporal Adam Allston, who testified during the regiment's mission up the St. Mary's river,

> When I heard de combshell a-screamin' troo de woods like de Judgment Day, I said to myself, "If my head was took off tonight, dey couldn't put my soul in de torments." . . . And when de rifle bullets came whizzin' across de deck, I cried aloud, "God help my congregation! Boys load and fire!" (71)

Allston's ability to fuse the individual "me" with a collective "we" permeated the practices of the regiment that often referred to themselves as the "First Souf" or the "Gospel Regiment."[37] They regarded the religious songs of slavery as a valuable resource. They combined black music making techniques with military language and practice to inspire a "spiritual militancy." At the same time, they sang about the "many thousands gone," those who lived on, in the land of spirit. The gone were no longer present in the body, but they were not to be forgotten. The circle could thus incorporate both the living and the deceased who became undead through memory and memorialization. The regiment created a black alternate universe in which freedom itself had to be reinvented anew constantly at the crossroads of slavery and freedom, Africa and America, servitude and soldiering, life and death. They held in dynamic tension the desire to transform the racial realities of the U.S. nation and their disciplined determination to continue to draw from the resources of their African-derived culture.

Music making and soldiering may appear to be activities conducted on two completely different planes of seriousness. Yet in the Afro-diasporic tradition that permeated the culture of the 1st South Carolina Volunteers, the practical activities of everyday life were part of a unified totality that integrated the spirit and regarded the collective as sacred. Musicologist Christopher Small argues that the first premise of African culture is "an absence of separation between aspects of life which Europeans are inclined to keep apart: the political, the economic, the religious and the aesthetic."[38] The propensity for blending diverse aspects of experience into a new synthesis permeated the efforts of the regiment to constitute themselves as a new totality made up of different parts. Sacred songs for the members of the regiment were instruments of interpellation, individuation, and collective formation. Marching steps created an embodied and kinetic unity among soldiers ambling down the road. Song lyrics calling out each member of the regiment by name mixed

---

37. These references are from Higginson, *Army Life.* I will use "1st South" throughout the book.

38. Small, *Music of the Common Tongue,* 22.

individual affirmation with collective obligation, similar to the manner that later shaped the jazz ensemble and other African American expressive forms. The call and response form (antiphony) of sacred songs was not only a musical device, but also a practice that leveled differences and taught the sharing of authority and responsibility. This sensibility endured over centuries, appearing in the liberatory strategies of Harriet Tubman in the 1860s and in the mass organizing tactics of Fannie Lou Hamer and Bayard Rustin in the 1960s. Through singing, men who had been slaves *heard* themselves as free before they *saw* themselves as free. The practices of collective singing as a strategy for organized protests pervades the narratives of slave revolts and mass demonstrations in the twentieth century. This tradition of using music to conjure an unseen power in this way demonstrates what Paul Gilroy calls, "the politics of fulfillment: the notion that a future society will be able to realize the social and political promise that present society has left unaccomplished."[39] The regiment was a fighting unit of the U.S. Army, but it was also what I deem here as a Black Communal Conservatory. Like the "invisible academies" that Robert Farris Thompson cites as important crucibles of black visual art, the Black Communal Conservatory is not so much a site of community based art making as it is a locus of art-based community making.[40] Yet these long and honorable traditions of resistance might have remained latent had it not been for the events of the Civil War and the possibilities they provoked. The 1st South inaugurated a tradition of black military music and their example was performed again years later in the twentieth century in legendary bandleader and conductor James Reese Europe and the Harlem Hell Fighters during the First World War. This black military and music tradition extended further in the 372nd National Negro Guard Infantry Regiment. The De Paur Infantry Chorus, as it was called, was led by Leonard De Paur, a premier black choral conductor and arranger.[41] At a moment when whites in the North and whites in the South were deeply divided, a time when the North desperately needed an infusion of disciplined troops and the South was uniquely vulnerable to slave refusals to work and ability to run away, black people like the members of the 1st South Carolina Volunteers knew what to do. They conjured new forms of freedom, social membership, and citizenship as fighting between the Union and the Confederacy made it possible for them to move from slavery to "contraband" to soldiers to citizens.

---

39. Gilroy, *The Black Atlantic: Modernity and Double-Consciousness*, 37.

40. Thompson, "Bighearted Power," *Flash of the Spirit*. For a discussion of art-based community making, see Lipsitz, *Footsteps in the Dark*, 123–24.

41. McGee, "The Historical Development."

Thomas Wentworth Higginson's memoir *Army Life in a Black Regiment* (1870) remains a central primary source in scholarship about this regiment. It forms a focal point of critique in this book[42] through an "against the grain" reading of Higginson's writing that reveals it to be part of the discourses of white sentimentality and sympathy that Jodi Melamed rightly describes as channeling the history of anti-racist resistance toward celebration of "the exceptional humanity and benevolence of anti-slavery whites."[43] Higginson was a white abolitionist placed in command of black troops. He had the opportunity to observe the activities of the regiment and was greatly moved by what he saw. Yet his life history, social location, and epistemological tools led him to craft a condescending and distorted picture of black self-activity and subjectivity. What is lacking in scholarly source materials is written documents from the soldiers themselves. This creates the risk of reinscribing the authority of Higginson's voice, of accepting his framework in the process of examining the evidence he presents. It is not the authenticity of *what* Higginson saw and recorded that is being disputed here, but rather *how* he saw and interpreted culture, the ways in which he obscured elements that were critical to the regiment's humanity. Challenging the authority of Higginson's voice and the dominant narrative of the victor entails making the aural episteme of the soldiers the center of this conceptual project. Doing so requires "postcolonial ears," a listening hermeneutics that accounts for the sonic politics at work in black music as an aural epistemology. I aim to reveal a view of black humanity that Higginson, and the hermeneutical legacy that followed him, have chosen to avoid. Through a vigorous reinterpretation of the soldiers' engagement with religion, music, and gender I will demonstrate that the soldiers took up national ideas of race, masculinity, and citizenship to be sure, but they *also* went beyond these ideas to imagine a "cosmic vision of freedom" that informed expressions of black culture that continued long after emancipation.

∾

An official emancipation ceremony that took place early in the life of the regiment provides an ideal point of departure for this book. On January 1, 1863,

---

42. I also engage primary source materials such as the first published collection of spirituals, Allen, Ware, and Garrison, *Slave Songs of the United States*; Suzie King's memoir, *A Black Woman's Civil War Memoirs* (King served as nurse and teacher in the regiment); and the *Letters and Diaries of Laura M. Towne*. The primacy of sources in the book are further supported by information gathered from the national archives, the Slave Narratives Collection at the University of North Carolina Chapel Hill, and the Houghton Library at Harvard, which houses the personal papers of Colonel Higginson.

43. Melamed, *Represent and Destroy*, xii.

a large gathering of black and white people gathered in a covering of shade provided by a massive oak tree dangling with strands of Spanish moss. Black women and young girls exuded an air of royalty, their heads crowned with colored handkerchiefs wrapped in turban-like fashion. The sweat and toil of slave life had dulled the brilliance of these hand-made crowns, but the light of the day's expectations illuminated their beaming smiles. The black men and young boys also looked regal in their fitted vests, pressed pants, and starched white shirts. Wearing hand-me-down field shoes that did not fit their feet, the men and the boys marched with dignity and determination toward the populated grove. A band from the 8th Maine Infantry had been commissioned to play accompanying music for the momentous occasion. When the band struck up their marching tune the crowd fixed their eyes on the nation's first black regiment, proceeding proudly with military precision to the stage.

A reading of the Emancipation Proclamation was followed by the passing of regimental colors to the First Regiment of South Carolina Volunteers, known as the "1st South." These ceremonies converted what had been known previously as the Smith plantation into a "hallowed ground." The regiment no doubt felt a sense of solemn consecration in this pageantry. Their memories of slavery informed their excitement in seeing the words stitched on their new flag donated by a New York church congregation. "To the First Regiment of South Carolina," the inscription read, "The Year of Jubilee Has Come."[44] The flag was handed to Colonel Thomas Wentworth Higginson, who called Corporal Robert Sutton and Sergeant Prince Rivers to the platform to receive the colors from Rev. Mansfield French, a Methodist missionary from New York who had arrived in the Sea Islands months earlier. Immediately following remarks by Reverend French, Higginson waved the flag, which must have been interpreted as a conductor's cue as an elderly black man opened his mouth in the true spirit of call and response to sing:

My Country tis of thee
Sweet Land of liberty
Of thee I sing

The organic nature of black singing was further displayed when two black women harmonized with the man who raised the anthem. Higginson was struck by the ways these African Americans took ownership of their citizenship and reflected: "some whites on the platform began . . . I motioned them

---

44. From *Liberator,* January 16, 1863, and *New York Daily Tribune,* January 14, 1863, in Ash, "Firebrand of Liberty," 23.

to silence."[45] The scene and sound of the slaves being transformed into soldiers and citizens through the nation's ceremonial ritual of bearing military colors produced a powerful symbol of embrace and acceptance. Amid this celebration of progress and national recognition, however, the regiment followed with the "John Brown Song." As a song collectively composed by slaves in honor of Brown's martyrdom, the song raised on this occasion functioned to keep Brown as a central element in black culture and the national culture. This scene served as a harbinger that the ensuing citizenship they would secure would motivate blacks to change the nation even as they entered it.

Scenes like these made an impression on many whites. As chronicled in Higginson's memoir and reported in the national press they helped establish for northern white readers especially the legitimacy of black claims for recognition and citizenship. An exasperated W. E. B. Du Bois noted the effectiveness, but also the injustice, of connecting black dignity to valor in combat. "How extraordinary, and what a tribute to ignorance and religious hypocrisy," he wrote, "is the fact that in the minds of most people, even those of liberals, only murder makes men. The slave pleaded; he was humble; he protected the white women of the South, and the world ignored him. The slave killed white men; and behold, he was a man!"[46] This transformation of slaves into soldiers marked a transformative moment in the construction of black masculinity. In a society that equated manhood with agency and citizenship, soldiering enabled black men to experience an alternative to the white supremacist fantasy of black adults as child-like and to protect themselves from the sexual racism and racist sexism that would later lead sociologist Robert Park to describe the African American as the "lady of the races."[47] The account of the 1st South authored originally by Higginson, has influenced subsequent retellings of black Civil War soldiers. These accounts vary in quality, but almost all of them foreground the benevolence of white liberalism and background the story of black agency.[48] *Conjuring Freedom* applies contemporary theo-

---

45. Higginson, *Army Life*, 31.

46. Du Bois, *Black Reconstruction*, 11.

47. Ferguson, *Aberrations in Black*, 58.

48. A succession of scholarly accounts has chronicled the history of black Civil War soldiery, from Joseph T. Wilson's *The Black Phalanx: Black Troops in the Union Army 1863–1865*, published in 1888, through McPherson's 1967 *Marching Toward Freedom*. The 1989 film *Glory*, directed by Edward Zwick, told the story of another black regiment in a manner that replicated the framework provided by Higginson. The 2004 exhibition *No Man Can Hinder Me: Black Troops in the Union Armies During the American Civil War* was hosted at the Beinecke Rare Book Manuscript Library at Yale University. In a slight departure from the traditional empirical approach to black Civil War studies, Wilson's *Campfires of Freedom* is a broad study of culture in the camp life of black regiments. Perhaps the most recent installation in black Civil War soldier studies, Coddington's *African American Faces of the Civil War* and Wallace and Smith,

ries of gender and culture in concert with religious studies, American studies, postcolonial studies, and musicology.[49] My own musical sensibilities inform the book's interpretive tone and shape, echoing Richard Wright's challenge that in writing about black life, the manner should reflect the matter.[50] The intensely musical character of the regiment enables us to read its history (and all African American history) as a progression of harmonic "changes" and syncopated "rhythms" that at times move forward while gesturing toward the past and often with repetition. The circular progression of the regiment's production of culture reflects that of a cosmogram, and the book reflects this circular motion.[51] The soldiers are "dead" and no longer here to tell us what they felt, but we need to listen to them anyway. As Walter Benjamin reminds us, inside the dominant constructions of history, "not even the dead will be safe from the enemy."[52] The 1st South Carolina Volunteers, like all other black regiments' soldiers, fought valiantly and courageously to help bring down the U.S. house of slavery. *Conjuring Freedom* does not set out to explain how individual members of the regiment felt, though "feeling" is intentionally invoked throughout this text. I am interested in affect as a social and political force, not as isolated personal experience. Through their musicking, the soldiers did indeed tell us how they felt, and those feelings live on in contemporary black culture.

This book is appreciative of, but resistant to, the traditional historical narratives about African Americans and the Civil War. These studies claim

---

Pictures and Progress are noteworthy monographs that expand black Civil War soldier studies to include visual studies.

49. In terms of method, I tell the story of the regiment using the lens of a cultural historian. For sure, Clifford Geertz's phrase "thick description" comes to mind as I reveal the regiment's interrelated narrative of manhood, music, and religion as a "cosmic vision of freedom." But this approach does not labor in isolation from my personal training both as a classically trained musician whose professional career has involved years of experience as a choral director along with the musical training I received as a child reared on a gospel blues tradition in St. Louis, MO. I bring an integrated sense of vocalist, choral director, music historian, and academically trained historian of culture—all to bear on the interdisciplinary hermeneutics presented here.

50. Kinnamon and Fabre, *Conversations with Richard Wright*, 67.

51. My "ear" as a musical artist, my "expertise" as a scholar, and my pedagogical impulse for teaching African American history as a kind of "musical progression" is the basis of the book's stream of hermeneutics. *Conjuring Freedom* presents cultural history as a sustained ensemble of voices that engage questions of race, religion, music, masculinity, and freedom. The general historical and theoretical tone of the book joins the chorus of American studies scholarship such as Cruz's *Culture on the Margins*; Gordon's *Ghostly Matters*; and Moten's *In the Break*. It is a work of intense interdisciplinarity that frequently presents the "unease of classification" and the "epistemological slide" described by Roland Barthes in his familiar work *Image, Music, Text*.

52. Benjamin, *Illuminations*, 255.

repeatedly that black men fought with equal valor as white men, that black religion was always a Protestant phenomenon, that black freedom has been imagined always solely in terms of national inclusion and progress. These overriding assumptions are not merely specters that haunt us, they have direct bearing on how we live in the present moment. My work in *Conjuring Freedom* reflects on the regiment in order to ask pressing questions about the current moment. Given the example of Higginson's activism in chapter 1, what can we learn about our own current approach to advocacy? If we consider the profile of the United States as a model democratic nation, what is the link between historic racial violence and racial progress? What is the substance of a people's "freedom dreams" inclusive of and beyond the juridical confines of the nation? How can we come to terms with the "both/and" dimensions of black music, especially black sacred singing. Black forms of music express a blackness that is *of* the blood but not reducibly *in* the blood. It allows for a radically democratic idea of "we" who have "tread our path through the blood of the slaughtered" as the lyrics of the black national anthem, "Lift Every Voice And Sing," reflect. And yet, this music did not emerge simply out of what Victor Anderson calls an "ontological blackness, but rather was created collectively through shared dialogue and deliberation."[53] As the first black regiment of the Civil War, the 1st South represents an additional dimension in the black communal conservatory: black music in the black military experience. Following the 1st South, a tradition of black music in the U.S. military continued in the example of James Reese and the Harlem Hell Fighters during WWI and again in WWII with the previously mentioned esteemed choral maestro Leonard De Paur and the De Paur infantry chorus.[54]

∾

Conjuring Freedom opens with an engagement with the regiment's commander. This chapter explores the politics of race, desire, and the hermeneutical legacies of Higginson's "possessive investment in whiteness" that finds him boasting about his professional activism while clinging tightly to racist tropes of human difference. I argue that Higginson's descriptive interpretation of the soldiers and their music corresponds to the nineteenth-century culture of anthropological scientism and a kind of American Orientalism. Higginson takes great "pleasure" in observing and describing the soldiers in essentially racial terms. Higginson silenced the soldiers' voices and carica-

---

53. Anderson, *Beyond Ontological Blackness.*

54. For a biography on James Reese, see Badger, *A Life in Ragtime,* and for Leonard De Paur, see Southern, *The Music of Black Americans,* 470, 536.

tured their humanity. We need to learn how to listen to their songs again in order to learn.

Chapter 2 explores the creative quality of religion in the regiment. As a unit composed of men from a variety of regions with distinctive religious backgrounds the regiment created a diverse blended religiosity as they referred to themselves as a "gospel army." Their "gospel" however, was both an embrace of Jesus as a soldier in the righteous army and as an unstoppable deity in the cosmic pantheon of gods and prophets. The religious "mix" of the regiment presents a rich and vibrant portrait of black religion that in many ways captures the often-occluded spirit of Afro-Atlantic religious eclecticism. Through my reading we see a U.S. black military aggregation in a syncretic moment. Every night in the "ring shout," this gospel army collectively conjured the spirit based on their diverse communal affinities and their disciplined hopes for freedom, reveling in a unity that had to be forged through practice rather than merely found from the consequences of their linked fate.

Chapter 3 takes up the nature of the manhood expressed in the spirituals sung and composed by the regiment. I argue that the pervasive music making of the regiment was a retention of slave culture, blending military training tactics with concepts of rhythm, singing, drumming, and oration, all of which emerged out of their nightly ring shouts. The regiment chose selections from the slave repertoire of songs and improvised on the language and disciplinary strategies of the military to create an alternate collectively gendered notion of selfhood—a "collective black masculinity." Although we might see this construction as merely musical, as black men making glorious sounds about black manhood, my reading takes up specific songs about fear, grief, and loss as being essential to a humanity that went far beyond the strictures and confines of racial and national constructions of manhood. Their musical approach to soldiering was both an embrace of traditional military valor and an invention of a new social group—"black singing soldiers." The musical example of the regiment would go on to inform subsequent forms of black music making and community making in the late nineteenth and early twentieth centuries when black barbershop quartets and jubilee quartets not only borrowed from the regiment's repertoire, but these ensembles also restaged similar versions of black musical masculinity through their choreography and uniform dress.

Chapter 4 presents an extended reading of the tripartite tropes of death, water, and freedom as expressed in the regiment's cosmology. This chapter reveals how the regiment created an alternate black universe through the themes of crossing and water. These practices continued in the ways in which references to water permeated art and activism in the twentieth century.

Chapter 5 brings the book "full circle" with my reading of the 1989 Hollywood blockbuster film *Glory*. Although the movie is based on the famed 54th Massachusetts Regiment and not the 1st South, the script borrowed several scenes from Higginson's memoir. As a representation of black Civil War soldiers *Glory* has a political investment in a particular kind of historical narrative. This chapter examines the politics of race, religion, violence, masculinity, and music presented in *Glory*.

The book's postlude attends to the racial violence enacted against the Emmanuel AME Church in Charleston, SC, in June 2015. While the book's prelude offered a meditation on my observation of the watch-night service held on the 150th anniversary of the Emancipation Proclamation, the postlude sadly attends to the massacre that took place in that very same sanctuary. Historically, Emmanuel had been a house of *refuge* and *resistance* for the black South Carolina Community. This both/and theme of refuge and resistance was absent in the media's coverage of the event as well as the first black president's eulogy of the pastor, who was also one of those murdered among his parishioners. The South Carolina black community, with its Gullah roots, represents a powerful embodiment of creative historical black culture that is sorely needed in the present.

∾

CHAPTER 1

A Strange Fulfillment of Dreams

Racial Fetish and Fantasy in
Thomas Wentworth Higginson's
Army Life in a Black Regiment

MOST OF what is popularly known about the 1st South Carolina Volunteers originates with the eyewitness account of its activities presented by Colonel Thomas Wentworth Higginson's *Army Life in a Black Regiment*. As a result, the historical sound bites of information about the regiment are often distorted by Wentworth's condescending paternalism, racial obsessions, and Orientalist perceptions about the Georgia Sea Islands and its black residents as innately exotic and foreign. Yet as the foundational text exerting formative influence for more than a century on subsequent scholarly studies in history, music, and racial studies as well as providing the core assumptions and guiding logic for the commercial motion picture *Glory, Army Life in a Black Regiment* is a valuable source of information, not so much about the actual practices and beliefs of black soldiers, but more about their erasure from the public record.

Army Life is not simply a document about the nation's first black regiment; it is also an autobiographical record that locates the author within a particular social, historical, and cultural context. Higginson proceeded confidently with a set of racial assumptions that betrayed his liberal abolitionist ideals. His intellectual confidence concerning black matters and his racial assumptions of black inferiority prohibited him from seeing the creative ways the regiment used religion, militarism, and masculinity in a way that would fit *their* world-

view, their "cosmic vision of freedom." The absences and excesses in Higginson's memoir require analysis and interpretation, if only to remove them as
impediments to understanding the complicated interplay of race, nation, masculinity, and religion in the cosmic vision of freedom authored by black Civil
War soldiers in music and military maneuvers. Higginson's memoir is a primary source document that corresponds with other sources of evidence about
black culture in the nineteenth century. It is primarily a document, however,
about its author, specifically his contradictory views on race, culture, and the
nation. It reveals little about the great black river of resistance encapsulated
in the regiment's activities. Yet encased within Higginson's racial fantasy and
fetish are examples of how the regiment used black cultural practices to subvert and invert meanings of race, nation, masculinity, and nation to offer alternative ways of imagining these categories.

Higginson's appointment as the leader of the 1st South Carolina Volunteers
came about because of his own personal history and connections in the wake
of the war's disruption of the slave system in South Carolina. On November 3,
1861 the U.S. Naval Fleet and Army Corps attempted to penetrate Confederate fortresses along the rim of the Georgia Sea Islands near the mouths of the
Santee and St. Johns Rivers along the coasts of South Carolina, Georgia, and
Florida. Just as the fleet was assembled for battle, a vicious rainstorm battered
the troops so badly that they were not able to fulfill the mission as planned.
The scale of loss due to the storm led to an alternate strategy of attack based
solely on the naval fleet. This attempt to revise the assault proved futile immediately as uncooperative weather sent more storms. On November 7, Admiral
Samuel Francis Du Pont ordered more ships to intervene in the expedition,
directing them to bomb Fort Walker and Fort Beauregard. This strategy faced
unforeseen challenges, but by evening the nation's flag was raised to proclaim
the Union's victorious possession of Port Royal.

Though the Battle at Port Royal may have seemed endless for the soldiers on the ground, the transfer of land and human property that followed
was rapid. White planters swiftly abandoned their plantations. This evacu-
ation resulted in the escape of over 10,000 slaves to safety alongside Union
troops. U.S. Secretary of the Treasury Salmon P. Chase viewed these humans
as property rather than people, describing them as "contraband," a term
used to describe goods imported illegally. Chase delegated his friend, former
Private in the 3rd Massachusetts Regiment, Edward L. Pierce, to assess the
"Negro situation." Anticipating that the war might abolish slavery, the federal
government enlisted several philanthropic and missionary organizations and
individuals to establish the "Port Royal Experiment," a war program designed
to prepare the "contrabands" for emancipation.

PORT ROYAL SOUND AND THE
PORT ROYAL EXPERIMENT

I see the sign of the judgment
I see the sign of the judgment
I see the sign of the judgment
Time is drawing nigh

Can you hear God talking
He's talking through the thunder
He's got the world in a wonder
Time is drawing nigh

For the enslaved Africans in the Sea Islands, the bombs decimating the Confederate fortresses were the signs and the sounds of the judgment, the wrath of God on the unjust, the fulfillment of God's promise of freedom. The military vessels wading their way through the outer rim of the Charleston Harbor may have been a conventional naval force in the eyes of their commanders, but in the apocalyptic imagination of the slave in the Civil War, these vessels symbolized the ship of Zion, coming to carry them to freedom. This vision of freedom was ritualized in the dramatic pageantry of victory that followed. The Confederate flags were pulled down and the banners of the Union were raised up. A slave boy named Sam Mitchell recalled,

> Dat Wednesday in November w'en gun fust shoot to Bay Pint (Point) I t'ought it been t'under rolling, but dey ain't no cloud. My Mother say, "son, dat ain't no t'under, dat Yankee come to gib you Freedom."[1]

The "day of the big gun shoot" set off a new chain of events. White planters loaded house slaves and a few possessions into wagons, thereby leaving many field hands behind. To spite the Yankee victory, the planters set fire to countless bales of cotton. White flight left those slaves who remained to decide whether they should destroy the material property of their owners or welcome Union soldiers as liberators and hand it over to them. As the slaves contemplated their new status, the *Atlantic* steamer pulled into Beaufort with missionaries, teachers, and anti-slavery sympathizers from Boston and New York on board. This was the first time a band of northern abolitionists would come face to face with the "slaves" whose cause they championed. Beaufort had been

---

1. "Sam Mitchell," 202.

the home of Carolina white aristocracy with its conspicuous wealth and captive human property. But the air and the soil in Beaufort were also rich with
African-derived black culture. The Sea Islands proved to be fertile ground
for the *Sankofa* practices of African culture through which enslaved Africans
drew on their fragmented memories of African rituals and worldviews as a
resource for creating something new on American soil. The state-sponsored
convoy of northern sympathizers could not have imagined the ways black cultural practices enabled a sense of survival and community that would enhance
black people's status as citizens. The missionaries embarked on an ambitious
experimental project of "teaching" black people on the islands how to live
together as citizens in a "free" society.

The Port Royal Experiment was an exercise that prefigured Reconstruction—a rehearsal of sorts. Following the Union Army's seizure of the Sea
Islands, a largely white cohort of educators and clergy occupied the area in
order to provide the freed people with what the newcomers deemed to be the
skills of citizenship.[2] Like the activities of the 1st South Carolina Volunteers,
the Port Royal Experiment created a black community whose collective oneness was anchored by an African-inspired worldview of ritual, behaviors, and
beliefs.

The emergence of black regiments owed much to the energy and activism
of the most visible black abolitionist of nineteenth-century America, Frederick Douglass. He waged a passionate public campaign on behalf of black
enlistment in the Civil War. In the early months of the conflict President
Lincoln responded negatively to any suggestions to include "slaves" in the
army. "To arm the Negroes," Lincoln argued, "would turn 50,000 bayonets
from loyal Border States against us that were for us."[3] Lincoln's position did
not persuade many military officials whose sense of urgency on the battlefield led them to recruit black regiments independent of federal support. In
late October of 1862, for example, James Henry Lane, a partisan abolitionist during the "Bleeding Kansas" conflict, recruited and raised a regiment of
black men from Missouri and Kansas to form the 1st Regiment Kansas Volunteer Colored Infantry.[4] Around the same time a militia of "free negroes" in
New Orleans formed the *Corps d'Afrique* also known as the Louisiana Native
Guards. Although the government did not officially recognize these two regiments, they took to the battlefield. It is important to note that while these
regiments were refused official status by General David Hunter, the Union
Army's Commander in South Carolina, he did make his own attempt at black

2. See Rose, *Rehearsal for Reconstruction.*
3. Basler, *The Collected Works of Abraham Lincoln,* 357, 423.
4. McPherson, *The Negro's Civil War,* 164–65.

regimentation as a way of resuscitating an ailing Union army. With no official order to do so, Hunter established an early version of the South Carolina Volunteers in May of 1862. With the exception of one company, this entire operation was disbanded within three months. Given the strain on the Union army because of its occupation of enemy territory in and around Charleston, Hunter once again took up his quest to enlist black men as soldiers. With the assistance of a respected black minister in Hilton Head named Abraham Murchison, Hunter organized a secret meeting with approximately two hundred black men on the evening of April 7, 1862.[5] Murchison presented a compelling case for enlistment, but the numbers of enlistees trickled in very slowly. In the face of the disbanding of the earlier regiment along with the suspicion held by many slaves that they could be sold to Cuba as part of the Port Royal Experiment, General Hunter was considering the draft technique used previously. Instead, on May 9, 1862 he issued his own emancipation proclamation as a gesture aimed at encouraging enlistment: all slaves within his jurisdiction were declared free.

Hunter's unofficial and unauthorized proclamation sent a charge of anger through the War Department as it upstaged President Lincoln's own agenda. A quintessential politician who considered timing to be the ultimate factor, Lincoln hesitated to respond until May 19, when he issued *his* proclamation, invalidating Hunter's declaration. In the midst of competing sources of military authority, strong public weariness concerning the loss of life in the war, and racial ambivalence on the northern side about the desirability of mobilizing black soldiers, three legal measures combined to set a new course. First, the Confiscation Act of 1861 authorized the seizure of all Confederate property, "including slaves." This meant that when slaves were "confiscated" by the Union army they were free to be employed in military service. Second, this legislation institutionalized the term "contraband" to establish a new liminal category of racial difference designating blacks as no longer slaves but not yet free. Third, the Militia Act of 1862 repealed the militia act of 1792 and authorized the employment of soldiers of African descent. Despite this triple wave of legal adjustments the general sentiments toward black enlistment remained unabashedly hostile. The looming risk of losing the war, however, compelled the War Department to make a strategic move on August 25 and give General Rufus Saxton the authority to officially raise and muster into service black troops from the Sea Islands. His orders specified that he could revive Company A from Hunter's initial South Carolina Volunteers. The second provision was that these regiments were to have white officers.

---

5. Mohr, *On The Threshold of Freedom*, 84.

Saxton had been born into a Massachusetts abolitionist family. His father was a Unitarian and a transcendentalist. Given his abolitionist commitments and social standing, it was no coincidence that he responded to his mandate to raise a black regiment by asking his friend and fellow abolitionist Thomas Wentworth Higginson to command the unit. Higginson had extensive involvement in anti-slavery activism, but his military experience was limited to his service as captain in the 51st Massachusetts infantry. Nonetheless, on November 5, 1862, General Saxton wrote to Higginson:

> My dear sir, I am organizing the First Regiment of the South Carolina Volunteers. . . . I take great pleasure in offering you the position of Colonel in it and hope that you may be induced to accept it.[6]

Higginson accepted Saxton's offer and on November 7, 1862 the 1st South Carolina Volunteers were officially mustered into service. Arriving in Beaufort, Higginson wrote his first journal entry on November 24, 1862 in the form of a reflection on his new "recruits" at Camp Saxton. This former plantation turned into a military camp featuring pitched white tents spread across the grounds was a constant reminder of the Civil War as an epoch-making moment in the path of black people from plantation property to complex personhood. Higginson seemed pleased by his appointment as colonel of the nation's first black regiment. In a journal entry he noted, "all looked as thoroughly black as the most faithful philanthropist could desire."[7]

Higginson came from a prominent Massachusetts family composed of clerics, entrepreneurs, and English aristocracy. Higginson's early life infused him with interests in music and cultural difference, which would later influence his account of life in the black regiment. Higginson understood himself to be a "child of the college," referring to Harvard College on whose faculty his father served. His father died when he was eleven years of age and his older siblings moved away, so he was reared in a female household that consisted of his mother, an aunt, and his two younger sisters. Music and literature dominated the Higginson household as it reflected the tastes of his mother and aunt. One of his sisters was an exceptional pianist, which pleasured Higginson's ears to the point that he made sure his bedroom door was opened just enough to hear her play as he drifted to sleep.

Informed by the fiery abolitionist climate in Massachusetts, Higginson was ordained as a Unitarian Universalist clergyman, but he was soon frustrated

6. Higginson, *Army Life*, 1–2.
7. Higginson, *Army Life*, 6.

by the timidity of the church and the organized abolitionist movement. He did not have to wait long, however, for an opportunity to become physically involved with the anti-slavery cause. In 1853, a fugitive Baptist slave preacher named Anthony Burns landed in Boston and was arrested and slated to be returned to the South. Higginson led a small militia attempting to rescue him from the local jail, was arrested and shortly released. Higginson's essays frequently reflected his on-the-ground activism. He considered himself a well-informed authority on nature, fitness, literature, and black revolts. His memoir reveals a strong sense of confidence in these areas, but it *also* reveals distinct perceptions about race.

In college, Higginson was introduced to systematic study of cultural difference. He took courses in literature from Edward T. Channing, and he was also very active in the college's Natural History Society. Channing edited the March 1818 issue of the *North American Review and Miscellaneous Journal*, which claimed to reveal secret aspects of the Hindu religion. As religious historian David Weir explains, this publication reflected an American departure from "the old Chinese Orient that the French had discovered; instead they [American intellectuals] turned their attention to the 'new' Sanskrit East that was beginning to excite their British contemporaries."[8] Channing was part of this shift to promoting a distinctly American "gaze" on the East. As a student of Channing and as an acolyte of the larger transcendentalist movement of the era, Higginson thought and wrote within this intellectual frame that resonates with some features of what twentieth-century scholar Edward Said would come to call "Orientalism."[9] Higginson maintained a lifelong interest in eastern civilizations, as evidenced by his participation in the work of the *Journal of the American Oriental Society* in 1891.[10]

Higginson published *Army Life in a Black Regiment* to document his military experience as an officer. But the memoir was equally a work of ethnographic cultural observation. *Army Life* is one of the most widely cited sources in nineteenth-century African American history, music, and culture. Higginson's book has been engaged as a text that fits a number of genres: military memoir, cultural criticism, and black music studies. Higginson's approach *also* places his work inside another genre: travelogue writing. Higginson had "studied" and supported the cause of Abolitionism before his posting to the Georgia Sea Islands, but he had never personally journeyed to the South. He was typical of northern sympathizers whose arrival (and writing) as travelers to the Georgia Sea Islands marks what Mary Louise Pratt calls perception of

---

8. Weir, *American Orient,* 14.

9. Said, *Orientalism.*

10. See the front matter of *Journal of the American Oriental Society* 18 (1897): 391–401.

a "contact zone" where travel facilitates an ethnographic interest in people designated as exotic and other.[11] Although Higginson considered himself to be an authority on black culture, an anxious sense of *racial difference* pervades his memoir.

Higginson was also enthusiastic about spending time outdoors with nature. He joined the Natural History Society and worked as an aide to Thaddeus William Harris, a Linnaean scholar who specialized in the classification of fauna.[12] The naturalist Louis Agassiz, who headed the Lawrence Scientific School in 1847 and founded the Museum of Comparative Zoology in 1859, likely influenced Higginson. Agassiz popularized a variant of scientific racism, "polygenism," which held that the different races had clear, distinct, and separable lineages as if they were different species.[13] This particular practice of racial classification is vibrant in Higginson's memoir, so that the genealogy of abolitionism, transcendentalism, and polygenism are combined to create an aesthetically colorful but troubling text. Higginson's naturalist and "orientalist" tropes pervaded his text, reflecting his intellectual formation. For example, he writes:

> Numerous plantation-buildings totter around, all slovenly and unattractive, while the interspaces are filled with all manner of wreck and refuse, pigs, fowls, dogs, and omni-present Ethiopian infancy. All this is the universal Southern panorama. . . . All are purer African than I expected . . . strange antics from this mysterious race of grown-up children with whom my lot is cast.[14]

The Georgia Sea Islands comprise a spread of over one hundred small bodies of land connected by several tributaries that flow along the coast of the Atlantic Ocean. They display precisely the kind of visual natural splendor that a transcendentalist and amateur botanist such as Higginson had only "dreamed" about. As such, the exotic feel of the Sea Islands was an ideal location of otherworldliness for him. It provided picturesque elements for a travelogue. When he describes the soldiers in natural settings outside of military training and the battlefield, Higginson clearly manifests his investment

---

11. Pratt, *Imperial Eyes*.

12. The biographical details put forth in this introduction, unless otherwise cited, are drawn from several of the excellent biographies of Higginson. See Edelstein, *Strange Enthusiasm*; Higginson, *Thomas Wentworth Higginson*; Meyer, *Colonel of the Black Regiment*. In addition to Higginson's *Army Life*, see additional autobiographies, *Cheerful Yesterdays* (Boston, 1898) and *Part of a Man's Life* (Boston, 1905).

13. See Nott and Gliddon, *Types of Mankind*.

14. Higginson, *Army Life*, 3–13.

in racial difference. For example, in the initial entry in Higginson's diary, he describes his arrival in Beaufort, South Carolina, the regiment's headquarters, as a "strange fulfillment of dreams" that found him "sitting where John Brown only wished he could have been."[15] His writing advanced a white perspective on African Americans as exotic and childlike, but it also stood as a confessional representation of his own preoccupation with these perceptions. His self-proclaimed expertise on black culture and his leadership over the nation's first black regiment played a key role in the ways he configured his own racialized manhood. Higginson used his position as colonel of the nation's first black regiment to advance his rivalries over the mantle manhood between himself and other white men such as John Brown and later Walt Whitman, whom Higginson loathed. These rivalries were part and parcel of Higginson's "fulfillment of dreams." This competition over white masculine honor required a backdrop of racial difference that romanticized the "rawness and savagery" of blacks compared to white Americans. Racial difference in this case disallowed full and equal humanity for African Americans, yet contained an explicit dimension of erotic desire.[16] He wrote, "I had always looked for the arming of the blacks, and had always felt a wish to be associated with them."[17] Higginson's use of racial stereotypes, loaded with feelings of desire and demeaning terminology, reveals what Sharon Holland calls "the erotic life of racism," which, in Higginson's case, emerges from a complex blend of abolitionism, paternalism, and his expressed *desire* for a political relationship with African Americans.[18] John Saillant provides specific comment on the eroticism of the black body and the republic: "White men eroticized black men in anti-slavery writings because in American ideology sentimentalism and republicanism grounded their vision of the body politic in a fundamental likeness that produces benevolence."[19] Like his fellow northern abolitionists, Higginson's well-intended sojourn in the Sea Islands and his offer of assistance to Africans on the threshold of legalized freedom was compromised not by a lack of zeal and sincere effort, but by the absence of a shared sense of humanity between himself and those he attempted to help.

The description of the soldiers as a "mysterious race of grown up children" in Higginson's memoir corresponds with the broader system of race language that appeared earlier in (among other places) Harriet Beecher Stowe's

---

15. Thomas Wentworth Higginson, *Army Life*, 3.
16. Looby, "As Thoroughly Black."
17. Higginson, *Army Life*, 2.
18. Holland, *The Erotic Life of Racism*.
19. "The Black Body Erotic," 89.

anti-slavery novel, *Uncle Tom's Cabin,* published in 1852.[20] Stowe and Higginson share in common a depiction of blacks as "childlike" and both were also prominent figures in the northern anti-slavery movement. The assumption that this racial perception only characterized the southern plantation and its white owner is here proven false. For as Ron Takaki writes in a now classic text, *Iron Cages,* "the racial ideology of the black 'child-like savage' served both caste and class functions in an increasingly complex way in the North as well as the South."[21] In Higginson's memoir, the "childlike" trope functions as part of a dense discursive formation, a system of statements concerning race, desire, philanthropy, pigment, music, and religion.

Higginson's choices of language in constructing racial difference for a presumed white readership can be illuminated by Edward Said's discussion of Orientalism. The connection is not exact: Higginson was not writing from the context of an "Orient" that existed outside the continental boundaries of America. But when he writes, "I had not allowed for the extreme remoteness and seclusion of their lives, *especially among the Sea Islands*" [emphasis mine], he reveals that he had constructed his own version of an Oriental subject within the nation. As Said states, one important aspect of Orientalism derives from an outside account of existing inside a particular context.[22] Higginson's abolitionism was his "deeply felt and urgent project," borrowing a phrase from Said, but his "orientalist" framework allowed him to maintain a clear racial difference between himself and those for whom he was advocating.

Said describes three elements in the construction of Orientalism that depend on the residential status of the observer.

1. Personal experience and testimony authorize Orientalism as a particular science of knowledge.[23]

In his memoir, Higginson writes,

> I had in my profession of literary man, made their wars & insurrections a special study, & in my profession of Abolitionist had tested well their quality.

---

20. Higginson, *Army Life,* 13.
21. Takaki, *Iron Cages,* 110.
22. Said, *Orientalism,* 323.
23. Ibid., 157.

In one of the most perilous positions of my life a fugitive slave had stepped in before me and intercepted the danger. . . .[24]

Here, Higginson appeals to personal experience in a way that is consistent with Said's frame. His firsthand encounter with a fugitive slave, together with his "study" of wars and insurrections, helps to "authorize" his memoir as a kind of official document produced by an "informed" observer. Even more confidently, in his essay "The Negro as a Soldier," Higginson says of his experience of former slaves in the Georgia Sea Islands, "I had always had so much to do with fugitive slaves, and had studied the whole subject with such interest, that I found not much to learn or unlearn . . ."[25]

Indeed, as his publishing record proves, Higginson had already made a "study" of slave insurrections, having published the essay "Nat Turner's Insurrection" in the August 1861 issue of the *Atlantic Monthly*. Higginson's study of insurrections is clearly personal, as documented in his first memoir entry: "I had always looked for the arming of the blacks, and had always felt a *wish to be associated with them*."[26] Higginson's front-line abolitionism, his "study" of insurrections, and his training as a naturalist enabled the particularized science of race, culture, and writing in his memoir. In particular, Higginson's combined use of racial terms and naturalist terms amounts to a classification of "otherness" informed by his understandings of black songs. He writes, "The words of the song, I have afterwards carried it to my tent, like some captured bird or insect. . . . I have completed the new specimen by supplying the absent parts."[27] Note that Higginson does not refer to the music he hears as simply "music." Instead, what he hears is something from the world of dreams. What is fulfilled here is the orientalist's quasi-scientific yearning to experience and to document the utterly exotic. Higginson classifies what he hears in naturalist terms, i.e., a "specimen." Only a few lines later, he states, "I could now gather on their own soil these strange plants."[28] Music is rarely considered part of Said's Orientalist framework, but here Higginson's description shows that he considers the classification of black music to be a "particular science of knowledge." The sounds Higginson heard in his home would have corresponded to the more general definitive aspects of "music" in the culture

---

24. This quote is taken from a group of unordered writings in the Houghton Library, Harvard University, MS Am 784 [858–879–927]. Several of these "scattered notes" are reprinted in the volume edited by Looby, *Civil War Journal*, 12.

25. Higginson, "The Negro as a Soldier," 2.

26. Higginson, *Army Life*, 2.

27. Ibid., 149–50.

28. Ibid., 149.

of Cambridge in the nineteenth century. Classical music *was* "music," and for a self-identifying "faithful philanthropist" such as Higginson, "spirituals" were something he heard about, but now encountered as "specimens" to be "captured." This tripartite subjectivity as abolitionist, observer of nature, and documentarian contributes to Higginson's own sense of racial difference and separation, which is the second installation in Said's frame.

2. The "resident" always writes from an intentional consciousness of being set apart from the environment, which serves a professional task.[29]

Higginson writes:

> Camp life was a wonderfully strange sensation to almost all volunteer officers, and mine lay among eight hundred men suddenly transformed from slaves into soldiers, and representing a race affectionate, enthusiastic, grotesque, and dramatic beyond all others. Being such, *they naturally gave material for description* [emphasis mine].[30]

> . . . I am reminded that my own face is not the color of coal.[31]

> . . . I found myself adrift upon a horse's back amid a sea of roses[32]

> . . . my black statues looked so dream-like[33]

> . . . I was the enchanted center.[34]

These statements from Higginson's memoir join together his "particular science of Knowledge" based on racial classification and his naturalist vocabulary. He notes that he is not of those whom he describes. He is among them but not of them, a sentiment expressed pervasively throughout his diary. Higginson makes frequent use of color designations to distinguish the soldiers, not simply as a category within racial classification, but also as different from himself. The fact that he is reminded that his "own face is not the color of

---

29. Said, *Orientalism*, 157.
30. Higginson, *Army Life*, 3.
31. Ibid., 7.
32. Ibid., 116.
33. Ibid., 118.
34. Ibid., 119.

coal" harks back to his initial days in the Sea Islands when he is struck by "their extreme blackness."[35] As if he were shopping for a particular color, he describes his initial reaction to seeing them upon his arrival: "all looked as thoroughly black as the most faithful philanthropist could desire; there did not seem to be so much as a mulatto among them. Their coloring suited me."[36] Drawing on a naturalist but now animalistic descriptive science, Higginson confesses that while he was "suited" by their color, he was not so much so by their legs: "all but the legs, which were clad in a lively scarlet, as intolerable to my eyes as if I had been a turkey." As described in Suzie King Taylor's memoir, *A Black Woman's Civil War Memoirs,* the regiment's initial uniform reflected the "bright and rather exotic zouave uniforms" prescribed to some other Union regiments.[37] This means that the soldiers' pants would have been red. These distinctions are based on "color," but when viewed in the context of Higginson's formal training, they are also a matter of racial difference. The soldiers were concerned about being conspicuous in a time of war, but Higginson seems unable to avoid relying on naturalist and biological tropes to frame race.

The relationship between race and space is a key element in the aesthetic feel presented in Higginson's memoir. Not only does Higginson portray expressions of black music as racial phenomena to be studied like specimens in nature, but he situates black bodies as a "natural" element within the geographical location. Higginson's snippets of poetry (e.g., "the watch-lights glittered on the land, the ship-lights on the sea") are part of a repertoire of Sea Island images that permeate his diary. But his further details about the population within the Sea Island region are repeatedly tropes of racial difference and distance. Higginson's application of the term "Ethiopian" on several occasions serves a dual function. On the one hand he writes of an "omnipresent Ethiopian infancy," which he says is exemplary of a "Universal Southern panorama."[38] This poses a faraway region, "Ethiopia," as the realm of infancy. Similarly, Higginson makes a racial construct when he remarks on the "childlike" quality of these adult black soldiers. But in terms of his sense of separateness as an author-observer, Ethiopia functions as a regional and racial trope that constructs the Sea Islands as an exotic place, so exotic that for Higginson it's somehow too otherworldly to be included within the purview of America.

Higginson admits to having dreamed about African Americans and the Georgia Sea Islands. Even after his arrival and during his continued writing, his way of approaching his experience creates an even larger gap between his

35. Ibid., 3.
36. Ibid., 6.
37. Taylor, *A Black Woman's Civil War Memoirs,* 48.
38. Higginson, *Army Life,* 7.

own sense of humanity and that of the people he writes about. Higginson's longing to be with these "others" in the name of abolitionism leads to the third part in the application of Said's framework.

3. The trip to the Orient is the "fulfillment of some deeply felt and urgent project."[39]

Higginson writes:

> I had been an abolitionist too long, and had known John Brown too well, not to feel a thrill of joy at last on finding myself in the position where he only wished he could be.[40]

> I had always had so much to do with fugitive slaves . . .[41]

> I did not seek the command of colored troops, but it sought Me.[42]

> The war brought to some of us, besides its direct experiences, many a *strange fulfillment of dreams* . . .[43]

Higginson's biography tells the story of a budding Bostonian abolitionist whose social and intellectual circles include several luminary figures across multiple genres. The Civil War represented a culmination of things gone wrong with the nation, but for Higginson the opportunity to serve as colonel of the nation's first black regiment placed him on the right side of history. General Saxton's letter to Higginson is dated November 5, 1862 and on November 9, 1862 Higginson wrote to his mother, Louisa Storrow Higginson, "ours will be a splendid regiment."[44] He exults at being in the position where John Brown "only wished" he could have been.

Higginson's objectification of the soldiers' music was a scientific exercise that took on the nomenclature of nature. His description of spirituals attests to the "elsewhere" quality that he heard in black music: "I could now gather on their own soil these strange plants, which I had before seen in museums

---

39. Said, *Orientalism*, 157–58.
40. Higginson, *Army Life*, 3.
41. Ibid., 189.
42. Ibid., 2.
43. Ibid., 149.
44. Higginson, "To Louisa Storrow Higginson, November 9, 1862," 243.

alone."[45] In providing his own ethnographic details about a particular song, he wrote that he "completed the new specimen by supplying the absent parts."[46] Despite the lack of any formal training as either a musician or musicologist, Higginson's interpretive comments on the singing of black soldiers parallels the cultural hegemony exercised by musicologists writing about Indian music in the late eighteenth and nineteenth centuries. In 1792 Sir William Jones published one of the earliest scholarly works on Indian music entitled "On the Musical Modes of the Hindus."[47] Jones used Western systems of musical notation to transcribe Hindu music. These transcriptions were later criticized because of the dissonance between the tonal structures of Hindu music and Western music. In 1834, N. August Willard published his "Treatise on the Music of Hindostan." Referring to Jones as an "eminent Orientalist," Willard was adamant that "It is impossible to convey an accurate idea of music by words of written language."[48]

As Jones, Willard, and other British musicologists debated their "romantic representations of British India,"[49] Napoleon Bonaparte's colonial conquest of Egypt in 1798 enabled the French monarch's official musicologist, Guillaume-André Villoteau, to create his own discourse of "Orientalism." *Description de l'Egypte,* published from 1809 to 1829, replicated the trend in British musicology studies on India in Villoteau's "description" of African music in Egypt. Villoteau remarked, "If the songs of the Copts were as pleasant as they are monotonous and boring, we could compare them to those hymns sung by the ancient priests celebrating Osiris, singing with seven vowels."[50] Villoteau's use of the term "monotonous" coincides with Higginson's description of the soldiers, singing "one of their quaint, monotonous, endless, negro-Methodist chants."[51] For Higginson and Villoteau, the repetitious qualities of African music were somehow "monotonous" in the negative sense of the word, a characteristic that would fit quite well with the perception of Higginson's description of the soldiers as "childlike." In this instance, the music making of Africans, whether in the U.S. or in Egypt, was being heard through an aural epistemology of Orientalism. This way of hearing music performed by non-white persons suggests that plaintive music and repetitious chanting were reflective of an underdeveloped exotic people who exist as interesting objects/

---

45. Higginson, *Army Life,* 149.
46. Ibid., 150.
47. Jones, "On the Musical Modes of the Hindus."
48. Zon, "From 'Very Acute and Plausible' to 'Curiously Misinterpreted.'"
49. Ibid.
50. Villoteau and Jomard, "Description de l'Égypte."
51. Higginson, *Army Life,* 13.

subjects for study and interpretation. They assumed that these people and their culture required a paternalistic and sympathetic translator.

The production of literary works from the British and America Empires in the nineteenth century coalesced with the sanctioned musicological work of Villoteau of the French Empire. All of these imperial regimes have in common a particular preoccupation with race, which Higginson fully shared. His particular preoccupation arises from the fact that his abolitionism requires race or specifically "blackness" as the primitive but grateful recipient of his philanthropic largesse. As seen in his racialized descriptions of music his epistemological lens coincides with the racial ideas of Orientalism circulating in the nineteenth century. For example, he writes, "I was startled when I first came on such a flower of poetry in the dark soil"; "when the dusky figures moved in the rhythmical barbaric dance the negroes call a 'shout.'"[52] Higginson considered himself an expert on black cultural matters, and his choice of language throughout the memoir suggests that his perception of the singers and their music amounts to a kind of scientific experiment. He describes his own process of transcription as "Writing down in the darkness, as best I could, ... I have afterwards carried it to my tent, like some captured bird or insect."[53] This metaphorical identity as the naturalist exploring in the wild distinguishes him from the French and British musicologists of the period.

The production of American literature in the nineteenth century frequently positioned the writer as a tourist exploring a foreign exotic land. This literature coincided with travel writing, which, in the nineteenth century, was a genre of writing that contributed to the Orientalist view of strange places and exotic peoples in the Eastern Hemisphere of the world. Higginson's *Army Life* parallels this genre of travel writing with one clear exception: he (re)positions the Georgia Sea Islands as a locale "within" the boundary lines of the (soon to be) United States, while at the same time imagining the people of the place as a "mysterious race of grownup children." This racial paradox manifests a form of "domestic orientalism," in that the perceptions used in the construction of Orientalism as an East-West paradigm are deployed here. Just as the exotic others in Said's Orientalist paradigm functioned as objects of sexual desire, so too is this the case in Higginson's memoir.

Higginson attempts to fulfill his scopophilic fantasies of race through writing. Higginson's poetic sensibilities implicitly contradict his political ambitions as an abolitionist, as his erotic gaze confesses a deep investment in maintaining the superior status of whiteness. Higginson's abolitionist project depended on the racial difference that maintained his own whiteness as intrin-

---

52. Ibid., 160, 146.
53. Ibid., 149.

sically superior to the blackness of his soldiers, which was innately inferior. This sense of difference was, in this military context, a gendered and even a sexual difference.

Throughout his memoir Higginson resolidified his investment in his whiteness by using racial distinctions of skin complexion to draw connections between race, primitivism, and intelligence. Following his initial introductory encounter with members of the regiment, Higginson reflected that those who were "thoroughly black" were suited to his taste and that "there did not seem to be so much as a mulatto among them."[54] In another section of the memoir he writes, "I notice that some companies, too, look darker than others, though all are purer African than I expected."[55] Higginson's expectation and attention to the varied skin tones of the regiment was also a matter of race and intelligence: "the men brought from Fernandina the other day average lighter in complexion, and look more intelligent."[56] Did the lighter skin men look "more intelligent" because their skin color was closer to white? Higginson tellingly writes that he became accustomed to "seeing them go through all their daily processes, eating, frolicking, talking, just if they were white."[57] This passage suggests that the leisure interactions between the soldiers is something that is reserved for those who are white, and as such, Higginson's description reenforces a view of the soldier's "color" or race as ontologically inferior.

Higginson's "possessive investment" in his own racial superiority is not merely a disembodied intellectual exercise that lives only in his imagination. It reveals itself as well in the corporeal dimensions of Higginson's racial writing, which are explicitly homoerotic. In his essay "A Night in the Water," which appeared in the *Atlantic* in 1864, Higginson located his body in a panoptic position of pleasure, allowing his gaze to fix the soldiers for his nocturnal ephemeral fantasy:

> I found my men couched, like black statues, behind the slight earthwork there constructed. . . . The night was so still and lovely, my black statutes looked so dream-like at their posts behind the low earthwork, the opposite arm of the causeway stretched so invitingly from the Rebel main, the horizon glimmered so low around me, for it always appears lower to a swimmer than even to an oarsman,—that I seemed floating in some concave globe, some magic crystal, of which I was the enchanted centre.[58]

---

54. Ibid., 6.
55. Ibid., 8.
56. Ibid., 8.
57. Ibid., 7.
58. Higginson, "A Night on the Water," 118.

By placing himself in the "centre" of a floating water fantasy, Higginson embodies what Mary Louise Pratt calls the "seeing man," a "European male subject . . . whose imperial eyes passively look out and possess."[59] The scene is staged in a way that disallows the soldiers any resistive agency, given that Higginson perceives them as mere statues "possessed" by Higginson's imperial gaze. As is typical throughout Higginson's memoir, such scenes depend on a romantic nocturnal vision of loveliness in which black male bodies are situated as adornment in a larger racial fantasy and erotic fetish. The objectifying language of Higginson's descriptions border on the pornographic, so that there is almost no need to read between the lines when he writes, "Never did I see such objects—some stripped to their shirts, some fully clothed, but all having every garment literally pasted to their bodies with mud."[60] Higginson's use of terms like "stripped" and phrases like "pasted to their bodies with mud" is, when read through a Freudian lens, a partial "fulfillment of dreams." Similar to the ways women are objectified solely as erotic objects, Higginson's racial fetish for black soldiers uses race and fetish to infantilize them in order to maintain a racial sense of superiority.[61]

In addition to the erotic functions of Higginson's preoccupation with black masculinity, there is also the competitive dynamic at work in Higginson's writing about his white male peers. Thomas W. Higginson's credentials as an abolitionist, clergyman, and literary expert were well known to the northern political intelligentsia in the nineteenth century, but it is worth considering that Higginson had not previously expressed any military ambitions. Higginson was a captain in the 51st Massachusetts Infantry during the early years of the war but his biographers have not noted any particular careerist ambitions or abilities with regard to Higginson's potential as a military leader. Despite this, he was selected to lead the nation's first official black regiment. Given the impassioned campaign on the part of Frederick Douglass to admit black men into the Union army, as well as the unofficial attempts by figures such as General David Hunter, why was Higginson, an abolitionist, clergyman, literary critic, and cultured gentleman with very little military experience (or ambitions), solicited for such a task? Higginson's liberal leanings may have rendered him sympathetic to the racial mission within the war-making effort, a mission that held no interest for President Lincoln, although he eventually signed the order to officially admit black men into the Union army. Higginson's limited military experience suggests a lack of expectation in the hierarchy of the U.S. War Department that the 1st South Carolina Volunteers would

59. Pratt, *Imperial Eyes*, 7.
60. Higginson, *Army Life*, 108.
61. Mulvey, "Visual Pleasure and Narrative Cinema."

or could achieve anything of more than symbolic significance in the war. Nevertheless, this did not affect the ways Higginson seized the opportunity to create competition between himself and his white male peers.

Military masculinity has always been a symbol of America's desire to project itself as a democratic empire. Higginson's mentality fits well within the ethos of the military as he undertakes to initiate the former slaves-turned-soldiers into what Robyn Wiegman calls the "province of the masculine."[62] The paradox implied by black men fully inhabiting this province in the U.S. military existed not simply as a contradiction at the societal level. Higginson's personal dependence on racial difference inevitably expressed itself in ways symptomatic of the larger, seemingly irreconcilable, problem of race, nation, and equality in the nineteenth century. To exacerbate matters even further, Higginson created masculine rivalries between himself and other white male activist-leaning figures of the nineteenth century, including William Sloane Kennedy and Walt Whitman.[63] Higginson's disdain for Whitman's writing was made obvious in his published reviews on Whitman's work, but he was equally disdainful of Whitman's presentation of working-class masculinity. As an astute critic of American literature, Higginson was well familiar with the poet's work and he was keenly aware of Whitman's Civil War activities. In a later memoir, *Cheerful Yesterdays,* Higginson recalled his first face-to-face encounter with Whitman:

> I saw before me, sitting on the counter, a handsome, burly man, heavily built, and not looking, to my gymnasium-trained-eye, in really good condition for athletic work. . . . The personal impression made on me by the poet was not so much of manliness as of Boweriness . . . a dandy roundabout.[64]

Higginson's use of the term "Boweriness" is significant in this context, given the Bowery's fall from grace as an eighteenth-century highbrow neighborhood of spatial design, elite entertainment, and gentlemen's-club respectability. During the Civil War, the Bowery transitioned to an area replete with lowbrow German Beer Gardens and brothels, a transition that no longer identified the Bowery as a social space where respectable masculinity was constructed through participation in high literary culture and arts. In *Gay New York: Gender, Urban Culture, and the Making of the Gay Male World 1890–1940*, George Chauncey writes that starting in the early nineteenth century the Bowery "had been the epicenter of a distinct working-class public culture, with its

---

62. Wiegman, *American Anatomies.*
63. Nelson and Price, "Debating Manliness."
64. Higginson, *Cheerful Yesterdays,* 230.

own codes of behavior, dress, and public sociability."[65] The working-class male "degenerates" and their sexual resorts that pervaded the 1870s Bowery would certainly have disturbed Higginson's normative masculine sensibilities of respectability and culture.

For Higginson, Walt Whitman, working-class men of the Bowery, and black Civil War soldiers all exemplified the *impossibilities* of manhood. Race and class were intrinsic to the Higginsonian definition of manhood as quint-essentially white, cultured, and credentialed.[66] Higginson's abolitionist politics *required* race and class to be sustained in order to maintain his "possessive investment in whiteness." As such black men were feminized based on racial difference, and working-class white men were dismissed as un-masculine due to their class status.

In addition to making note of Whitman's "Boweriness," Higginson also wrote, "It is no discredit to Walt Whitman that he wrote 'Leaves of Grass,' only that he did not burn it afterwards and reserve himself for something better."[67] Though not exclusively, themes of sexuality are prominent in Walt Whitman's *Leaves of Grass,* which he self-published in 1855. Immediately following the book's publication, Whitman was fired from the Department of the Interior. Secretary of the Interior James Harlan, a former college president and Methodist minister, was offended by the book's obscenity. Most biographers agree that he was responsible for Whitman's discharge.[68] In *Leaves of Grass* Whitman integrated same-gender love, intense physical passion between men, and spirituality in a way that upset the genteel American literary establishment of the nineteenth century. Given his role as a volunteer nurse during the Civil War, Whitman's dismissal serves to illustrate what Eve Kosofsky Sedgwick calls an "important American ambivalence toward pragmatic politics" that is unable to reconcile any one individual social issue.[69] On the one hand Whitman, like Higginson, performs a "service" to the nation in his role as a volunteer nurse. Yet, similar to Higginson, Whitman's service frames the social problem of race in ways that further solidify blackness through philanthropic acts and language itself. Between these white masculine liberal figures lies a paradox of race and even class: if racial difference and class status marked the necessary distinctions for Higginsonian masculinity, then it was Higginson's own

65. Chauncey, *Gay New York,* 34.

66. My use of the phrase "impossible masculinity" is inspired by Jennifer Devere Brody's *Impossible Purities.*

67. Higginson, "Literature as Art."

68. See Miller, *Walt Whitman.*

69. Sedgwick, *Between Men,* 204–5.

inability to access blackness that conditioned his rivalry with his abolitionist colleague and peer John Brown.

In the trajectory of Higginson's activist career, John Brown was the oldest of his rivals. Yet comparatively, the musical memory of John Brown as it was written into the collective conscience of slaves—compared to that of Higginson's memoir—makes for an interesting irony, recalling the phrase, "the first shall be last and the last shall be first." When Higginson writes that he felt the "thrill of joy" on "finding himself in the position where he [John Brown] only wished to be," his statement coincides with his earlier reflection, "I had always looked for the arming of the blacks, and had always wished to be associated with them."[70] Here Higginson constructs another rivalry, as he presumes that *his* fantasy of black militarism was also John Brown's. He does not seem to consider that the "unofficial" aspect of John Brown's raid on Harper's Ferry was much more in keeping with the tradition of black-led insurrections such as those by Gabriel Prosser, Denmark Vesey, and Nat Turner. The account of John Brown's planning and raid reveals no evidence that Brown "wished" to serve as colonel of an officially state-sanctioned army. On the contrary, Brown would likely have argued against it, as his project involved the self-arming of African Americans in opposition to the state. The raid and death of John Brown was perceived by enslaved Africans as a landmark event in the insurrectionist tradition, resulting in the song of tribute composed by slaves "John Brown's Body." This song was a popular selection for the 1st South Carolina Volunteers regiment and for slaves throughout the Civil War. Higginson was thus constantly reminded of blacks' regard for John Brown, although he mentioned the song only casually throughout his diary. Despite this constant reminder of Brown through the music in the regiment, Higginson did not present the lyrics to the song about him in his account.

The specific details as to how "John Brown's Body" was composed are fittingly sketchy, given the collective compositional processes of slave music, but the tune is thought to have emerged from a folk hymn in the camp meeting style of the mid-nineteenth century. Musically, the plaintive folk melody and march-style rhythm of the song enabled it to spread quickly throughout the South, but when it reached the North the lyrics were considered a bit radical even for northerners who were sympathetic to the abolitionist cause. While there were many variants of the John Brown Song, Julia Ward Howell's "Battle Hymn of the Republic" attests to the catchy nature of the melody of "John Brown's Body," but also to the liberal erasure of the radicalism from which it originated.

---

70. Higginson, *Army Life*, 2.

Thomas Higginson's legacy of abolitionism was both complemented and complicated by his literary ambitions. It is true that his memoir is one of the most important records of black cultural history to emerge out of the Civil War, but it is *also* true that his project of writing was a racial exercise that furthered the distance between himself and those for whom he advocated. Unlike Higginson, John Brown's abolitionism was not anchored in a purely abstract and intellectual knowledge of African Americans and their culture. Brown lived and died in direct relationships with those he tried to liberate. It is this relational aspect of his activism that distinguishes him from Higginson. Even Frederick Douglass expressed admiration for John Brown's ruthless sincerity when he wrote:

> His [John Brown's] zeal in the cause of my race was far greater than mine—it was as the burning sun to my taper light—mine was bounded by time, his stretched away to the boundless shores of eternity. I could live for the slave, but he could die for him. The crown of martyrdom is high, far beyond the reach of ordinary mortals, and yet happily no special greatness or superior moral excellence is necessary to discern and in some measure appreciate a truly great soul.[71]

The martyrdom of John Brown resonates with a Christological aspect of slave religion during the Civil War in which Jesus was portrayed as a soldier who not only suffered at the hands of imperial power, but who willingly died in the name of freedom. The ritual theater of John Brown's execution bears strong resemblance to the events leading up to Jesus's crucifixion. John Brown faced his sentencing in the Circuit Court of Jefferson County, Charles Town, Virginia on Wednesday, November 2, 1859. After hearing his pronouncement of death Brown declared,

> Now, if it is deemed necessary that I should forfeit my life for the furtherance of the ends of justice, and mingle my blood farther with the blood of my children and with the blood of millions in this slave country whose rights are disregarded by wicked, cruel, and unjust enactments, I say let it be done.

Trial records state that after Brown's speech and sentencing, a man who was not a resident of Jefferson County offered applause, which was quickly sup-

---

71. Nicholas Buccola, ed., "The Essential Douglass: Selected Writings and Speeches" (Indianapolis: Hacket Publishing, 2016), 261. Originally published as "John Brown, An Address by Frederick Douglass at the Fourteenth Anniversary of Storer College, Harpers Ferry, West Virginia, May 30, 1881" (Dover, NH: Morningstar Job Printing House, 1881).

pressed. While the compositional origins of the John Brown song have yet to be proven, it is not difficult to imagine that the lone supporter of John Brown took his confession out of the courtroom and into the surrounding Charles Town African American community. This act of transmission would fit appropriately with the "orature" of slavery, which transmitted historical events orally and turned them into histories of mythological importance. The song "John Brown's Body" fully demonstrates this process. Slaves would have received the news of Brown's willingness to forfeit his life for theirs in the context of their cosmology, which would have engendered a relationship completely unlike that between Higginson and the men of the 1st South.

Higginson's presence was that of an abolitionist but also an observational scientist. In the first pages of his introduction, he reflected, "I had been an abolitionist too long, and had known John Brown too well, not to feel a thrill of joy at last on finding myself in the position where he only wished to be."[72] Higginson was one of the secret six who funded Brown's efforts, and while the other five sponsors fled in the wake of Brown's capture, Higginson was very visible, assisting Brown's wife during the interrogation and trial proceeding. Higginson believed that his assignment as commander was a matter of providence. He wrote, "I did not seek the command of colored troops but it sought me."[73] Higginson may have shared the popular sentiment that John Brown's insurrection was a failure, and this sentiment would have been affirmed when he was selected to serve as colonel of the regiment. However, John Brown was honored by black people in a way that would trump Higginson entirely through the composition and singing of "John Brown's Body" in his honor.

Higginson's credentials and his status as the colonel of the nation's first black regiment earned him a place in American history that is undeniable. His significance has been further affirmed in the ways that scholars have come to rely on his memoir as a primary source document. The slaves' own musical tribute to John Brown remains a salute that Colonel Higginson did not receive. Given the ways music was the primary expression of the slave's heart and soul, and considering the popularity of the "John Brown Song" during the Civil War, it is worth asking what might have been the effect of this song on Higginson's sense of confidence having arrived at the position where John Brown only "wished to be?"

As a commander of black troops, Higginson took up residence in a "special" separate quarters designated for the highest-ranking officer of the regi-

---

72. Higginson, *Army Life*, 3.
73. Ibid., 2.

ment. He lived among his regiment of black soldiers but more as a scientific observer than as a comrade. John Brown in contrast shared his farm at North Elba with members of the colored settlement nearby. Gerrit Smith was a wealthy pro-abolitionist who inherited several tracts of land from his father. In 1846 Smith opened up his land to create one of the country's first "colored settlements" made up of African Americans who had escaped from slavery. When Brown heard of Smith's project, he purchased land on the settlement to assist with the farming. He developed strong ties with those on the settlement, attending church services with the exile community. These refugees admired his strong will and courage in the fight against slavery. The patriarch of the Epps family, Lyman Epps, attended the special memorial service held on Brown's farm. At one point in the service the elderly man lifted up his voice to lead the gathering in one of John Brown's favorite hymns, "The Year of the Jubilee."[74] Epps and his family had sung this song often with John Brown. The pure tenor voice of Epps was a fitting reminder of the ways John Brown situated his abolitionism *inside* the African American freedom struggle in the creating of relationships.

The ritual, theater, and final confession of John Brown's hanging demonstrated his willingness to be a martyr for the cause of abolitionism. While many of his fellow non-violent abolitionists scrambled to disassociate themselves from what the general public perceived as a fanatical radicalism, others helped to manufacture Brown's status as a martyr. At the hour of John Brown's hanging church bells were rung across the nation from New England to Kansas, and several clergy used Brown's final words in their homilies and sermons.[75] Higginson noted the consistent singing of the John Brown song throughout the regiment. Nonetheless, despite his sense of entitlement to interpret the cultural activities of the regiment, he drew no real connection as to the "why" and "how" of the song's function in the lives of the soldiers. Higginson wrote about the insurrections of Denmark Vesey and Nat Turner, but the construction of masculinity in these narratives is not detached from his own fetish of black masculinity. John Brown's achievement in such a high place in the pantheon of anti-slavery revolutionaries was not simply a signification on race, but it also signified on blackness and masculinity. As Daniel C. Littlefield writes, John Brown's "bold act capped nearly three decades of tensions between black and white abolitionists, and within the black com-

---

74. Donaldson, *A History of the Adirondacks,* 3–19.
75. Oates, *To Purge This Land with Blood.*

munity itself, about wide held views of race and slavery and about the relationship between manhood and violence."[76]

Higginson's failure to include the John Brown song in his transcribed catalogue of the regiment's repertoire is significant. For while Higginson believed himself to have occupied the position John Brown "wished" to have, the pervasive singing of the John Brown song in the regiment served as a reminder of the revolutionary bond between African Americans and John Brown. Ultimately, such a musical tribute was not made on Higginson's behalf, and the constant singing in honor of John Brown reminded him of the soldiers' affection for John Brown.

John Brown's Body lies a-mouldering in the grave
John Brown's body lies a-mouldering in the grave
But his soul goes marching on.

Glory glory hallelujah, glory glory hallelujah
Glory glory hallelujah his soul goes marching on

The stars in heaven are looking kindly down
The stars in heaven are looking kindly down
His soul goes marching on

Given Brown's own remarks in response to his death sentence, remarks that suggest political and spiritual as well as biological understandings of race, it seems that Higginson incorrectly understood himself to be where Brown "wished" to be. On the contrary, John Brown was exactly where he "wished" to be, in the heart, soul, and memory of African Americans. The phrase "his soul goes marching on" fits perfectly into the black sacred cosmology of slavery as it marks Brown's veneration. According to this cosmology, John Brown would have transitioned seamlessly to the status of an ancestor in the pantheon of black revolutionaries invoked early in the war by Frederick Douglass—names such as Gabriel Prosser, Denmark Vesey, and Nat Turner. More critical to Higginson's rivalry with John Brown is how Brown's transition from death to ancestor marks a transcendence of race, which contrasts sharply with Higginson's own implicit choice of positionality. Higginson uses race to retain racial difference, whereas Brown transcends race in order to blur the lines of racial difference.

---

76. Littlefield, "Blacks, John Brown, and a Theory of Manhood."

The veneration of John Brown was reflected in the newly composed music in the regiment. Brown could have inspired the following lyrics from the regiment's repertoire:

If you want to die like Jesus died
Lay in de grave,
You would fold your arms and close your eyes
And die wid a free good will [1st South Carolina Volunteers]

CONCLUSION

Higginson maintained a "war journal" that stands apart from his well-known published *Army Life in a Black Regiment.*[77] While there is overlap between the war journal and the published memoir they are distinct in ways that are critical to the cultural studies nature of this book. This lengthy but insightful description by Christopher Looby helps to illuminate the need to tell the story beyond the story provided by Higginson:

The diary is . . . a peculiarly uncensored record of the cultural unconscious of Civil War America: its revelations about the deep structure of Higginson's (and others') fundamental assumptions about such aspects of social identity as race, gender, ethnicity and class.

Army Life in a Black Regiment represents a modern technology of interpreting African American culture. Higginson attempts to commit to pen and paper that which his own orientalist ears and political worldview of racial difference could not translate. The tensions between sound, writing, race, and modernity collide in Higginson's memoir. Jon Cruz calls Higginson "a prototype in the terrain of American cultural interpretation," yet there are alternate ways of reading the terrain and thus interpreting what he recorded.[78] The actual cultural practices of the South Carolina Volunteers stand in sharp contrast to the picture of them presented by Higginson's Orientalism, racial fantasy, and erotic fetish. Their cultural labors reveal what is obscured by Higginson. His mode of interpretation need not be the final word on how to see and hear a black regiment. The "hidden transcripts" of history and culture

---

77. A collection of letters, correspondence, and various notes written by Higginson are maintained at the Houghton Library, Harvard University, MS Am {928}, 2–3. His "Civil War Journal" is recently published in Looby, *The Complete Civil War Journal.*

78. Cruz, *Culture on the Margins,* 149.

encoded in the regiment's practices of soldiering and sacred singing reveal the humanity of the soldiers and their community.[79]

Thomas Wentworth Higginson's *Army Life* has been a critically important primary source for scholars across the disciplines. Other diarists, such as Laura Matilda Towne, Charlotte L. Forten, and William Francis Allen, published accounts of their long-term visitations to the Sea Islands. While their descriptions were not as detailed as Higginson's, their accounts will be engaged in the coming chapters. Higginson's description of the ring shout stands out among these historical documents for two reasons that hold significance to this book. First, *Army Life* is the primary record of the 1st South Carolina Volunteers, which requires a deference to Higginson's record as a primary source document. And second Higginson, unlike Forten, Towne, and Allen, was not only an abolitionist, but he was also a credentialed literary intellectual, which granted him a farther reach of literary readership and cultural authority more so than other diarists. His reach and authority continued even after the war when he published the work of Emily Dickinson posthumously in 1890.

Higginson's own intellectual pedigree and his record of witnessing continue to situate him within the academic production of knowledge. And yet, this location is *not* where John Brown wished to be. Inside the songs created and sung by black soldiers and the struggle that produced them was precisely where he wanted to be, embraced in the hearts and minds of those alongside whom he fought. As John Brown lived on in the singing of the regiment, his presence was part of a cosmology that was reflected in the regiment's religiosity, which emerged from the ability of African Americans to mix several religious frames simultaneously in pursuit of a freedom that demanded an end to slavery in *this world* but embraced a cosmic vision freedom beyond its material and legal dimensions. Higginson's interpretive comments framed African American religion as static, fixed, and bound by the categories of denomination and doctrine. Indeed, Africans in America embraced the structures of Christianity imposed on them. However, these same Africans improvised on the structures of Christianity by demanding justice and freedom "now," while at the same time conjuring their ancestors for spiritual militarism.

It was not mere coincidence that the freedom-fighting "soul" of John Brown was summoned in the singing of the 1st South (and other black regiments): the John Brown song was given a marching tempo, which denoted tribute and spiritual militancy. To Higginson's eye, the religion of the regiment could only exist as either the master's religion or not. But the regiment expressed an African American religion that was both/and, for they conjured

79. Scott, *Domination and the Arts of Resistance.*

Jesus as a "mighty man" that no man could hinder. The regiment turned a military march into a freedom march and called it "John Brown's Body."

Even as the Sea Islands community celebrated the limited freedom of legal emancipation, a "cosmic vision of freedom" was being forged as religion, soldiering, and singing were blended to conjure the militant spirit of John Brown on behalf of black freedom. The regiment's installation of black religion was not merely a black version of white Christianity. The creative and dynamic tradition of African American religion was enabled by Black Communal Conservatories, the "invisible institutions" of black musicking that house the often hidden transcripts of wisdom, similar to the *konesans* of Haitian Vodou. On record, and in the eyes of a benevolent state, they were granted membership in the Union army, but they referred to themselves as "a gospel army."[80] But to *become* a "gospel army" the regiment met nightly in the ring shout where they engaged in a "collective will to conjure."

---

80. Higginson, *Army Life,* 41.

CHAPTER 2

The Collective Will to Conjure

Religion, Ring Shout, and Spiritual Militancy in a Black Regiment

The God of the white man inspires him with crime, but our God calls upon us to do good works. Our God who is good to us orders us to revenge our wrongs. He will direct our arms and aid us.

—DUTTY BOUKMAN, *VODOU CEREMONY, HAITIAN REVOLUTION*[1]

But when I reflect that God is just, and that millions of my wretched brethren would meet death with glory—yea, more, would plunge into the very mouths of cannons and be torn into particules as minute as the atoms which compose the elements of the earth, in preference to a mean submission to the lash of tyrants, I am with streaming eyes, compelled to shrink back into nothingness before my Maker, and exclaim again, thy will be done, O Lord God Almighty.

—DAVID WALKER, *APPEAL TO THE COLORED CITIZENS*

If each of us was a praying man, it appears to me that we could fight as well with prayers as with bullets, for the Lord has said that if you have the faith even as a grain of mustard-seed cut into four parts, you can say to the sycamore-tree, Arise, and it will come up

—CORPORAL THOMAS LONG, 1ST SOUTH CAROLINA VOLUNTEERS[2]

I mean to fight de war through, an' die a good sojer wid de last kick, dats *my* prayer

—NAME UNKNOWN, 1ST SOUTH SOLDIER[3]

---

1. Dubois, *Avengers of the New World*.
2. Higginson, *Army Life*, 198.
3. Higginson, *Army Life*, 19.

Ride in, kind Saviour
No man can hinder me
O, Jesus is a mighty man!
No man can hinder me
We're marching through Virginny fields
No man can hiner me
O, Satan is a busy man
No man can hinder me
And he has his sword and shield
No man can hinder me
O, old secesh done come and gone!
No man can hinder me

—1ST SOUTH CAROLINA VOLUNTEERS, "RIDE IN, KIND SAVIOUR"

DURING THE first Great Awakening in the first half of the eighteenth century, masses of enslaved Africans converted to Christianity.[4] Through their embrace of the Old Testament narrative of Exodus and the promises of deliverance in the New Testament book of Revelation, slaves expressed an action-oriented hope that the nation would one day be purged of slavery, that America would become the New Jerusalem of biblical prophecy. The Civil War seemed to them to be the moment of decision and resolution of the contestation between a purportedly Christian nation and its enslaved population. They believed that God had sanctioned the war as the means through which the captives would be set free.

The introduction (and imposition) of Christianity in the slave quarters was central to the history of the U.S. and to the history of African American religion. Slave owners deployed the Christian religion as a form of social control over their chattel, but the slaves attempted to transform the religion they had been given into a means of envisioning, enabling, and enacting their liberation. Drawing on Afro-diasporic beliefs about the importance of willingness and work, they collectively conjured a religion that transcended the slave owners' conventional religious categories, structures, and denominations. Enslaved Africans summoned the spirit as a source of empowerment in the struggle for freedom. The religion that was intended for the slave's destruction had been radicalized for their reconstruction.

The slave rebellions and revolutions enacted throughout the African diaspora demonstrated a collective yearning to be free. As government officials and abolitionists debated whether they should arm black soldiers to fight for

---

4. Raboteau, *Slave Religion,* 66.

the Union, they could not help but be aware of the histories of armed and organized insurrections incited by slave eschatology: an imagined and active intention to "end" slavery through life-risking violence. Slave eschatology held that in the divine will of God all should be free. Yet that did not mean they should wait for this end to be delivered to them. Instead, the slaves believed they had to take action to bring about freedom and trust God to show up and empower them for a victorious outcome. In particular, as Gayraud Wilmore argues, the "pervasive radicalism just under the surface of black religion in the antebellum period"[5] expressed a self-activating "spiritual militancy." Similarly, Robert Farris Thompson describes a "fiery militance of the *vodun* realm" and the "spiritualized militancy" at work in the "attack medicines" of Bas-Zaire. Joseph Murphy extends this idea further in his discussion of Rastafarianism's "eschatological militancy toward the sinners against Africa."[6] The regiment creatively blended Christian theologies cultivated in slavery, themes of nation and liberty from the civil war, their African cosmology, and the nation's military structure to express an African American religion that demanded justice through military means. At the same time, the creator God, the spirit, and the ancestors were integrated into a cosmology that constituted a cosmic vision of freedom that was both here and now and beyond.

In their pursuit of a cosmic vision of freedom, the 1st South drew on this diasporic spiritual militancy in their collective conjuring of *ashé,* the power to make things happen. "Spiritual militancy" in this case combined spirituality with militarism to form a supernatural weapon that enabled the regiment to identify itself as the "gospel army" of the Civil War. Even Frederick Douglass, in his crusade for black Civil War soldiers, invoked the lineage of "glorious martyrs" in his famous speech, "Men of Color, To Arms!" Douglas asked his listeners to "Remember Denmark Vesey of Charleston; remember Nathaniel Turner of Southampton; remember Shields Green and Copeland, who followed noble John Brown . . ."[7] The common link between these "glorious martyrs" and the regiment was an organized militarism based on the spiritual force of religion. Given the close proximity between Vesey's plot in Charleston and the regiment's campground in Beaufort, Douglass's invocation of Vesey would have particular resonance to their own spiritual militancy. For it was Denmark Vesey, along with his co-conspirator Gullah Jack, who plotted and assembled an army of approximately "3,000–9,000 blacks ready to move on signal."[8] Echoing Douglass, Gayraud Wilmore describes Gabriel Prosser,

5. Wilmore, *Black Religion and Black Radicalism,* 69.

6. Thompson, *Flash of the Spirit,* 180; Murphy, *Working the Spirit,* 231–45.

7. Douglass, "Men Of Color, To Arms!," 527.

8. As quoted by Wilmore, *Black Religion,* 60.

Denmark Vesey, and Nat Turner as "Three Generals in the Lord's Army," a historical caption that corresponds with the regiment's self-identification as a "gospel army." When viewed in the African American tradition of spiritual militancy, the 1st South was the gospel army with Prosser, Vesey, Turner, and even John Brown as their gloriously martyred generals.

The religious sentiment voiced in the epigrams of this chapter by Dutty Boukman, David Walker, and Corporal Thomas Long of the 1st South locate the struggle for freedom in a "collective will to conjure" the spirit as a resource for a military mission. For Africans scattered throughout the New World, a variety of religious experiences have been central to creating cultures of resilience and resistance. The surveillance and supervision of the southern plantation regime did not allow African religious systems to survive in their entirety. This did not mean, however, that all traces of an African past or the enduring African-derived practices in the present were completely suppressed.[9] The collective and creative use of African derived religiosity by the members of the 1st South Carolina volunteers involved both determined African retention and dynamic New World invention. Albert Raboteau explains that the Africanisms that constitute the black religious tradition "have continued to develop as living traditions putting down new roots in new soil, bearing new fruit as unique hybrids of American origin."[10] Despite the traumatic break of the Middle Passage, Africans in America retained and further developed religious sensibilities and perceptions celebrated collectively in song, drum, and movement. As it was the case throughout the Black Atlantic, Africans in North America employed a diverse mix of folk, institutional, and traditional religions in their attempts to "make sense" of their existence.[11] Charles Long notes that the tripartite dynamics of New World democracy, black bondage, and religious violence meant that "the slave had to come to terms with the opaqueness of his condition and at the same time oppose it. He had to experience the truth of his negativity and at the same time transform and create *an-other* reality."[12]

During the Civil War, slaves became soldiers in a way that was guided by this tradition of opposition (i.e. slave insurrections). They transformed a conventional Amy unit into a "gospel army," one that relied on a collective

---

9. The following scholars have mediated the presence of *Africanisms* in the New World: Herskovits, *The Myth of the Negro Past*; Frazier, *The Negro Family in the United States*; Barrett, Soul-Force; Levine, *Black Culture and Black Consciousness*; Sobel, *Trabelin' On*; Asante, *The Afrocentric Idea*; Murphy, *Working the Spirit*; Pitts, *Old Ship of Zion*; Gomez, *Exchanging Our Country Marks*. Ultimately I agree with Albert J. Raboteau that "homogeneous African cultures were transmitted to the New World" (*Slave Religion*, 328).

10. Raboteau, *Slave Religion*, 4.

11. Long, *Significations*.

12. Long, "Perspectives for a Study of African-American Religion," 27.

will to mix and combine the diverse regional and religious experiences of its members. Echoing Catherine Bell's discussion of ritual, the regiment's ring shout activities served as an integration of thought and action.[13] The mustering of the 1st South into the Union army was part of the politicking of President Lincoln, who understood the outcome of the war in transactional and *ordinary* legal terms. But for those black men and women who enlisted in the 1st South, religion and music conjured the spirit for *extraordinary* means. Black soldiering embraced traditional notions of masculinity and valor, but it also meant becoming a "gospel army" where they conjured the spirit for combat. The presumed incongruences between the enslaved African's embrace of Christianity, the ways in which this embrace could be a source of militant revolution, and the collective will to demand freedom for themselves as well as others "throughout the civilized world" are the elements that explain how the ring shout functioned as a ritualistic site of making sense in a senseless world.[14] In this sense "ritual," as Jonathan Z. Smith writes, "gains force where incongruency is perceived and thought about."[15] The will to meet "night after night" in the ring enabled a collective will toward "one-ness" to serve the goal of freedom.

Challenging Frederich Nietzsche and Michel Foucault's familiar discussion of the dangers latent in a "will" to power, Andrius Bielskis argues that the creation of meaning is an important product of the will. He explains that "meaning is the will. . . . The social world is not only about power relations, it is also about human solidarity and empathy."[16] A collective will to conjure pervaded the actions of the 1st South. The *collective will to conjure* is defined here as the communal pursuit of ultimate meaning and purpose by summoning *ashé*—the supernatural power to make things happen.[17] Theophus Smith describes conjure as "a magical means of transforming reality." Similarly, Yvonne Chireau argues, "Magic is a particular approach or attitude by which humans interact with unseen powers or spiritual forces." Conjure, with magic as its basis, enabled the regiment to make collective and creative use of spiritual forces to transform or empower their military actions on the road to freedom. Music

---

13. Bell, *Ritual Theory, Ritual Practice.*

14. "Address of the Colored State Convention to the People of the State of South Carolina." State Convention of the Colored People of South Carolina. *Proceedings of the Colored People's Convention of the State of South Carolina.* Zion Church, Charleston, November, 1865 (Charleston: South Carolina Leader Office, 1865), 23–26.

15. Smith, *To Take Place,* 109.

16. Bielskis, "Power, History and Genealogy."

17. My discussion of conjure and that of *"ashé"* here is informed by the following scholars: Thompson, *Flash of the Spirit*; Smith, *Conjuring Culture*; Murphy, *Working the Spirit*; Albanese, *America Religions and Religion*; Chireau, *Black Magic.*

functioned in the regiment as a form of magic. Specifically, the singing of the soldiers was an intentional act of conjuring the spirit through sound. In their responses to the racist and dehumanizing realities of slavery, enslaved Africans recreated collectives that used a variety of religious expressions to summon their African deities and reconnect to their ancestors. They created a sense of community that would retain Africa as an anchoring symbol.[18] They conjured the spirit as a way to undermine the bondage of colonialism on the mind, body, and spirit. Hence, the *collective will to conjure* became a critical part of the Afro-Atlantic religious tradition of importing extraordinary power into ordinary contexts by mixing magic with diverse religious frames.[19] The enslaved Africans' endeavor to confront and transcend their condition was concerned with summoning the spirit in such a way that would result in an encounter with what Charles Long, reflecting on Rudolf Otto, called the *mysterium tremendum*. For slaves, the eschatological tone of the Civil War mandated human "manpower," but it also required that "supernatural" power, which was called forth in the collective conjuring of Old World Gods, New World Deities and Saints, and ancestral spirits. Seeing the Civil War as a Holy War, the regiment used the ring shout as a circle of conjure that would result in form of "collective effervescence" as a strategy of spiritual militarism.[20]

> Last night I was at the "Praise House" for a little time and saw Miss Nelly reading to the good women. Afterwards we went to the "shout," a savage heathenish dance out in Rina's house. Three men stood and sang, clapping and gesticulating. The others shuffled along on their heels, following one another in a circle and occasionally bending their knees in a kind of courtesy. They began slowly, a few going around and more gradually joining in, the song getting faster and faster, till at last only the marked part of the refrain is sung and the shuffling, stamping, and clapping get furious.[21]

Laura M. Towne, a northern educator and abolitionist peer of Higginson, recorded the above description of a ring shout at the "praise house." Early in her diary Town described the ring shouts she witnessed as "the remains of some old idol worship."[22] Towne's use of terms like "savage," "heathenish," and "idol worship" correspond with the literature produced by northern white visitors to the Sea Islands. As discussed in the previous chapter, their

18. Stuckey, *Slave Culture*. Also see Long, "Perspectives."
19. Joyner, *Down by the Riverside*.
20. Durkheim, *The Elementary Forms of Religious Life*.
21. Towne, *Letters and Diary of Laura M. Towne*, 23.
22. Ibid., 20.

way of seeing and hearing was racially particular. Colonial white Christianity underpinned "how" they saw the religious and cultural practices of African Americans. However, this perception was not the truth of black religiosity and cannot be taken for granted. The collective will to "conjure" in the ring shout was not in conflict with African Americans' embrace of Christianity. The ring shout was a primary means by which black people Africanized Christianity. Chireau illustrates this in her discussion of magic and conjure, "from slavery days to the present, many African Americans have readily moved between Christianity, Conjure, and other forms of supernaturalism with little concern for their purported incompatibility."[23] Conjuring the spirit through song and dance may have conflicted with the diarists' religious sensibilities, therefore they had to describe what they saw in terms of "civilization." And yet, in the context of black religion the ring shout is a critical aspect of what Albert Raboteau describes in naming black sacred practices as "danced religions."[24]

Although Afro-Atlantic religious history often proceeds through isolated inquiries about Christianity, Islam, and "other" religions, these divisions do not capture the "syncretic complexity" of Black Atlantic religiosity.[25] Charles Long observes that "the religion of any people is more than a structure of thought; it is experience, expression, motivations, intentions, behaviors, styles and rhythms."[26] The diverse regional religiosity of the 1st South Carolina Volunteers produced religious polyrhythms as well as musical ones. Multiple religious expressions coexisted simultaneously but unevenly. The presumption of black religion as univocally Protestant has parallels to the reliance on the downbeat in European music criticism. Just as black music cannot be heard productively without acknowledging its polyrhythms, the religiosity of the 1st South needs to be approached as a kind of syncopation with hidden beats and rhythms that might be obscured by listening only for the downbeat. The solders' willingness to use the ring shout to conjure their regional religious histories through gesture, song, and rhythm coincides with what Rachel Harding describes as the ways enslaved Africans "absorb, carry, wrestle with, and yield to the history and its ghosts, the experience of slavery and survival that sustains an ancestral connection to Africa."[27] This absorption and wrestling with the past and present produced a way of knowing in which the present is both haunted by the past and filled with a determining but disciplined hope. The regiment's diverse religiosity constituted an embodied knowledge, a com-

---

23. See Chireau, *Black Magic*, 12.
24. Raboteau, *Slave Religion*, 13.
25. Gilroy, *The Black Atlantic*.
26. Long, *Significations*, 7.
27. Harding, "É a Senzala."

munal epistemology in which blended religious experience took precedence over discrete religious identities and the strict doctrines attached to them. Their vision was both otherworldly and this-worldly, aiming to change the order of the present world while embracing a cosmological view of the universe that included the spirits of the living dead. The regiment's regular return to the ring, "night after night," as Higginson writes, is a performance *strategy* of ritual and music, critical to their practice of envisioning and enacting freedom. Of course, the discipline of military life aims to create docile and obedient bodies, but in this case the regiment's nightly ring shout entailed what Michel de Certeau describes as the "manipulation of power relationships that becomes possible as soon as a subject with will and power can be isolated."[28] The ring shout became the place and the practice through which the soldiers managed and made meaning of the war, the history of slavery, and freedom dreams for the future.

THE FELLOWSHIP OF THE RING

The circle enlarges, louder grows the singing, rousing shouts of encouragement come in, . . . "Wake 'em, brudder!" "Stan' up to 'em brudder!"— and still the ceaseless drumming and clapping, in perfect cadence, goes steadily.

—THOMAS WENTWORTH HIGGINSON, *ARMY LIFE IN A BLACK REGIMENT*

A drum throbs far away in another—wild killdeer-plover flit and wail above us, like the haunting souls of dead slave-masters—and from a neighboring cook-fire comes the monotonous sound of that strange festival, half pow-wow, half prayer meeting, which they only know as a "shout." . . . The hut is now crammed with men, singing at the top of their voices, in one of their quaint, monotonous endless negro-Methodist chants, with obscure syllables recurring constantly, . . . all accompanied with a regular drumming of the feet and clapping of the hands, like castanets . . . inside and outside the enclosure men begin to quiver and dance, others join, a circle forms, winding monotonously round some one in the centre; some "heel and toe" tumultuously, others merely tremble and stagger on, others stoop and rise, others whirl, others caper sideways, all keep steadily circling like dervishes; spectators

---

28. de Certeau, *The Practice of Everyday Life*, 36.

applaud special strokes of skill. . . . And this not rarely and occasionally,
but night after night . . .

—THOMAS WENTWORTH HIGGINSON, *ARMY LIFE IN A BLACK
REGIMENT*

The ring shout and the music-making practices of the regiment attest to a
range of religious expressions at work simultaneously. They provide an ideal
site for examining the combination of diverse religious sensibilities—the tex-
tures, sensations, rhythms, and choreographies—embodied in the communal
religious ceremonies of an exiled people. The ring shout promoted a dynamic
capacity for religious improvisation and, as such, it functioned as an expansive
sanctuary that embraced the regional and religious diversity of the regiment
whose enlistees came from diverse locations that were immersed in particular religious affiliations. The African's encounter with the colonial religious
doctrines and denominations created particular histories that are animated
through performance. In his discussion of "circum-Atlantic" performance
Joseph Roach argues, "performances so often carry within them the memory
of otherwise forgotten substitutions—those that were rejected and, even more
invisibly, those that have succeeded."[29]

The African syncretic religions of Cuban Santeria, Brazilian Candomblé,
and Haitian Vodou, as well as Africanized Christianity in America, all have
in common the ceremonial combination of song, dance, and drum. The West
African tradition of counterclockwise dance, song, and drum (percussion
broadly considered) embodied in the "ring shout" aimed to bring the *orishas*
into human presence. The ring shout functioned as a primary vehicle for the
"collective will to conjure" throughout the African diaspora. The diasporic
currents of black religion as ritualized in the ring shout meant that multiple
religious frames coexisted. In this instance, elements from Islam and Christianity were syncretized as Africanisms: "She kneel down on duh fib. She bow
uh head down tree time and she say 'Ameen, Ameen, Ameen.'"[30]

Higginson's memoir and other published diaries by northern visitors contain clues that African Americans had the capacity to embrace many religious
expressions simultaneously. Higginson framed his descriptions of his troops
in Orientalist terms, not recognizing that the Islamic terms he deployed
described a people whose history contained actual connections to Islam, especially in the Georgia Sea Islands. The worldview of the 1st South encompassed
Islam, herbal-faith practices, Protestantism, and Catholicism, all of which had

---

29. Roach, *Cities of the Dead*, 5.
30. Patience Spaulding, as quoted in Austin, *African Muslims in Antebellum America*, 98.

already been blended together in the Afro-Atlantic religion of the Sea Islands.
The varied religious expressions among enslaved Africans contained anchoring commonalities rooted in ceremonial, ritualistic, and religious approaches
to what Joseph Murphy calls "working the spirit." Percussive music and choreography combined to make the spirit's presence felt and known. The spirit
is "worked" in ceremony and ritual in order to "empower the community and
praise the spirit."[31] The 1st South Carolina Volunteers reveal themselves as a
microcosm of the larger "circum-Atlantic" practice of sense-making, as they
combine song, drum, and dance to conjure the spirit. Circum-Atlantic practices were not only the result of syncretic expressions of Catholicism and/or
Protestantism, but Islam is part of the repertoire of African diasporic religion.
While diarists such as Higginson and Towne would not have recalled the history of Islam in the lives of enslaved Africans in the Sea Islands, their use of
terms such as "Mohammaden" and "beads" suggests the lasting influence of
Islam on Sea Island culture.[32]

Edward Curtis's *Encyclopedia of Muslim American History* related that one
Mohammed Ali ben Said joined the 54th Massachusetts Colored Regiment
of Volunteers in 1863 and was mustered out in South Carolina in 1865.[33] It
is also quite likely that among the "rebels of guerillas" on St. Simon Island
were descendants of a Muslim patriarch named Salih Bilali.[34] Bilali, a Muslim slave who lived and worked on Sapelo Island during the mid-nineteenth
century, was recalled in several WPA interviews under President Roosevelt's
"New Deal" project from 1936 to 1938.[35] In terms of creating an archive of
slave narratives, the oral histories collected as part of President Roosevelt's
Works Progress Administration project document the variations of Bilali's
name. Given the ignorance of Islamic slave names that was common among
whites, it is not surprising this would happen. Still, Bilali is the most consistently traceable version of the patriarch's name. He is taken up here because
his family was remembered by their distinctive *dress,* religion, and language.
Georgia Conrad, a white Sea Island neighbor, wrote:

> On Sapelo Island near Darcen, I used to know a family of Negroes who wor-
> shipped Mohamet [*sic*]. They were tall and well-formed, with good features.

---

31. Murphy, *Working the Spirit,* 7.

32. See Higginson's description: "Their whole mood is essentially Mohammaden," (*Army
Life,* 41) and Towne's: "She was enchanted with the beads 'Miss Rosie' sent her . . ." (*Letters and
Diary,* 212).

33. Awad and Curtis, IV, "Autobiography," 73.

34. Higginson, *Army Life,* 213.

35. Savannah Unit of the Georgia Writer's Project (WPA), *Drums and Shadows.*

They conversed with us in English, but in talking among themselves they used a foreign tongue that no one else understood. The head of the tribe was a very old man named Bi-la-li. He always wore a cap that resembled a Turkish fez.

Higginson could not have known that the exotic Islam he read about in other parts of the world had already existed in America for nearly two centuries. The very soil on which he stood in South Carolina had been tilled by Muslim slaves.[36] The enslavers' ignorance of Islam did not erase the slaves' cultural memory of Islamic practices, nor did it prohibit the creative means by which Muslim slaves maintained their distinctiveness. As revealed in the testimony by Conrad, clothing played a key role in the ways Muslim slaves expressed their religious identity, particularly through coverings. One of Bilali's great-daughters, Katie Brown, remembered her grandmother wearing a white veil that hung loosely around her shoulders.[37] In addition to the gendered distinctions of the veil and fez, African Muslims were also distinguished by the wearing of turbans, which represented various levels of clerical status. As Sea Island Muslim slaves maintained the distinctions of Islamic dress across generations, Laura Towne's special attention to the "grand turbans" suggests the blending of Muslim attire within black Protestant culture. The prior presence of turbans may well have influenced the head wrap culture of black women in the Sea Islands, as "women, old and young, quite commonly wear kerchiefs around the head and tied at the back."[38]

The distinctiveness of enslaved African Muslims was noted in the ways they were placed within the hierarchy of the slave system. For example, the Muslim patriarch Bilali was strategically placed in the position of "driver" because of the ways Muslims were noted for their discipline and character.[39] Sylviane A. Diouf writes, "There is some indication that the Muslims succeeded in the slave structure, that they were promoted and trusted in a particular way. Both Bilali and Salih Bilali, for example were drivers."[40] According to James E. Bagwell's biography of plantation owner James Hamilton Couper, Bilali, to whom Couper referred simply as "Old Tom," was the "head driver. A

---

36. Austin, *African Muslims*, 29.

37. Diouf, *Servants of Allah*, 75.

38. Herskovits, *The Myth of the Negro Past*, 140.

39. Austin, *African Muslims*; Turner, *Islam in the African-American Experience*; Diouf, *Servants of Allah*; Gomez, *Exchanging Our Country Marks*.

40. Diouf, *Servants of Allah*, 102.

man of superior intelligence, he was the son of a prince of the Foulah tribe in Africa. . . . He had been a strict Mohammedan."[41]

Between 1720 and 1740 South Carolina witnessed its longest period of unrestricted slave importation, with large numbers of Africans brought from Islamic regions such as Senegal, Gambia, and Guinea.[42] The cultivation of rice in South Carolina and the importation of Africans from Islamic regions created concurrent histories of religion and economic exploitation. Diouf explains, "In the United States, South Carolina planters had a predilection toward Senegambians because of their skills in rice and indigo cultivation."[43] Thomas Spaulding's inherited commercial empire reveals evidence of these intersections of race, religion, and labor. Born in 1774, Thomas was the only offspring of one of the wealthiest families on the coast of Georgia. He developed a lucrative but diversified portfolio of crop production that included sugar, cotton, and rice, which, when combined, made for an expansive enterprise that required a specialized labor force. Spaulding personally supervised some of his slave laborers, but his second in command was an African Muslim named Bu Allah, who was considered the "patriarch of the Sapelo Slaves."[44] Sapelo Island holds the most traceable ancestry of African enslaved Muslims in the Georgia Sea Islands. Richard Brent Turner notes the many versions of Bilali's name: Bu Allah, Ben Ali, Bilali Mahomet, and Bilali.[45] The style of dress, diet, and discipline practiced by Muslim slaves distinguished them from their peers, and it was the perception of this character that caught the attention of Higginson in his observation of the regiment.

Hurrronje notes, "It was a Dutch Scholar, H. Reland, the Utrecht professor of theology, who in the beginning of the eighteenth century frankly and warmly recommended the application of the historical justice even towards the Mohammedan religion."[46] Nineteenth-century scholarly literature on Islam and Africans in America features the phrase "Mohammedan" and sometimes "Mohammetan" as a descriptor used by whites to characterize enslaved Muslims. Higginson uses the phrase the "Mohammedan mood." The longlasting presence of Islam in the Sea Islands did not create a homogenous Muslim identity, but the imprint left by enslaved Muslims in the 17th and 18th centuries can be discerned in several aspects of Sea Island culture. For example, in addition to the Mohammedan mood sensed by Higginson there was also his

41. Bagwell, Rice Gold, 133.
42. Rowland, Moore, and Rogers, The History of Beaufort County South Carolina, 128.
43. Diouf, Servants of Allah, 47.
44. Juengst, Sapelo Papers, 7.
45. Turner, Islam in the African-American Experience, 32.
46. Hurgronje, Mohammedanism, 14.

use of the term "dervish" ("Then the excitement spreads . . . all keep circling like *dervishes*), which has resonance with the choreographic sensibilities performed by Africans throughout the larger diaspora, especially in the syncretic Afro-Islamic version of whirling dervishes found in Morocco.[47] As Higginson writes in one of the epigrams at the beginning of this chapter:

> This hut is now crammed with men, singing at the top of their voices, . . . all accompanied with a regular drumming of the feet and clapping of the hands, like castanets. Then the excitement spreads . . . all keep steadily circling like *dervishes*.[48]

Scholars working across a number of fields including African American folklore, religious history, cultural history, and linguistics have devoted significant attention to the presence of Islam among imported Africans in the Georgia Sea Islands, specifically in South Carolina.[49] With few exceptions these studies tend to focus on readings of textual evidence that, when taken in isolation, occlude the embodied epistemological repertoire in performances of ritual and pleasure. For example, the ring shout mirrored the ritualistic counterclockwise walk around the Kaaba in Islamic ritual.[50] The customary formation of the ring shout consists of a group of singers and dancers performing *counterclockwise* in a circle, while others stand outside the circle singing and clapping, encouraging those in the ring, thereby enabling a collective conjuring of the spirit. The dance form imitates a wheel in the middle of a wheel, or a moving spiral within a circle, its circulating currents of power corresponding to the movement of the cosmos as a whole. As Robert Farris Thompson observes, "the spiral emphasis of the Kongo cosmogram moves through the ring shout."[51] While the ring was a ceremonial circle of culture with the capacity to accommodate any number of religious expressions, the dervish-like quality described by Higginson resembles the Moroccan Gnawa trance music developed originally by slaves from sub-Saharan Africa. Similar to the "spiritual militancy" of the 1st South, Gnawa musicians blend religion, ritual, music, and militarism. According to Deborah Kapchan, Gnawa musicians, also known as the "brotherhood," have a patron spirit named "Baba

---

47. Higginson, *Army Life*, 41.
48. Ibid., 41.
49. Herskovits, *The Myth of the Negro Past*; Turner, *Islam in the African-American Experience*; Wood, *Black Majority*; Stuckey, *Slave Culture*.
50. Turner, *Africanisms in the Gullah Dialect*.
51. Thompson, "Big Hearted Power," 37–64.

Mimum" who is the *Moul al Sieff*, the "master of the swords."[52] Baba Mimum is also a gatekeeper deity, similar to Papa Legba in Haitian Vodou. The Gnawa were ritual musicians imported into Morocco during the 15th and 16th centuries. Their descendants fell victim to the transatlantic slave trade. Ritualistically, Gnawa was a syncretic cult that blended African spirituality with Islamic Sufi mysticism. As such Gnawa ritual musicians were in synch with the larger ceremonial currents of the African diaspora in which song, dance, drum, and gesture served as the channels by which colonized African communities conjured the spirit for hope, healing, and transformation.

The relevance of the Gnawa ritual musicians for the 1st South Carolina Volunteers lies in their shared combinations of race, religion, ritual, and militarism and a strikingly similar repertoire of ring shout practices aimed at working the spirit that generated a wheel in the middle of a wheel. Given these choreographic ingredients, the circular character of the "whirling dervishes" in the tradition of the Sufi mystic Rumi could easily have blended into the dance aspect of the ring shout. Through their nightly engagement with the ring shout, and through the diverse religious affiliations of its members, the regiment was, like its fellow Gnawa constituents, engaging its own particular forms of syncretism. The circle of the dance as a choreographic function of syncretism is shared between the two, but for the regiment, it is not the case that one religious tradition is being fused with another, but rather a remixing of many religious elements is taking place out of the blending of the members' collective will to conjure the spirit.

In addition to the whirling dances established by the Turkish dervishes, Gnawa dervishes "whirled" themselves inside the larger "circle" procession with an additional group singing, clapping, dancing, and encouraging the dervishes who, along with the drummers, invoked a trance state of possession.[53] The common properties between the Gnawa ritual musicians and the ring shout in the regiment share West African uses of drum, song, and dance. In addition, both the regiment and Gnawa constitute male performing ensembles. The Gnawa musical tradition existed before their enslavement in Morocco, and while historical evidence does not suggest that this specific tradition (at least by name) was imported into the New World by Africans from the sub-Saharan regions, this absence of evidence does not negate the ways the soldiers' ring shout allowed for a dance that led to trance. The dervish signification on the Sufi-trance dance was being deployed elsewhere by Africans in Morocco who, like their North American counterparts, were engaged in

---

52. Kapchan, *Traveling Spirit Masters*, 116.
53. See Hunwick, "*The Religious Practices of Black Slaves.*"

the *collective will to conjure* that used the multiple points of contact available to them.[54] The emphasis on the collective aspect in this section corresponds even further with the "brotherhood" dimension in the Gnawa tradition, which constitutes a mystical healing sect in the Afro-Morrocan Islamic practice. Furthermore, the intersection of music, spirituality, and masculinity has generalizable significance.

Islam exerted influence on Gullah culture. Higginson made note of the regiment's speech dialect as evidence of Gullah influences, but did not know that Gullah culture is a densely textured worldview that permeates all of life. William S. Pollitzer reveals the influence of Islam on Gullah language, "Islamic influence is present in several words. . . . Various African legends enrich Gullah names: *Akiti* is a famous hunter in Mandinka folkore who, by conquering the elephant, became king of the bush."[55] The "cosmic vision of freedom" of the 1st South Carolina Volunteers embraced an "earthly" idea of goodness, one that complemented the established expressions of religion. The soldier's cosmic sense of freedom was enriched by the historic presence of Gullah culture on the Georgia Sea Islands. As Higginson observed, "Their philosophizing is often the highest form of mysticism; and our dear surgeon declares that they are all natural transcendentalists."[56]

That he refers to the soldiers as "natural transcendentalists" in this context of healing corresponds to Higginson's connection to transcendentalist figures such as Emerson, Thoreau, and Henry James who were advocates of what Catherine Albanese describes as "nature religion." She explains, "the transcendentalists expressed their religion of nature, sometimes through solitary walks in the woods and sometimes through the gathering of like spirits in common." Specifically as it pertains to Ralph Waldo Emerson, Albanese puts forth three anchoring tenets of his published treatise on nature entitled *Nature*. Accordingly, nature was the satisfying source for all physical needs, the visual beauty of nature was a healing source for the mind and body, and lastly, nature helped to shape metaphors in language.[57] While Higginson's transcendentalism was learned via literary texts, the soldiers' embrace of nature was, for Higginson "natural." He did not see that the regiment's engagement with nature was part and parcel of an embodied knowledge framed in their cosmology.

The regiment did not require a system of doctrines and texts in order to contemplate the presence of the spirit in the natural world because their cosmology integrated nature, spirit, individual purpose, and community. As such,

---

54. El Hamel, "Constructing A Diasporic Identity."

55. Pollitzer, *The Gullah People and Their African Heritage*, 113.

56. Higginson, *Army Life*, 41.

57. Albanese, *America: Religions and Religion*, 486.

they did not invent, nor could they use, a category such as "transcendentalism." Nevertheless, their belief in a larger universal energy did not conflict with the ways they used the master's book to subvert the master's power. In order to accomplish this, an entire new way of being would have to be created. The result would be both a *new* heaven and a *new* earth. The slave-holding empire called America could become the New Jerusalem.

De Nyew Heaben and de Nyew Wol

Atta dat, A see one nyew heaben an one nyew wol. De heaben an de wol wa Been dey fus done been gone away. An de sea ain been dey no mo. Den A see God City, de nyew Jerusalem, da come down outta heaben fom God. De city Been all ready, like a bride git all ready an dress op fine fa go ta e husban. A yeh a loud boice wa come from de shrone say, "Look yah! From now on, God da mek e home wid e people! E gwine lib wid um an dey gwine be e people. God esef gwine be dey wid um all de time, an e gwine be dey God. E gwine wipe ebry teah outta dey eye. Dey ain neba gwine cry no mo. Dey ain neba gwine dead no mo, an ain nobody neba gwine git hebby haat. Dey ain neba gwine suffa no pain.

—Revelation, 21:1–4, *De Nyew Testament*[58]

And I saw a new heaven and a new earth: for the first heaven and the first earth were passed away; and there was no more sea. And I, John saw the holy city, new Jerusalem, coming down from God out of heaven, prepared as a bride adorned for her husband. And I heard a great voice out of heaven saying, Behold, the tabernacle of God *is* within men, and he will dwell with them, and they shall be his people, and God himself shall be with them, and *be* their God. And God shall wipe away all tears form their eyes; and there shall be no more death, neither sorrow, nor crying, neither shall there be any more pain: for the former things are passed away.

Brudder, keep your lamp trimmin' and a-burnin',
Keep your lamp trimmin' and a-burnin'
Keep your lamp trimmin' and a-burnin'
For dis world most done.

—1st South Carolina Volunteers, "This World Almost Done"

---

58. *De Nyew Testament.*

In traditional Christian eschatology, the book of Revelation is considered the definitive word on the "apocalypse." The book narrates the second coming of Jesus Christ, which will mark the end of "this world." In accordance with the "slave eschatology" discussed earlier in this chapter, the apocalypse is not only a matter of theology about the next world, but also pertained to "this world," a material and physical world of bondage, terror, torture, and death. The regiment's collective will to conjure drew on the tradition of black spiritual militancy to insist that another world (a New Jerusalem) was possible. In fact, the slaves' very existence as humans demanded that the world that tried to reduce them to the status of tobacco, sugar, cotton and other commodities be brought to an end. The poetics of the Gullah dialect served important purposes for that goal, especially in the regiment's words of encouragement to "keep your lamp" burning for this "world almost done." The burning lamp here captures the quality of slavery as a form of worldly darkness that imposed itself on dark people. Three hundred and fifty-eight soldiers enlisted from Georgia, which had a long rich history of black Baptist Churches who influenced Gullah culture.[59] Vincent Wimbush describes the work of recovering these historical and religious traditions as an exercise in "Reading Dark Peoples Reading the World Darkly."[60] He contends that "coming to terms" with the Gullah "scripture" does not solely concern the master's religion, but instead coming to grips with an action-oriented expansive black religious imaginary, one that produces an alternate reading of the Christ who brought light into the dark world of the Roman Empire. This interplay of darkness and light also alludes to the hypocrisy of John Winthrop's 1630 description of America as a "city upon a hill," which was taken from Jesus's Salt and Light Sermon on the Mount. To the slaves, the "big gun shoot," the 1st South's existence as the nation's "gospel army," and the songs of black singing soldiers were all signs of what W. E. B. Du Bois called "The Coming of the Lord." Du Bois captures well the sense of apocalypse expressed in the regiment's prediction that "this world almost done" when he wrote: "It was all foolish, bizarre, and tawdry. Gangs of dirty Negroes howling and dancing; poverty-stricken ignorant laborers mistaking war, destruction and revolution for the mystery of the freedom human soul; and yet to these black folk it was the Apocalypse."[61] This reality did not remove them from the paradoxes of a racist democracy, but it provoked them to insist on "freedom now," an idea that has been the driving force inside black humanity and culture for centuries.

---

59. Raboteau, *Slave Religion*, 139–40. See also Creel, *A Peculiar People*.
60. Wimbush, *African Americans and the Bible*.
61. Du Bois, *Black Reconstruction*, 84–128.

The determination to reach for fragments of an African past to create something new is an important dimension of Gullah culture and an important reason for its influence on the regiment. For Higginson Gullah culture was merely a matter of "dialect," but to the soldiers, the Gullah culture was blended into the regiment's "collective will to conjure." What we know as Gullah culture was the product of a process. As the transatlantic slave traders plundered the Central and West regions of the African continent, various tribes and ethnicities, including Djola, Wolof, Werer, Mandinga, Mende, Temne, and Ibo, created a mixed and syncretic yet distinct culture of shared language, religion, music, cuisine, textile manufacturing, and worldviews that came to be known as "Gullah." In the Georgia Sea Islands where Gullah culture touched every form of existence, folk beliefs in magic and root work coexisted alongside vestiges of Islam and versions of Christianity. The spirit could be conjured or summoned through the *creolization* of multiple sources, including natural substances from the earth. The soldiers' use of tobacco, for example, entailed conjure as a "pharmacopoeic tradition of practices."[62] The regiment's collective will to conjure drew on Gullah sensibilities of herbal folk healing, which became all that much more valuable given the army's disregard of the regiment's medical needs.

Margaret Humphreys explores the racial disparities in the medical establishment's treatment of black soldiers.[63] The few black Civil War soldiers who did receive official medical treatment were marked as abnormal and were treated as laboratory subjects—inherently diseased but perfectly suited for experimentation. The faith in herbal culture among former slaves turned soldiers was particularly significant for the South Carolina Volunteers, many of whose members came from the Georgia Sea Islands. Despite his racially essentialist leanings, Higginson made an astute observation that linked the soldiers to their climate and culture of curing when he wrote:

> But their weakness is pulmonary; pneumonia and pleurisy are their besetting ailments; they are easily made ill, and *easily cured* . . . [my emphasis].
> But then it is to be remembered that this is their sickly season, from January to March and that their healthy season will come in summer, when the whites break down.[64]

---

62. Smith, *Conjuring Culture*, 5.
63. Humphreys, *Intensely Human*.
64. Higginson, *Army Life*, 42.

They love passionately three things besides their spiritual incantations; namely sugar, home, and tobacco.[65]

Though Higginson claimed that his soldiers were "easily cured," the official medical literature collected from the bodies of black soldiers by white surgeons and nurses demonstrated that

> black soldiers in the American Civil War were far more likely than their white comrades to die of disease. Many of them entered the war disadvantaged by a lifetime of malnutrition and the immunological naïveté engendered by their rural pasts.[66]

Higginson's racial essentialism obscured any recognition of the ways the regiment's use of tobacco was an element within the larger slave herbal healing culture of the Sea Islands. In her discussion of female slaves and midwives, Deborah Gray White reveals,

> Any number of broths, made from the leaves and barks of trees, from the branches and twigs of bushes, from turpentine, catnip, or tobacco were used to treat whooping cough, diarrhea, toothaches, colds, fevers, headaches, and backaches.[67]

Along with many other northern white clerics, teachers, and activists who encountered the exotic swamp climate of the Georgia Sea Islands, Higginson held distorted beliefs about race, region, culture, and conditioning. Preexisting Enlightenment racial discourses coupled with regional lore about blacks in the Sea Islands formulated by the whites who inhabited the area shaped these views. A local physician named Langdon Cheve confessed, "I have never allowed a white mechanic or other white workman to stay on the plantation after the 20th of May," the date that Higginson declared that the "whites break down."[68] Popular and philosophical racial discourses of the nineteenth century espoused the idea of an inherent African genetic defense against the "fevers" that plagued the Sea Islands, although whooping cough led to the deaths of at

---

65. Ibid., 14.

66. Humphreys, *Intensely Human*, xiii.

67. White, *Ar'n't I a Woman*, 124.

68. James Hamilton Jr. to Langdon Cheves, November 12, 1838, Langdon Cheves I Papers, South Carolina Historical Society, as quoted in Rowland, Moore, Rogers, *History of Beaufort County*, 324.

least fifty slaves owned by plantation owner James Hamilton.[69] The pharmacopoeic culture of Gullah spirituality in the immediate Georgia Sea Islands enabled the soldiers to develop methods of self-care that combined the philosophical, practical, and spiritual. This is strongly suggested in the following comment by Higginson: "Their Philosophizing is often the highest form of mysticism; and our dear surgeon declares that they are all natural transcendentalists" (41).

~

The health of black soldiers was not a priority for the Union army. This meant that the soldiers had to take the initiative in respect to their own care. Even though the 1st South had the benefit of official surgeons in the persons of Seth Rogers, Wm. B. Crandall, J. M. Hawks, Thos. T. Minor, and E. S. Stuard, the soldiers' interaction with nature was a matter of faith, a collective conjurational spiritual practice that harked back to their slave folk culture of herbal healing.[70] Higginson considered the soldiers' use of "sugar, home, and tobacco" to be elements "beside" their "spiritual incantations." In fact these elements enabled a communal spirituality within the regiment's eclectic religious context that supported their negotiation of self-care, healing, and survival. The presence and function of the "herbalist faith healer" in Gullah culture is well documented by scholars of folklore, history, religion, and cultural studies.[71] Gullah culture treated the spiritual causes of disease and did not perceive the role of "root doctors," "conjurers," or "medicine men" as standing in conflict with their faith, since religion, magic, superstition, and conjure were "mixed up" together.[72] This is an essential aspect of Gullah culture that allows room for an expansive pharmacopoeia in the enterprise of health and wellness, one that draws reverently on the earth's natural resources as a gift to humanity. Since, in the nineteenth century, the combination of medicine, religion, and spirituality seemed contradictory to the untrained eye, "plantation journals refer to the practitioners as simply 'slave doctors.'"[73] But, just as was the case with the larger Sea Island diaspora, the will to conjure one's healing and wellbeing through the use of roots, herbs, and various other natural resources found a normal place in daily camp life activity. Although Higginson does

---

69. Ibid.
70. As documented in Higginson, *Army Life*, 207–8.
71. Pinckney, *Blue Roots*.
72. Chireau, *Black Magic*, 12.
73. Pinckney, *Blue Roots*, 49.

not draw the connection between the soldiers' self-manufactured remedies he does comment that the regiment had "learned to take care of themselves."[74]

Tobacco was a staple in black slave pharmaceutical culture. Given its role in native culture, it is likely to have been an herb earlier generations of enslaved Africans inherited from their contact with the Indians. According to Herbert Covey's comprehensive study on slave herbal and plant treatments, "Lobeli was also known as Indian *tobacco,* pukeweed, asthma weed, emetic herb, emetic weed, vomitwort, eyebright, wild tobacco or *comfort root.* . . . Folk practitioners used this plant as a muscle relaxant [emphasis mine]."[75] It is not surprising that Higginson as a Harvard trained clergyman and botanist did not associate the soldier's passions for "tobacco" and "sugar" with their religious sensibilities, since his observations were always filtered by his limited understanding of recognizable religious traditions. Nevertheless, the anxieties of war and separation from "home" make the *effects* of tobacco a likely herbal resource for such ailments. It is also worth noting that the soldiers' love of sugar was not simply a matter of its taste. Covey's study reveals "African American folk practitioners have used sugar to stop bleeding," a practice that would have certainly been useful for soldiers in battle.[76] Sugar, in the context of slave folk medicine (as well as in traditional Western medical research), has been proven to have an antiseptic quality.

That Higginson would have noted the soldier's use of sugar and tobacco is probably due in part to his early childhood interest in horticulture and his transcendentalist affiliation. This may help to explain, in part, an exchange between the surgeon and Higginson that resulted in the soldiers being described as "natural" transcendentalists. One of the founding tenets of the transcendentalist movement was its disenchantment with modernity and slavery in particular. Yet while the transcendentalists saw the divine in nature, the West African sacred cosmos permeating slave culture meant that they viewed nature as only one of many resources made available by the gods. For the self-identified transcendentalists of New England, transcendentalism was a formalized system of belief, thought, and identification, but for the soldiers and larger community of Sea Island African Americans, the elements of transcendentalism were an organic part of their worldview. As Jon Cruz writes with regard to enslaved Africans, "these natural black transcendentalists were not absorbed as partners into the institutions of utilitarian liberalism" associated with Higginson's more formal transcendentalist leanings.[77] Yet the fact

---

74. Higginson, *Army Life,* 27.
75. Covey, *African American Slave Medicine,* 102.
76. Ibid., 141.
77. Cruz, *Culture on the Margins,* 147.

that the colonel would describe them as "natural transcendentalists" suggests
the ease and normalcy with which the soldiers articulated such beliefs—even
to a white surgeon. For the regiment, tobacco and sugar were earthly elements to use in their collective will to conjure. From the Gullah cosmological perspective, the universe generously provided for their needs.[78] Gullah
culture emerged out of the struggles of New World Africans to hold on to
their cultural identity in the context of slavery. They achieved this by incor-
porating African sensibilities into daily activities, such as weaving, medicine,
agriculture, arts, work, and rituals of religion.[79] In doing so, what an outsider
would consider a mundane and meaningless task was for the enslaved African
a meditative spiritual practice. Yvonne Chireau notes that "from slavery days
to the present, many African Americans have readily moved between Christianity, Conjure, and other forms of supernaturalism with little concern for
their purported incompatibility."[80]

JESUS AND MARY IN THE "GOSPEL ARMY"

Ride in, kind Saviour
No man can hinder me,
O, Jesus is a mighty man!
No man can hinder me
We're marching through Virginny fields
No man can hinder me
And he has his sword and shield,
No man can hinder me

——1ST SOUTH CAROLINA VOLUNTEERS, "RIDE IN, KIND SAVIOUR"

In keeping with the slave's images of biblical characters, Jesus was portrayed
as a king riding on a "milk-white horse" with an abiding and unstoppable
power to lead slaves in their conquest over slavery. In the song "Ride in Kind
Saviour" Jesus is represented as a prophetic paradox: both a "kind savior" and
a "mighty man" with "sword and shield." The specific location in this spiritual is also significant. References to "we're marching through the Virginny
fields" find the regiment circling back along the trails of enslavement, a speci-
ficity that could have been initiated by any of the twenty soldiers who enlisted

---

78. Smith, *Conjuring Culture*, 143.

79. Turner, *Africanisms*. Pollitzer, *The Gullah People*, 113; Cross, *Gullah Culture in America*,
6.

80. Chireau, *Black Magic*, 12.

from Virginia.[81] With King Jesus "riding in the middle of the air" the "Gospel Army" was confident that "no man can hinder me." Certainly, the theology of slave religion embraced Jesus as the deified son of God. In the slave's experiential context it was *necessary* to reimagine Jesus in his Roman context. Although not attributed to the 1st South Carolina Volunteers, a similar version of the same spiritual supports the slave's militarized Christianity:

> He is the King of Kings, He is the Lord of Lords,
> Jesus Christ the first and last, no man works like him
> He pitched his tents on Canaan's ground
> And broke the Roman Kingdom Down[82]

These spirituals represent visual-musical themes that permeated the culture of slave resistance. One account describes an elderly slave woman preparing her Sunday dinner on a Virginia plantation in 1861. Hearing the occasional roar of the cannon, "the old 'mammy' greeted each 'boom' with, 'ride on Massa Jesus.'"[83]

Soldiers in the "gospel army," saw themselves collectively as God's agents chosen to bring about a new world order in the present, but their "spiritual militarism" involved a longer fetch of history. In the context of Afro-Christianity, biblical figures and images came to be incorporated symbolically as adopted ancestors who, when conjured, would assist the "gospel army" in their battle for freedom. Led by the soldiers who enlisted from the historic black parish in St. Augustine, Florida, the regiment's singing conjured the Catholic deity "Mary" from the pantheon of ancestors to assist them in battle, in a close analogue to the Vodou ceremony that began the Haitian Revolution.[84] The spirituals performed by the 1st South reveal the multiple layers of expression embedded in black religion. As such, a song such as "Hail Mary" expresses both the religious significance of Mary as well as the soldiers' special sense of valor.

> One more valiant soldier here,
> One more valiant soldier here,
> One more valiant soldier here,

---

81. National Archives, RG 94.

82. Lovell Jr., *Black Song*, 253. Further discussion on various versions of this spiritual are found on pages 231, 232, and 253 in Lovell's text. Unless reflected in the song quoted from the 1st South Carolina Volunteers, some quotations are taken from these pages in Lovell.

83. As documented in Wiley, *Southern Negroes*, 19.

84. Thylefors, "Our Government Is in Bwa Kayiman."

To help me bear de cross.
O hail, Mary, hail!
Hail, Mary, hail!
Hail, Mary, hail!
To help me bear de cross.

Due to his pre-Civil War abolitionist activism, Higginson prided himself as an expert on black cultural interpretation. Concerning "Hail Mary" he wrote: "I fancied that the original reading might have been 'soul' instead of 'soldier,' with some other syllable inserted to fill out the metre, and that the 'Hail Mary' might denote a Roman Catholic origin, as I had several men from St. Augustine" (152). These "several men" would have included the 196 soldiers who enlisted from Florida.[85] The "illegal" exodus of slaves from South Carolina continued into the eighteenth century when nearly one hundred slaves from St. Helena Parish arrived in St. Augustine in 1715. Hence, St. Augustine became a sanctuary for slaves seeking both religious refuge and community. But the freedom aspiration of slaves in South Carolina was not simply a matter of fantasy and escapism. As Peter Wood demonstrates in his study of the presence of Africans in colonial South Carolina from 1670 up to the Stono Rebellion of 1739, this carefully planned and well organized uprising ushered in a new era of black slave resistance. It represented "the first time in which steady resistance to the system showed a prospect of becoming something more than random hostility."[86]

These Afro-Catholics held an intense desire for religious refuge, community, and liberation that eventually evolved into the Stono Rebellion. Thus the transition from *soul* to *soldier* in "Hail Mary" had historical and religious roots. Several aesthetic dimensions of the rebellion evidenced the Kongolese-Catholic roots of its organizers. Drumming provided the call to assemble the slave army. The singing, drumming, and dancing taking place in the Civil War resonated with the practices of the Stono Rebellion more than a century earlier. As one account reveals, "They [the rebels] increased every minute by new Negroes coming to them, so that there were Sixty, some say over a hundred, on which they halted in a field and set to dancing, singing and beating drums, to draw more Negroes to them."[87] John K. Thornton explains that South Carolina slaves imported from the Kongo originated not from "the Portuguese colony of Angola (as some accounts have implied), but from the kingdom of Kongo (in modern Angola)," a country steeped in its own tradi-

---

85. National Archives, RG 94.
86. Wood, *Black Majority*, 309.
87. "An Account of the Negro Insurrection in South Carolina."

tion of Catholicism that boasted a high level of literacy, excellent schools, and a large number of churches.[88] The civil wars in the Kongo led to the development of military training spreading notable expertise in handling firearms, a specialized skill that was well documented in the follow-up reports to the Stono Rebellion. As one of only two Christian countries in central Africa, the Kongolese were quite proud of their Catholic heritage. They identified *themselves* as Christians, and evidence of their devotion in this period became visible in the high-reaching wooden crosses adorning their chapels in regional provinces such as Nsundi, which remained in use up through the twentieth century. Moreover, some reports from the Stono uprising blamed "the black Christians of the Congo" for leading the rebellion.[89]

Mark Smith takes up the specific Catholic influences of the Stono Rebellion. Drawing on previous scholarship, Smith argues that the very date of the event—Sunday, September 9, 1739—demonstrated the rebel army's identification with the Kongolese Catholic calendar. The rebels met on Saturday for "contemplation, planning, and preparation, as Saturdays, for the Kongolese, were sacred days to revere the Virgin Mary."[90] The rebels made their actual strike on Sunday, which not only coincided with the slaves' day off, but, as Smith argues, Saturday allowed them a day of preparation that coincided with their veneration day.[91] Smith draws a series of important connections between the rebellion and Afro-Catholic theologies of temporality, place, and space, since Mary would have been an ideal patron saint and/or "ancestor" to be conjured in order to provide protective intervention. Given her utility to previous generations of Afro-Catholics, Mary showed up again in the Civil War as an icon of the South Carolina Volunteers, a "gospel army" whose Catholic sensibilities were integrated into the regiment's repertoire by the soldiers from St. Augustine.[92] Reading "Mary" in this genealogical context locates the South Carolina Volunteers within the tradition set forth by the Stono Rebellion in which the regiment was linked to their Afro-Catholic ancestors' freedom dreams. Given the soldier's mixture of religious militarism and musicality, the Stono legacy also attests to the importance of music in setting the stage for moments of battle. The fervor of the Stono Rebellion was intensified by the singing, dancing, and drumming of the militants who organized the event in the West African oral tradition of "call and response."[93]

88. Thornton, "African Dimensions of the Stono Rebellion," 1103.

89. Ibid., 1103.

90. Smith, *Conjuring Culture*, 527.

91. Ibid., 513, 518.

92. Toni Morrison, *Beloved*, 36.

93. Wood, *Black Majority*, 316.

Higginson noted, "We have recruits on their way from St. Augustine, where the negroes are chiefly Roman Catholics; and it will be interesting to see how their type of character combines with that *elder* creed [emphasis mine]."[94] Here, not only does the exchange between generations suggest a mixing of musical repertoires, but the claim that the "elder creed" embraced the Catholic religious sensibilities points further to the blended quality of the regiment's project of collective conjure. Higginson's evocation of the "elder creed" equally suggests, in relation to the communally improvised song "Hail Mary," that Mary was also perceived as an orisha, occupying the role of *Yemaya*, deity of the ocean and fierce protector. Situating Mary in an African-derived pantheon of "spiritual militancy" shows how St. Augustine's soldiers integrated their regional *and* religious roots into the larger musical repertoire and ritual practices of the regiment.

The conjuration of "Mary" in the soldiers' repertoire reflects the Catholic sensibilities of soldiers originating from St. Augustine, who were part of a long tradition of Afro-Catholics and religious militia. Despite the specifics of this genealogy, however, the Catholic conjuration of Mary, the Mother of God, was not the only Mary mentioned in the regiment's repertoire. The music-making enterprise of the soldiers, both within and beyond the ring, entailed a signification on their *multiple* religious affiliations, whereby such signifying practices witnessed the invocation of iconic figures such as Mary, figures in biblical narratives such as Mary of Bethany, and of course Jesus himself, who, "as much for American slaves as he was for the author of the book of Revelation at the end of the New Testament, was a man of war."[95] In this instance, the pervasive improvising around former slave spirituals did not restrict the use of all these figures. For example, the gospel narratives of Mary and Martha was also evoked in the regiment's repertoire:

Bow low, Mary, bow low, Martha
For Jesus come and lock de door,
And carry de keys away.
Sail, sail, over yonder,
And view de promised land[96]

Higginson did not offer any detailed interpretive comments on the above lyrics, except to say that the sound of the song was "graceful and lyrical,

94. Higginson, *Army Life*, 41.
95. Callahan, *The Talking Book*, 200.
96. "Bow Low, Mary."

and with more variety of rhythm than usual."[97] What he meant by "usual" is impossible to ascertain, given the absence of any singular sonic paradigm of slave spirituals suggested on his part. Nonetheless, his specific mention of the song's "variety of rhythm" can be theorized in terms of its performative context, given the possibility that Higginson heard the song as it was being composed. But, since this song appears later in the catalogue than "Hail Mary," "Bow Low Mary" provides an example of the value of communally composed spirituals. Its raw materials come from the scene of Mary and Martha grieving at the tomb of Lazarus. The song valorizes the implosion of the tomb that gives way to Lazarus's resurrection, a musical framing that marks the end of slavery as a march toward death and points to the expectation of the outcome of the Civil War as a symbolic resurrection and new life.

In his first published autobiography, Frederick Douglass described his victory over his overseer Mr. Covey as "a glorious resurrection from the tomb of slavery."[98] The metaphoric function of the term "tomb" in relation to slavery is striking in this black Civil War context. Far more than the tomb signifying death in battle, the archetypical resting place for the dead, in a profound double signification, the subject's resurrection from the slavery of death *and from the death of slavery* is reimagined in visual detail by the presence of Mary and Martha, followed by the presence of Jesus himself when, after the resurrection, "Jesus come and lock de door, and carry de keys away." This combination of music, biblical narrative as libretto, and choreography is a symbolically staged event portraying the death of slavery. It exemplifies an embodied black biblical hermeneutics that reenacts a "ritual event" in which music functions as a sign and symbol that gives voice to the unspeakable.[99] These are performances that rescue and render visible the obscure subject. In writing their own musical score within an oral culture where such biblical narratives were heard and passed down, the soldiers understood their shared enslaved pasts as a collective Lazarus or the "communally dead." Mary and Martha were conjured through the compositional process. When read through the biblical narratives of Mary and Martha the song's significance takes on a dramatic visual quality whose aim, temporarily, is "to achieve a virtual, rather than literal" meaning of freedom awaiting African Americans after the war.[100] Given this fluid presence of women in the soldiers' ecumenical repertoire, it is important to note

---

97. Higginson, Army Life, 159.

98. Douglass, *Narrative of The Life of Frederick Douglass*, 83.

99. Marks, "Performance Rules and Ritual Structures," Uncovering Ritual Structures." Here, I draw from Morton Marks's discussion of black music and language alternating through dance to establish certain rules of performance.

100. Smith, *Conjuring Culture*, 23.

the seemingly paradoxical logic of Mary being "hailed" on the one occasion, while on another Mary (sister of Martha) is asked to "bow low." From the perspective of a typical interpretation elevating doctrinal loyalty over embodied experience and sensuality, this pairing presents a contradiction. But the earlier salutation of Mary emerges out of the particular Afro-Catholic context, while the resting place, the chamber of death is, in their imagination, a "low" place. Therefore, both are true to their respective contexts. The presence of black women within and around the regiment symbolically embodied the roles of Mary and Martha in this eschatological context.

In the ring and beyond, the Catholic sensibilities of "recruits" from St. Augustine were added and mixed along with the Muslim, Baptist, and Methodist influences of Gullah religious music, which, in terms of lyrical phrasing, had been influenced by Methodist hymns and camp meeting songs. William Francis Allen, Charles Pickard Ware, and Lucy McKim Garrison note the specific influence of Methodism on spirituals in the Georgia Sea Islands: "Such expressions as 'Cross Jordan,' 'O Lord remember me,' 'I'm going home,' 'There's room enough in Heaven for you,' we find abundantly in Methodist hymnbooks; but with much searching I have been able to find hardly a trace of the tunes."[101] Even Higginson noted the regiment's "negro-Methodist chants" sung in their nightly ring shouts.[102] The "Afro-Baptist" tradition put forth in Mechal Sobel's *Trabelin' On* includes strong data on black Baptist membership. Despite their influences and their valiant efforts, the Methodists present in the Sea Islands made less of an impact than did the Baptists, who not only outnumbered the Methodists in terms of outreach and mission work, but also counted among their members the wealthiest slaveholders. Walter F. Pitts's *Old Ship of Zion: The Afro-Baptist Ritual in the African Diaspora* traces the African influences of black Baptist ritual practice throughout the South.[103] Even more particular to Baptist success, was the absence of a hierarchical church structure and loose governance of liturgy, both of which allowed slaves to Africanize their Christianity. This freedom of structure gave rise to black societies on plantations in "praise houses" that emerged in the context of Gullah religion. Typically, a black elder was appointed as the leader responsible for rituals such as baptism and exhortation. The leader, often the elder of the community, carried out the codes of discipline. Slave culture was prone to rebellious behavior that could be dangerous to the community, so elders were responsible for monitoring lapses in moral conduct. As Margaret Washington explains in her study of Gullah folk religion, the elders of black societies were

---

101. Allen, Ware, and Garrison, *Slave Songs of the United States,* ix.

102. Higginson, *Army Life,* 13.

103. On this see also Sobel, *Trabelin' On.*

responsible for the ethical responses to "barn burning, hog stealing, Sabbath breaking and fornication."[104]

As a black religious sensibility was deeply influenced by African spirituality, Gullah religiosity blended theology from Christianity with forms of African mysticism in a way that was ceremonial, theatrical, and transcendent. The magical and miraculous imagery of biblical texts appealed to Gullah sensibilities. These permeated the cultural practices of the regiment. The connections between community, spirituality, and solidarity expressed in "spirituals" were not simply meditations on Christian conversion. Slave religious cultural practices signified on the material realities of slavery and the events of history. The song secured the memory of slavery's modes of production and the means of terror associated with forced labor. Elements such as corn, cotton, the whip, and lash were scripted into songs that ultimately remembered those "many thousands gone."

> No more peck o' corn for me,
> No more, no more,
> No more peck o' corn for me,
> Many tousand go.
> No more driver's lash for me, *(twice)*
> No more, &c.
> No more pint o' salt for me *(twice)*
> No more, &c.
> No more hundred lash for me, *(twice)*
> No more, &c.
> No more mistress' call for me,
> No more, no more,
> No more mistress' call for me,
> Many tousand go[105]

"Many Thousands Gone" represents the historical material realities in which slave music was composed. Even Higginson recognized this when he wrote, "peck of corn and pint of salt were slavery's rations."[106] Higginson included the song as part of the regiment's repertoire. Previously, Lieutenant Colonel Trowbridge wrote that the spiritual was "first sung when Beauregard took the slaves of the islands to build the fortifications at Hilton Head and Bay Point."[107] Gen-

---

104. Washington, "Community Regulation," 13.
105. 1st South Carolina Volunteers, "Many Thousand Go."
106. Higginson, *Army Life*, 169.
107. Allen, Garrison, and Ware, *Slave Songs*, 48.

erally speaking, "Many Thousands Gone" does not at all fit the unproblem-
atically Protestant identity often imposed on "spirituals." It demonstrates the
influence of Gullah culture on the regiment (as the dialect bears out), but the
song also attests to a West African sense of temporality that celebrates the end
of slavery's forms of deprivation and torture. Furthermore, the song acknowl-
edges the "many thousands gone," those lost to the labor and lash of slavery,
those who would not be crossing over into Canaan at the present time: they
are gone but not forgotten. Ultimately, the song honored the ancestors, and,
in the phrase "no more," informed them of the end of slavery. This announce-
ment included a litany of slavery's methods of oppression, e.g., "hundred lash,"
"mistress' call," "pint of salt," "peck of corn."[108]

Just as the regiment took up the ritualistic practices of Gullah religiosity, they also incorporated, along with the Islamic, Protestant, and Catholic
sensibilities, Gullah *theology* into the imagery of the music, as in the lyrics of
this song:

> I know moon-rise, I know star-rise
> Lay dis body down.
> I walk in de moonlight, I walk in de starlight
> To lay dis body down.
> I'll walk in de graveyard, I'll walk through de graveyard,
> To lay dis body down.
> I'll lie in de grave and stretch out my arms;
> Lay dis body down.
> I go to de judgment in de evenin' of de day,
> When I lay dis body down;
> And my soul and your soul will meet in de day
> When I lay dis body down.[109]

Higginson confessed that the above selection "surprised" him, writing, "with
all my experience of their ideal ways of speech, I was startled when first I came
on such a flower of poetry in that dark soil."[110] The poetic visual imagery of
the spiritual is indeed arresting. It reflects the Gullah belief that one travels
through various stations before death. The idea that the body must be put to
rest in order for the soul to travel back to God reveals the Gullah belief in a
transcendent soul that lives beyond the body.[111] In describing a funeral of two

---

108. Higginson, *Army Life*, 169–70.
109. "I Know Moon Rise."
110. Ibid., 160.
111. See Pinckney, *Blue Roots*.

soldiers, Higginson reveals how the traditional military burial rite was combined with the Gullah religious sensibility of funeral ritual:

> The men sang one of their own wild chants. . . . Just before the coffins were lowered, an old man whispered to me that I must have their position altered—*the heads must be towards the west*; so it was done—though they are in a place so veiled in woods that either rising or setting sun will find it hard to spy them [emphasis mine].[112]

Higginson's poetic phrase "veiled in the woods" reveals the ways the soldiers' songs influenced the texture of his own writing. Yet if for Higginson the "veil" of the woods is primarily a matter of concealment, for the soldiers the song expresses a visual metaphor in which the sunrise imitates the beginning of life and the setting of the sun marks its closure. The "position" of the body in this funeral scene reflects a specifically Gullah choreography of funeralizing. As documented in Elsie Clews Parsons's important collection, *Folk-Lore of the Sea Islands, South Carolina,* the soul was expected to travel to the destination of its maker:

> The "box" was placed on a farm-wagon; and the mourners followed on foot to the cemetery, a mile off—one of those ragged patches of live-oak and palmetto and brier tangle which throughout the Islands are a sign of graves within—graves scattered without symmetry, and often without head-stones or head-boards, or sticks, but invariably dug east and west, the *head to the west*.[113]

Despite the fact that these soldiers were several generations removed from their African origins, the choreographic staging of the deceased soldiers expressed the African-inspired Gullah belief that *The Sea brought us and the Sea shall take us back*.[114] It is likely that despite the generational distance, the "elder creed" may have insisted on staging the soldiers' funeral in such a way that secured their "crossing over" into the spirit world to become ancestors. The "gospel army" sang of their crossing as both an Exodus narrative, and the song of a "crossing" in the cosmic sense.

My army cross over,
My army cross over,

---

112. Higginson, *Army Life,* 34.
113. Parsons, *Folk-Lore of the Sea Islands,* 215.
114. Cross, *Gullah Culture,* 96.

O, Pharaoh's army drownded!
My Army cross over[115]

Several of the regiment's songs use the term "crossing" or "cross over" as a way of signifying on the past, present, and future. But the term "army" was further complicated and noted even by Higginson: "I hear our men talk about 'a religious army,' 'a Gospel army,' in their prayer-meetings."[116] In addition to its musicality, the phrases, "gospel army" and "religious army" are to be read in the context of the regiment's militarization of the Bible. As Corporal Thomas Long sermonized,

> It appears to me that we could fight as well wit prayers as with bullets,—for the Lord has said that if you have faith even as a grain of mustard-seed cut into four parts, you can say to the sycamore-tree, Arise, and it will come up.[117]

Given the initial failure of General Hunter's attempt to organize the South Carolina Volunteers, and the lack of recognition bestowed on the regiment even after they were officially mustered into the Union army, it is not surprising that Corporal Long chose the selected biblical text that deals with the potential power contained even within the smallest amount of faith. Long's reworking of the biblical passage from the Gospel of Matthew 17:20 demonstrates a certain rhetorical skill of oration that does not quote the passage exactly as it appears, but instead uses it more performatively as a script on which to improvise. By cutting the mustard seed into four parts, Long used the visual resources in immediate view and ignored the mountainous imagery in Matthew's version of the saying. His local imagery improvises on Luke's "sycamine tree" (Lk. 17:6, KJV), pointing to the similar-sounding *sycamore* tree that grew in abundance in the Sea Islands. The sycamore tree can stand anywhere between "seventy to one hundred and twenty feet in height," and the rich and swampy soils of the Georgia Sea Coast were ideal for their growth.[118] Here, Long sermonizes that the regiment, by putting its faith into fighting action, will rise up high like the sycamore tree.

Corporal Long's war homily is part and parcel of the regiment's collective will to conjure. He exhorts the men to a faith that "moves" objects—not simply a blind faith—but one of belief and action. The faith underpinning

---

115. "My Army Cross Over."
116. Higginson, *Army Life,* 41.
117. Ibid., 198.
118. Keeler, *Our Native Trees,* 63.

the regiment was supported by a richly diverse assembly of sensibilities held together by African syncretic religions and folk spiritualties. New arrangements of old songs, as well as new rhythms and choreography, were imported from their particular regional religious backgrounds. The diversity within this union meant that there were more opportunistic connections to access the points of power. In this instance, the regiment creolized their many religious sensibilities as the collective took priority over a single loyalty to one religious faith. The ultimate question of existence was taken up in the incantations, choreography, and polyrhythms of an army that viewed the Civil War as "one more river to cross."

Just as the blending of multiple black religious expressions was animated by the ring shouts practiced on the islands, so too was this blended quality of black religion active in the ring shout of the regiment. Accessing the spiritual power of this diversity required a conjurational strategy that mixed a variety of religious sensibilities from several backgrounds. The regiment's practices reveal that the liberation of a people was not effected by military might alone. It also involved working the spirit through a synthesis of diverse religious rituals and engagements with the sacred. The boundaries of religious identity and affiliation were both embraced and transgressed.[119] The members of the regiment brought with them to military service a variety of religious expressions, representing their diverse origins throughout the Georgia Sea Islands, and this resulted in a blended religious texture. As Higginson reflected comparatively, "The white camps seem rough and secular . . . [whereas] I hear our men talk about 'a religious army,' 'a Gospel Army' in their prayer-meetings."[120]

The Africans' attempt to make sense of the senselessness of slavery entailed a collective project in which song, drum, and movement were employed ritualistically to channel supernatural powers from ancestral spirits and gods. These rituals and the sensibilities borne out of them did not rely on any one particular doctrine or institution, but rather embodied a spirituality and immediate worldview emanating from the sensuous qualities of black religion—hearing, seeing, touching, and spirit possession. The embodied practices of song (hearing: call and response), dance (unified and improvised choreography), and drum (touch: the body's physical and intuitive relationship to the drum) opened up syncretic practices of sense-making not based on a mind/body division but on an incorporation of all of the senses.

For the approximately 10,000 abandoned slaves throughout the Georgia Sea Islands at the time of the Port Royal experiment, the quest for human

119. Haraway, *Simians, Cyborgs, and Women*, 181. Also see M. Strathern's mediation of Donna Haraway's "Partial Connections" in Strathern, *Partial Connections*.

120. Higginson, *Army Life*, 41.

meaning was taken up as a collective venture in the context of grossly unequal power relations. Meaning and power were entangled in relationships to land, property, race, religion, nation, and citizenship in the past, present, and future. The soldiers' nightly engagement with the ring shout provided the space in which to address the liminal space they inhabited and to perform the crossing between slave and soldier and person and citizen. It reimagined their community, but it also served as a means by which they sought to heal the psychic trauma of slave memories and the terrors of war. Amanda Porterfield underscores the "psychosocial dynamics" of shamanism "as a symbolic means of addressing psychological and social conflict."[121] Following Porterfield, Theophus Smith argues further for the need to recognize "corporate shamanism" in black culture as a generator of mass movements in African American history.[122] As Africans throughout the New World used the song, dance, and drum combination to conjure ancestral spirits, this "corporate" act of will also created a sense of oneness, a collective identity that fostered cooperation for the sake of community.

The making of a corporate subject required an attempt to reattach limbs of the imagined collective body. It meant refashioning a whole out of fragments, out of what had been dismembered, dislocated, and displaced by the "original sin" of the colonial encounter and the trauma of the auction block. The collective will to conjure on the part of the regiment expressed their attempt at reconciling the ambivalent peril of the Civil War, which was at the same time readable as a divinely staged event and also as an unfulfilled commitment on the part of a Christian nation to grant them their God-given freedom. Despite these mixed sentiments, a determination to participate in the making of their own freedom persisted and such determination enabled a cooperation that both embraced and transcended their regional/religious affiliations. How appropriate then that the South Carolina Volunteers would have named themselves a "gospel army," with *one more river to cross* before reaching freedom. They understood that they could not cross over simply with guns, bullets, uniforms, and material warfare alone, so they hammered out old slave songs in memory of the *many thousands gone* and those for whom there would be *no more auction block*. Summoning *Mary* and *Jesus riding on a milk-white horse*, Africans throughout the Black Atlantic would draw on their collective will to conjure when they encountered *one more river to* cross, though this river would rise many times over. The collective will to conjure in African American religion, and Afro-Atlantic religion in general, functions as an *act*

---

121. Porterfield, "Shamanism."
122. Smith, "The Spirituality of Afro-American Traditions."

of reorientation that maintains a cosmological vision of freedom. This notion of freedom is anticolonial in its embrace of "this-world" and "other-worldly" realities; it demands equitable human existence but resists being defined solely by nationalistic terms and/or colonialist conditions.

The nationalistic terms of freedom are inherently masculine, and the Civil War presented a prime opportunity by which black men could attempt to access a conventional manhood. However, the regiment's improvising of soldiering through religion and music demonstrates a divergent black masculinity that expressed an important part of their cosmic vision of freedom. The inherent connections between religion and conjure, music and masculinity are present in the regiment's lyrics, *"one more valiant soldier here, to help me bear de cross."* This phrase, which is followed by the refrain "Hail Mary," is replete with symbols and significance of religion, suffering, and soldiering. And yet, the phrase is not a text void of sound, as for the regiment singing was a serious component of soldiering. This phrase in the song, *one more valiant soldier,* is concerned with an economy of meaning: for these black singing soldiers music was not marginal to the economy of *their* military manhood, but the song was central to it. The songs of the nation's "gospel army" reclaimed the revolutionary spirit of John Brown in their constant singing of "John Brown's Body." The collective will to conjure enabled an integration of religion and revolution through music. As such, black music was key to their overall mission of black freedom because collective singing created a "Gospel army" with "more" meaning and purpose than the traditional soldier.

CHAPTER 3

One More Valiant Soldier

Music and Masculinity in a Black Regiment

Now we sogers are men—men de first time in our lives. Now we can look our old masters in de face. They used to sell and whip us, and we did not dare say one word. Now we ain't afraid, if they meet us, to run the bayonet through them.

—SERGEANT PRINCE RIVERS, 1ST SOUTH CAROLINA VOLUNTEERS[1]

One more valiant soldier here,
One more valiant soldier here,
One more valiant soldier here,
To help me bear de cross

—1ST SOUTH CAROLINA VOLUNTEERS, "HAIL MARY"

THE UNION army's chaotic occupation of the Georgia Sea Islands initially filled the slaves with fear. White northerners charged with the official task of creating the Port Royal Experiment were also assisting General David Hunter in recruiting volunteers for the nation's first official regiment of black men. Some slaves in the Sea Islands were suspicious that enlisting would result in their being sold as slaves to Cuba. Laura M. Towne, a northern educator who resided on St. Helena's Island during the Port Royal Experiment, wrote in her diary on May 5, 1862: "General Hunter has offered to arm the negroes and train them. But as they think it a trap to get the able-bodied and send them to Cuba to sell, they are not at all anxious to be soldiers."[2] Resistance to army service also emanated from fears that it would further fragment black family

---

1. *Report on the Proceedings of a Meeting Held at Concert Hall*, 22.
2. Towne, *Letters and Diary*, 38.

networks already ruptured by the long histories of the Middle Passage, the auction block, and the slaveocracy's utter disregard for familial ties. In the wake of the second attempt to establish a black regiment in the Sea Islands, northerners described scenes of children and wives clinging desperately to black males taking refuge in the woods, only to be "hunted" by Union soldiers who threatened to take them in by force. This initial fear, anxiety, and suspicion about military service reveals that joining the army was not so much a personal decision motivated by dreams of masculine military glory, but rather a political decision that developed gradually and collectively with the welfare of the entire community in mind.

When soldiers did enlist in the regiment, they could not take the meanings of masculinity and manhood for granted. For them, black masculinity could not be taken for granted, but had to be created from scratch under uncertain and perilous new circumstances. Necessity rather than ideology shaped the processes of subject formation in the black regiments. The forms of masculinity available to black men during the Civil War differed markedly from those available to white men. White men had never been slaves. They had never been called boys even when they were adults. White men could assume that men and women inhabited separate spheres, while black men and women had been treated in ways that placed them closer together than their white counterparts.[3] White men lived their entire lives in a country whose major institutions were structured to protect white male propertied power. Up until emancipation, both laws and customs deemed black men to be white men's property. White men could take for granted their own rights, identities, and interests as individuals and they constructed their military operations out of long histories of collective interactions in commerce and government. Black men found themselves forced to construct new identities as legally free men and to negotiate new social charters with other blacks and with white society at large. Negotiating a sphere of masculinity that was inextricably tied to race, nation, and citizenship entailed grief and anxiety for black soldiers and the women who were left to care for the children. As Jacqueline Jones reminds us, "Whether southern black men volunteered for or were pressed into Union military service, the well-being of their families remained a constant source of anxiety for them."[4] The music making activities of their regiments played an important role in forging the identities and fusing the solidarities needed by black Civil War soldiers to define and secure their new social roles and to help them arbitrate and negotiate the contradictions they faced.

---

3. Davis, *Women, Race and Class.*
4. Jones, *Labor of Love,* 48.

The men of the 1st South sang a song that called on each other to take on the role of "one more valiant soldier."[5] Their singing retained the solidarity and collective creativity of slave culture, but combined traditional spiritual singing with a new language of masculine soldiering that allowed for a multi-dimensional portrait of black masculinity. The category of "spirituals" in black music tends to be regarded as inherently gender neutral. Yet as Susan McClary notes, we pay a large price for not recognizing musical practices as activities that create rather than merely reflect gendered identities. McClary laments that "Music is generally regarded as neutral—a *neuter*—enterprise, again because of the desire not to acknowledge its mediation through actual people with gendered bodies."[6] The gendered bodies of the soldiers and the gendered dimensions of the racial oppression they faced inflected the music they made with challenges to prevailing gender norms. The regiment's improvising of soldiering through religion and music necessarily diverged from the scripts of race, gender, and nation and even the confines of a black masculinity that would impede their emergence as members of a newly freed yet still aggrieved and insurgent community. The divergent black masculinities that emerge reflect what José Muñoz named as the process of disidentification. In this case, the regiment combined singing and soldiering to conjure an alternate expression of black masculinity. Understanding the sonic forces that generated new understandings of gender require listening hermeneutics.[7] The vexed nature of race, slavery, and gender further complicates the role of singing in the construction of black Civil War masculinity and the musical imprint of this construction on the community at large. For example, the creation of this new black manhood involved boys and women as well. The presence among the troops of adolescent males enlisted into service as drummer boys rendered the creation of black musical masculinity as an intergenerational endeavor. In addition, because black women proved integral to black military survival and success—as evidenced by Harriet Tubman's military leadership—the soldiers created their own masculinity in dialogue with what J. Jack Halberstam calls female masculinity. Rather than simply expressing an already existing sense of latent or actual manhood, soldiers in black regiments had to create new forms of gendered affiliation and identification dialogically as they struggled for freedom and citizenship.

The Civil War held a powerful allure for young boys who aspired to make themselves into "men." Joining up with a regiment was a way for adolescents to escape from the violence of slavery as individuals, but it also compelled

---

5. Higginson, *Army Life*, 10.

6. McClary, *Feminine Endings*, 139.

7. In addition to Muñoz, *Disidentifications*, I draw from Anzaldua, *Borderlands/La Frontera*.

them to recognize their ability to author a new future for their people. When adolescent drummer boys affiliated with the regiment came across youths even younger than themselves, they greeted them with the prophetic phrase "Dem's de drummers for the nex' war."[8] The enlistment records of the 1st South Carolina Volunteers attest to the presence of young black males. They list Daniel William Wiggins, age 12; Charles Easton, age 14; John Wells, age 14; Lummas Allen, age 15; and June Hamilton, age 15.

Drummer boys comprised the rhythm section of the regimental band, but they also performed important military functions, on and off the battle-field.[9] In combat, a drummer boy was expected to drop his drum and assist a wounded soldier. Away from the battlefield, drummers set the pace for dress parades and drill exercises. The bass and snare drums helped to discipline the soldiers' bodies "in time." In addition to this military function, the drum also fulfilled a musical function as the synchronizing tenet, the emphasis on the *beat* in black music as a key to the making of a collective. John Mowitt, in *Percussion: Drumming, Beating, Striking* argues, "in possessing a body, a skin, a head, and a voice the drum has long represented the expressive interiority that we call the subject, the human being insofar as it intones 'I.'"[10] In their service as accompanists to military drills and exercises, black drummer boys enabled the "I" to become an intergenerational "we" in the regiment. Higgin-son noted the importance to the South Carolina Volunteers of what he called "grave little boys blacker than ink," describing a "jolly crew, their drums slung

---

8. Higginson, *Army Life*, 101.

9. Even after the official opening of enlistment to black men, black regiments were rarely afforded the luxuries of a regimental band. While the 1st South Carolina Volunteers was the first officially enlisted black regiment, they did not enjoy the kind of financial support that was garnered by the famed 54th Massachusetts regiment with its notable personnel and associations. Frederick Douglass, the leading black abolitionist and the most public spokesperson for the recruitment of black Civil War soldiers, was also the chief recruiter of the 54th Mass. Douglass enlisted his own sons Charles and Lewis Douglass (the latter served as the 54th's original Sergeant-Major). Special recruitment and fundraising events were held on behalf of the 54th Mass., which was being marketed as the nation's preeminent black regiment. Notable person-alities such as Ralph Waldo Emerson and Wendell Phillips gave speeches on behalf of the 54th Mass. Robert Gould Shaw, a member of the prominent Boston abolitionist family headed by Francis George and Sarah Blake-Shaw, and who would later be selected as colonel of the 54th, led a successful fundraising campaign that raised $500 to purchase instruments and instruc-tion for a regimental band. Corporal James Henry Gooding wrote, "The papers say we are to leave here the 20th. . . . We have got a band, or at least the instruments; there are fifteen men taken from the regiment to form a band." When compared with the zero dollars invested in a regimental band for the 1st South Carolina Volunteers, the nation's first black regiment, the capital raised from private (but notable) individuals and state funds reveals an investment in the representational politics of race and masculinity as continuously played out in the repre-sentational hegemony of the 54th Massachusetts regiment.

10. Mowitt, *Percussion*, 6.

on their backs, and the drum-sticks perhaps balanced on their heads. With them went the officer's servant boys, more uproarious still, always ready to lend their shrill treble to any song."[11] Similarly, Suzie King Taylor recorded a lively scene describing the playfulness of the drummer boys in the camps:

> I must mention a pet pig we had on Cole Island. . . . That pig grew to be the pet of the camp, and was the special care of the drummer boys, who taught him many tricks; and so well did they train him that every day at practice and dress parade, his pigship would march out with them, keeping perfect time with their music. The drummers would often disturb the devotions by riding this pig into the midst of evening praise meeting . . . [12]

The presence of drummer boys in the regiment gave an intergenerational dimension to its construction of black masculinity. Blessed with opportunities denied to their ancestors, the soldiers also saw by their side some of the boys who would eventually inhabit whatever form of manhood they constructed.

J. Jack Halberstam reminds us that throughout history, women contesting the practices that make agency, mastery, and subjectivity synonymous with manhood have created forms of female masculinity that challenge the isomorphism of men and power. Harriet Tubman's emergence as a woman commanding Union soldiers during the Civil War exemplifies this dynamic and reveals that the 1st South Carolina Volunteers constructed their masculine ideals in dialogue with it.[13] Even before the war, Harriet Tubman's activism as a chief architect of the Underground Railroad had already earned her a reputation for fearlessness, as well as a hefty bounty on her head in several states. Evidence strongly suggests that Frederick Douglass arranged a meeting between Tubman and John Brown in April 1858.[14] Following this meeting, John Brown paid tribute to Tubman in the pronoun he used to describe her in a letter to his son: "*He* is the most of a *man* . . . that I ever met with."[15] Tubman embodied the leadership qualities in the anti-slavery movement that had always been considered masculine. Joining the caravan of northern abolitionists who journeyed to the Sea Islands, Tubman was deployed to Beaufort, South Carolina, where she took charge of the Christian Commission House. There, she taught washing, sewing, and baking, while distributing books, clothing, food, and other supplies for soldiers. For her labor Tubman initially received $200 from

---

11. Higginson, *Army Life*, 101–2.
12. Taylor, *A Black Woman's Civil War Memoirs*, 92.
13. Halberstam, *Female Masculinity*.
14. Larson, *Bound for the Promised Land*, 157.
15. Ibid., 158.

the government and was allowed to draw rations like "other soldiers." Keenly aware of the inequities of pay for "other soldiers," she refused such privileges. Although washing, sewing, baking, and distributing supplies might seem to contain Tubman solely in a traditional domestic capacity, she was also actively involved in moments of combat as a strategist, scout, spy, and nurse.

Tubman led an expedition of soldiers from the 1st South up the Combahee River. When the expedition encountered people still in bondage, they announced to them that freedom had come. As Tubman later recalled on encountering one group, "I looked at them about two minutes, and then I sung to them."[16] Realizing that their Moses had come to set them free, the crowd joined Tubman in a call and response manner. As she stood on the shore beckoning the captives to board the ship she sang:

Of all the whole creation in the east or in the west
The glorious Yankee nation is the greatest and the best
Come along! Come along! Don't be alarmed,
Uncle Sam is rich enough to give you all a farm[17]

From the repertoire of the 1st South a similar sentiment is expressed involving water, ships, song, crossing, and freedom:

Come along, come along, and let us go home
O, glory, hallelujah? Dis de ole ship o' Zion
Halleloo! Halleloo! Dis de ole ship o' Zion,
Hallelujah!

Tubman's lyrics express an explicitly patriotic tone that is not apparent in this song by the regiment. However, the use of song to "collect" and create community is shared between the two songs in the phrase "come along." Not only does this suggest a destination, but also it enables an "us," a sense of how a notion of "we" was vital to the self-identification of members of the regiment.

Tubman's raids along the Combahee River were documented in Higginson's memoir, but he made no specific mention of Tubman, which is not surprising, given the degree to which Higginson disagreed with Tubman's "direct way of interpreting orders."[18] It may have been that Tubman's confidence about her own abilities disturbed Higginson's sense of authority. Tubman's history demonstrates how the economy of gender was in flux in the wake of the end

16. Larson, *Bound for the Promised Land*, 214.
17. Bradford, *Scenes in the Life of Harriet Tubman*, 53.
18. Bradford, *Scenes*, 217.

of slavery. Her combination of sewing and soldiering indicates how femininity and masculinity could exist along a continuum, rather than being seen as
incommensurable and opposite identities. As a woman, she performed a version of masculinity typically reserved for "men."

The new gender roles that emerged for black women during the Civil War
were not merely matters of private and personal concern. As Jacqueline Jones
argues, black women worked "to sustain family ties and preserve a vital group
culture."[19] Suzie King Taylor was one of the women engaged in that work. Born
into slavery on August 6, 1848 in Liberty County, Georgia, Taylor was fully
familiar with the sacrificial efforts black women made to maintain the bonds
of family. In her memoir she recalled:

> My grandmother went every three months to see my mother. She would hire
> a wagon to carry bacon, tobacco, flour, molasses, and sugar. . . . The profit
> from these, together with laundry work and care of some bachelor's rooms,
> made a good living for her.[20]

On an April morning in 1862, while traveling with her uncle in a rural section
of Georgia near Savannah, the Union army's attack on Pulaski, the main fortress for the Savannah harbor, provided the fourteen-year-old Taylor with her
chance for freedom. Her uncle hid her aboard a Union gunboat. As her family followed the route of exodus for slaves in the region, King-Taylor's uncle,
along with most of the men in her family, became some of the first enlistees
in General Hunter's initial but canceled experiment of black regimentation.
When the next opportunity to enlist in a black regiment arose, Taylor's male
relatives seized the opportunity. This inspired her to serve as the regiment's
official laundress and teacher. As a child-slave in Savannah, King-Taylor had
secretly defied the law to learn how to read and write. This enabled her to do
"as much teaching as washing and ironing" for the regiment. In most circumstances, the pressures of military mobilization meant that slave women had to
bear responsibility for caring for the children, the sick, and even the elderly
in isolation. King-Taylor chose to remain with members of her family while
serving in the regiment, combining her traditional familial gendered respon-
sibilities with public work alongside the men. Taylor's role in the regiment is
not reducible to a service to masculinity and manhood. Her labor was part of
the process through which soldiers constructed a military manhood based on

---

19. Jones, *Labor of Love*.
20. Taylor, *A Black Woman's Civil War Memoirs*, 26.

forms of affiliation and identification that reflected but also transcended the form of the family.

New gender roles emerging in social life were frequently first tried out, learned, and legitimated through music. For the 1st South Carolina Volunteers, music making called into existence a conservatory based on communal practices of teaching, listening, and learning, in an alternative academy from which new ideas and identities emerged. Higginson wrote that the soldiers returned to the ring shout night after night. The abundance of singing in the regiment suggests that the soldiers *listened* to themselves sing fairly consistently. The after-effect of hearing themselves singing is significant. They no longer *heard* themselves as slaves, but as soldiers transitioning further into manhood. Singing transformed the regiment into a musical ensemble in which the construction of gender was a collective venture, producing a "collective black masculinity" that was forged through collective and interactive singing.

Higginson admired the performance of his troops. "I do not as yet see the slightest obstacle in the nature of the blacks, to making them good soldiers, but rather the contrary," he wrote during the early weeks of their training.[21] Although Higginson held tightly to his racial fantasies and phobias regarding the "nature" of black people, his experiences enabled him to challenge the idea that white men alone possessed the biological and psychological properties in accord with "nature" that were needed to make men good soldiers. Had he been more attentive, he might have seen how the music of the soldiers helped equip them for their new roles. The regiment's communal process of composing and arranging repertoire represents the "oral" praxis of black song-making, a practice replete with structure, discipline, and intention. The mechanics of black musicking in the regiment—the song, dance, drum, and story—were intentionally alchemized to reflect an African retention, an African American invention, and the circum-Atlantic praxis of engendering free selves.

The device of call and response, known to musicologists as antiphony, permeated the music made in slave communities. A lead voice or instrument would "call" out a line, and the rest of the group would "respond." Repeated several times each day and every day, this practice provided participants with a model of relations between the individual and the group and between leaders and followers. The individual was always a social being, formed in relation to others. The regiment was not led by an individual expert who specialized in "conducting." Instead, an ensemble—in the communal sense of the word—

---

21. Higginson, *Army Life*, 12.

was constructed at the intersections where listening, identification, and the formation of selfhood met.[22] Voices blending together created compelling harmonies that could not be voiced by any one person. Group singing made a song proceed at a slightly irregular tempo composed collectively in the act of performance. Antiphony conceives of song and speech in dialogic ways, as an interaction that depends on both the solidarities of sameness and the dynamics of difference. Because voices are not alike, multiple and subtle harmonies are possible. A metronome can only mark out a single pulse, but humans singing together create polyrhythms, after beats, and syncopation. Although this mode of performance predates the transcribed and formal arrangements of "spirituals" in the post-emancipation era, the "musical intuition" that foregrounds this aural epistemology should not be underestimated. The collective capacity to make discriminating sounds is learned through the kinesthetic act of listening, a skill that is critical in Black Communal Conservatories.[23]

Call and response also informed relationships between expressly musical forms and other sonic sources and influences. In the black regiments, music making staged a relationship between the commands and the choreography of military drills. The *1862 U.S. Cavalry Tactics Instructions, Formations, and Manoevres* [*sic*] manual states, "The tone of command should be animated, distinct, and of a loudness proportioned to the troop which is commanded."[24] This animated tone of command served as a sonic resource to the troops, who heard it as a "call" that begged for a "response." Soldiers could call out answers to commands. They could move their feet and bodies to respond to the articulation of commands and the intervals between them. A command to march to the "route step" allowed individuals to set their own pace and to march in any order. White soldiers experienced the step as an escape from the demands of the group and the opportunity to become disassociated individuals. The black troops, in contrast, used the route step to fashion collectively new patterns of march and new rhythmic variations. For them music was a *verb* not a noun, a process not a product, an activity not an object. Listening, dancing, and singing served as nodes in an integrated network in their process of music making.[25]

Higginson's discussion of the soldiers' deployment of the "route step" provides an example of the pervasive presence and power of their choreographic impulses:

---

22. Cummings, *The Sonic Self: Musical Subjectivity and Signification*, 5.

23. Ibid., 55.

24. Cooke, "Cavalry Tactics or Regulations."

25. Small, *Music of the Common Tongue*, 50.

The "route step" is an abandonment of all military strictness, and nothing is required of the men but to keep four abreast, and not lag behind. They are not required to keep step, though, with the rhythmical ear of our soldiers, they almost always instinctively did so; talking and singing are allowed, and of this privilege, at least, they eagerly availed themselves.[26]

The regiment transformed what would have typically been a mundane exercise of military training into a sonic activity inscribed on the body. Military discipline and training are designed to dissolve individual bodies into one unit. In mastering this goal, the regiment also transcended it. As former slaves turned soldiers, the soldiers made music in a way that honored and cultivated their individuality while still authoring a collectively imagined and enacted performance. In applying Louis Althusser's concept of "interpellation" to music, John Mowitt argues that "the sonoric event of interpellation-qua-event is embodied. . . . [The] interpellative call strikes and moves the body, hailing it 'into position.' Thus, in addition to music's interpellative dimension, there is the matter of music's irreducibly percussive character."[27] Improvising on this percussive power enabled the 1st South Carolina Volunteers to create the kind of "sonoric event" that Mowitt describes. In the context of soldiering during the Civil War, the event had social as well as musical causes and consequences.

The song "Hold Your Light" exemplifies the ways in which singing helped black soldiers produce new identities that affirmed dialectically both individual and group concerns. One verse reads:

Hold your light, Brudder Robert
Hold your light,
Hold your light on Canaan's shore!

Higginson wrote that "This would be sung for half an hour at a time, perhaps *each person present being named in turn* [emphasis mine]."[28] The calling of individual soldiers' names in the song enacts a politics of time and space. For ex-slaves, owning one's own name was a source of joy. Their names were not simply being called, but through their voicing individuals were recognized as *persons,* as brothers, as members of a community. By calling out to each other in the song "Hold Your Light Brudder Robert" the men reveled in no longer being someone else's possession. Renaming themselves and each other, and repeating those names over and over, helped them to conjure their freedom.

26. Higginson, *Army Life*, 100.

27. Mowitt, *Percussion*, 58.

28. Higginson, *Army Life*, 150.

Individual articulations provoked collective responses. Individual negotiations with military masculinity were worked out collectively.[29] Musically, the call and response dynamic between the individual who leads the call through song and the collective response is one of listening and recognition, based on a communal sense of "feeling." Fred Moten refers to feeling as the "inspirited materiality" of sound and its reproductive value.[30] Singing was not just a way to imagine a new identity, but rather to experience it. It was a way of hearing freedom *before* seeing it. As Bernice Johnson Reagon contends,

> Songs are a way to get to singing. The singing is what you are aiming for and the singing is running the sound through your body. You cannot sing a song and not change your condition.[31]

The regiment's musical repertoire expressed a military and masculine identity, but it also displayed a yearning desire for full humanity that could not be contained within traditional notions of military valor, as evidenced in the phrase "One More Valiant Soldier" in the song "Hail Mary."

SINGING AND SEEING

Through sacred singing, soldiers in the 1st South Carolina Volunteers heard themselves hailed as free people. Yet it was important for them to see themselves and to be seen by others as free as well. The line of march was not only a military maneuver, but also a visual representation of their collective march to freedom. The uniform of the Union army identified them as authorized to exercise violence in the name of the state, but it also clothed them in common colors that underscored their linked fate and its attendant collective obligations.

The spectacle of the black regiment in uniform, however, is not simply a relationship between object and spectator. Black soldiers were transformed by looking at themselves adorned in military uniforms. The spectacle offered evidence that they were no longer slaves. The transition from slave to soldier via the U.S. military uniform is reflected in a song composed by a different black regiment with lyrics that proclaimed "We-e looks li-ike me-en a-a marching' on, we looks like men of war."[32] This song was transcribed by Henry Goddard Thomas, Colonel, of the 2nd Brigade of Colored Troops at St. Petersburg. The

29. Bakhtin, *Toward a Philosophy.*
30. Moten, *In the Break,* 11.
31. Walton, "Women's Ritual Music," 255.
32. As documented in Epstein, *Sinful Tunes and Spirituals,* 293.

chorus of the song captures the essence of how black soldiers would have felt in uniform:

We look like men
We look like men
We look like men of war
An army dressed in uniform
We look like men of war

The military uniform marked a rite of passage for black soldiers, but it would take years before the federal government would mandate equal treatment in the provision of clothing. Men who dressed alike could think of themselves as alike and that threatened white supremacy. So although military discipline required Congress to pass an law that in 1864 that mandated that "all persons of color . . . [in] the military service of the United States shall receive the same uniform, clothing, arms, equipment . . . as other soldiers of the regular or volunteer forces of the United States," an exception was made in respect to shoes.[33] The military insisted that shoes worn by whites were fundamentally different from those worn by blacks. One request made to the Secretary of War asked for a shipment of 10,000 pairs of "Negro shoes of large size" to Memphis, Tennessee.[34]

Like the uniform, the printed word was a visual symbol of agency and subjectivity. Enslaved Africans were keenly aware of how their bondage was sustained through the colonizer's manipulation of the printed word. In particular, "slave codes" prohibited access to the power of the printed word and it also disallowed them the capacity to bear witness to their own experience through writing. Members of the 1st South Carolina Volunteers eagerly sought to obtain spelling books so they could learn to write about their experiences and have their writing read by others. Literate soldiers made the orders of command easier to disseminate and literacy was a valuable preparation for masculine citizenship. Suzie King-Taylor, who played an important role as one of the regiment's teachers, later recalled, "I taught a great many of the comrades in Company E to read and write, when they were off duty. Nearly all were anxious to learn."[35] Higginson confirmed Taylor's perception, noting, "Their love of the spelling book is perfectly inexhaustible."[36] The law had long mandated that reading and writing be withheld from enslaved Africans. This act of power and subjugation was often misinterpreted by people who believed

33. In Lord, *Uniforms of the Civil War*, 76.
34. Ibid., 76.
35. Ibid., 52.
36. Higginson, *Army Life*, 19.

that illiteracy was the slave's inherent condition. The soldier's thirst for learning the English language was enormous, but not in opposition to their oral
culture of knowledge. Instead, learning to read and write contributed to the
"both/and" conjunction in the African American experience in the ability to
blend the written word and the spoken word.

BLACK COMMUNAL CONSERVATORIES

The Africanisms in black music comprise an extensive inventory of "jewels
brought from bondage," to invoke Paul Gilroy's apt phrase. These African
retentions in black music did not express an essentialist racial subjectivity,
but rather the ongoing work of group making inside an elaborate network
of teaching, learning, and training in the arts that constitute Black Communal Conservatories. The term "conservatory" is preferred here because of the
ways black music making serves as an intentional and critical element in black
epistemologies that have supported and sustained black performance both
within formal institutions and beyond them. Writer and performance theo-
rist Ngũgĩ wa Thing'o helps us see how practices of "orature" in African and
Afro-diasporic culture produce fluid interactions among music, drama, literature, history, and philosophy.[37] Black Communal Conservatories are historically dynamic in that the transmission of black musical culture changes over
time. As a regiment of black singing soldiers of the Civil War, the regiment's
combination of singing, soldiering, and drumming forged a new expression
in Black Communal Conservatories. Like the "invisible academies" that Robert Farris Thompson cites as important crucibles of black visual art, the Black
Communal Conservatory is not so much a site of community-based art making as a force for art-based community making. In accordance with this tradition, people develop collective epistemologies dedicated to the survival of
black communities. Traditional Euro-American aesthetic theory and practice
would not dignify the venues where newly freed slaves created diverse, plural,
and collective artistic expressions as conservatories. In the dominant culture
a conservatory is a formal institution run by credentialed gatekeepers that
nurtures and cultivates artistic practices. Black people emerging from slavery
controlled no formal institutions, but they had a great need for expressive
culture. Their networks of instruction, apprenticeship, and performance created a collective canon of signature works and preferred practices essential

---

37. My use of "orature" is inspired by the artist Ngũgĩ wa Thing'o. In particular, see his
article, "Notes towards a Performance Theory of Orature."

to the work of conjuring freedom. These conservatories transmitted musical mechanics and techniques, to be sure, but they also served as repositories of oppositional philosophies, styles, histories, and spiritual beliefs.

The lyrics of their songs gestured to collective memories of common experiences. For example when the regiment sang,

> No more peck o' corn for me, No more, no more
> No more peck o' corn for me, many thousand gone
> No more driver's lash for me, no more, no more
> No more driver's lash for me, many thousands gone

The terms "peck o' corn" and "driver's lash" evidence the material history of slavery. Almost Freireian in their pedagogical quality, Black Communal Conservatories cultivated musical devices and created a performance praxis that promoted reflections on slavery, soldiering, musicking, masculinity, and a cosmic vision of freedom.[38] Yet abolitionists such as Higginson reduced the mechanical aspects of black music making to racial essentialism. Observing what he described as his "mysterious race of grown up children," he was completely unable to recognize the soldiers' capacity to consciously compose music. When he heard the soldiers sing "Many Thousand Gone," Higginson wrote,

> I always wondered . . . whether they had always a conscious and definite origin in some leading mind, or whether they grew by gradual accretion, in an almost unconscious way.[39]

Higginson asked an oarsman—not one of the soldiers—to explain the song. The oarsman replied, "Some good sperituals . . . are start jess out o' curiosity. I been a-raise a sing, myself once." The oarsman's answer explains both the intentional and exploratory aspects of black singing. He did not say that only some persons are allowed to "raise a sing," but instead identified complex relationships between individuals and the group. Elders and griots played special

---

38. Freire, *Pedagogy of the Oppressed*. Freire's overall concern here is with a particular context of revolution as it pertains to the emergence of an uprising among the underclass in the society. While that is not so much the case with the regiment, Freire's emphasis on an alternative to the traditional system of teaching and learning, which is always invested in state forms of power and capitalism, is what concerns me here. Ultimately, the value of alternate academies of knowledge is the point made in my invocation of Freire.

39. Higginson, *Army Life*, 170.

roles, but they did not monopolize the creation of songs. Call and response was not simply a musical device but a technique that envisioned and enacted a celebration of democratic intersubjectivity.

The philosophical underpinnings of Black Communal Conservatories produce forms of expressive culture that bear witness to ancestral wisdom. They display reverence for the collective as sacred. They evidence the community's shared understanding of its historically inflected material conditions at any given time. Slaves' determination to find ways of self-empowerment through the search to find a meta voice articulating a sense of identity and freedom constitutes just one such important element in black music philosophy.[40] The calling of names in the ring shout, the musical mechanics of producing sound and its impact on the formation of self-hood, the inherently democratic practice of individual contributions to the collective process, and communal performance are all aspects of what William C. Banfield describes as "cultural codes," "principles, representations, practices, and conventions understood to be embraced."[41] These "cultural codes" express engagement with deep philosophical issues concerning the nature of knowledge and existence that are both visible and aural in black music. The early pioneers of transcribing black music did not take into account *how* the music they heard was learned, nor did they imagine the vast cosmological underpinnings of the music, a cosmology that layered temporalities, carrying history into the present. Moreover, they were unable to grasp the music as an epistemological framework on its own terms. The philosophical underpinnings of black music were articulated through its stylistic aspects. The expression of ideas proceeded through the accessorization and ornamentation of rhythms and melodies. The music that Higginson and others heard was grounded in an "orature" that could not be discerned solely from the reductionist exercise of musical notation. In the first anthology of *Slave Songs in the United States,* edited by William Francis Allen, Charles Pickard Ware, and Lucy McKim Garrison, the editors wrote:

> As the negroes have no part-singing, we have thought it best to print only the melody; what appears in some places as harmony is really variations in single notes.

In a use of language that bears a strong resemblance to Higginson they wrote:

---

40. Here, I use the phrase "meta voice" as an epistemological engagement. I intend to speak to the way enslaved Africans used singing as a way to connect themselves to the past, present, and future idea of an African collective. I realize for critical theory "meta" poses a problem in relation to the grand narratives embedded in literature. That is not what is being raised here.

41. Banfield, *Cultural Codes,* 9.

And what makes it all the hard to unravel a thread of melody out of this strange network is that, like birds, they seem not infrequently to strike sounds that cannot be precisely represented by the gamut, and abound in "slides from one note to another, and turns and cadences not in articulated notes." "It is difficult," writes Miss McKim, "to express the entire character of these negro ballads by mere musical notes and signs.[42]

Similarly Higginson offered the following disclaimer in the opening pages of his essay "Negro Spirituals": "The words will be here given, as nearly as possible, in the original dialect; and if the spelling seems sometimes inconsistent, or the misspelling insufficient; *it is because I could get no nearer* [emphasis mine]".[43] The early ethnographers of black music could not represent the music they heard in its own terms because the singing they heard emerged from techniques and trainings that resist being reduced to a text. In addition, they could not represent such music because they could not have "looked" for the aural epistemology that created it. For Higginson and his contemporaries who tried to access the soldiers' singing through colonized eyes and ears, the music was hidden in plain view. The regiment's music was part of the "invisible institution" of black musicking, the Black Communal Conservatory foregrounded by the African tradition of "orature" and tailored to the fit the military needs of the soldiers. In response, these early music ethnographers turned to racial essentialism, describing what they heard not as art, but as a transparent window into the peculiar souls of black people. They were unable to see their own epistemological limitations. A mystified appeal to black essentialism was their only recourse. On the contrary, however, the "slides," the "turns and cadences not in articulated notes," and the "odd turns made in the throat" were part and parcel of the skills of African-derived stylized singing that used the entire palette of sound rather than only the notes of the Western measured scale. This approach to sound was taught and learned through Black Communal Conservatories.

The structure of black music in the regiment takes up the call and response device as a particular kind of structure, one that depends on the cultivation of critical listening. The unstructured components of this revolve around the synthesis of individual and collective freedom through improvisation. Songs were started by a leader and then responded to by the collective. The song is composed in the process of this exchange. It is even further recomposed on each occasion of its performance. It is collectively authored, continuously developed, and creatively elaborated by new verses, choruses, and changes

---

42. Allen, Ware, and Garrison, *Slave Songs,* v–vi.
43. Higginson, *Army Life,* 150.

in the lyrics. It acquires new slides, bends, punctuations, riffs, rhythms, and a host of other improvisations that equally enhance the arrangement of the song. This form of learning creates an unofficial, alternative, and oppositional educational institution. Just as an individual is conditioned and constituted by the sonic vibrations of his or her own singing, so too is the collective transformed by the voluminous sounds of multiple voices. The collective body or ensemble is transformed by the coalescence of sonic vibrations shared by the musical community. These waves, however, are not simply thoughtless unconscious feelings, but rather articulations of what Raymond Williams calls "structures of feeling," which he describes as "not feeling but thought as felt and feeling as thought: practical consciousness of a present kind, in a living and interrelating continuity."[44] The soldiers were transformed by the sounds of their own voices as they vibrated through their own bodies and the bodies of others. The intense listening they learned in diverse Black Communal Conservatories made them conscious of the beauties of sound, but also trained them in ways of breathing, singing, and thinking together that proved vital for social and political practice.

Black singing soldiers created an alternative masculinity in music. They could not secure full inclusion by simply embracing military service as Frederick Douglass predicted and hoped. Instead, they had to perceive military masculinity as potentially both medicine and poison, as toxic as well as tonic. Like their contemporaries and ancestors who viewed the cross of Christianity as a crossroads, as emblematic of both the greatness of God and the lowness of man, they had to hone and deploy a sense of parallel construction to see the latent possibilities in surface appearances. Their communal conservatories had long nourished this capacity. Masculinity became another object to be manipulated, revised, and redeployed by singing as well as other means. Although Frederick Douglass overestimated the potential effect of the mere fact of military service in his "Men of Color to Arms" speech, he was by no means unfamiliar with the altering power of black singing. Reflecting on the "unmeaning jargon" and sorrow songs of his youth, he recalled:

> The hearing of those wild notes always depressed my spirit, and filled me with ineffable sadness. I have frequently found myself in tears while hearing them. The mere recurrence to [sic] those songs, even now, afflicts me: and while I am writing these lines, an expression of feeling has already found its way down my cheek.[45]

---

44. Williams, *Marxism and Literature*, 132.
45. Frederick Douglass, *Narrative*, 30

For Douglass, who mastered the white masculine enterprise of speech and text, the memory of "those songs" comes to him as an affliction. Through a sonic rememory, he carried unseen evidence of slavery in his body. Douglass believed that if the nation saw black soldiers in the U.S. uniform the nation would perceive black men as "persons." Douglass believed that the songs could evoke sympathy or pity, but he did not understand them as instruments for liberation. He explained "the mere *hearing* of those songs would do more to impress some minds with the horrible character of slavery, than the reading of whole volumes of philosophy on the subject could do [emphasis added]". Douglass instructs the reader to venture to Colonel Lloyd's plantation, and "in silence, analyze the sounds that shall pass through the chambers of his soul—and if he is not thus impressed, it will only be because 'there is no flesh in his obdurate heart.'" It is not the lyrics alone, according to Douglass but he advocates an analysis of "sound" that would reach the "chambers of the soul."

Douglass would thus not have predicted that a regiment of black soldiers could use singing to conjure their freedom. Black masculinity studies, as a field, has focused almost exclusively on black masculine subjectivity as an "individual" enterprise of exceptionalism, in which Frederick Douglass has been one of the most engaged figures. Yet his "musical affliction" can be read as an "ineffable" cry for an unconventional hermeneutics that would not rely solely on his own text as an ultimate authority about black manhood. Although Douglass did not articulate the power of music in his vision for black soldiery, it is precisely this absence that the music of the 1st South Carolina Volunteers stands to fill.

During and after the nineteenth century, the dominant culture's racial interests shifted away from racial justice and toward what Jon Cruz calls "ethnosympathy," a preoccupation with slave singing as the representation of an authentic but manageable black interiority. This approach obscured the social, political, and even spiritual critique of nationalism and power embedded in slave religious singing. In addition to these dangerously potent aspects of black music, there is also the "invisible institution" of learning and teaching involved in black music. Although northern white visitors to the Sea Islands were enraptured by what they considered both the beauty and "primitivism" of black singing, they could not see or hear some of the most important aspects of what they were looking at and listening to. They did not discern the intricate levels of teaching and learning embedded in black music through its philosophy of practice, its communal epistemology, and its capacity to express an alternate black universe.

The music made by the 1st South stands within the tradition of black song, a tradition of teaching, listening, and learning that produced new songs from old songs, a prophetic tradition that expressed the "realities of change" in black life.[46] When Douglass wrote that the "songs of the one and of the other are prompted by the same emotion," he contested the notion that black song could be reduced to an either/or binary of sorrow or joy. The coexistent convergence of sorrow and joy in black music, as passed down through Black Communal Conservatories, expresses the simultaneous lamentation and celebration of black song. An honest engagement with black song on its own terms must listen for its lamentation as a means by which African Americans articulate the social realities of change. But lamentation in black song is also a critique of the inequities of power that thrive in social practices: lament is, in this instance, necessary to a determining black humanity. Here, I am echoing Walter Brueggemann's position that "In the absence of lament, we may be engaged in uncritical history-stifling praise. Both psychological inauthenticity and social immobility may be derived from the loss of these" songs.[47] The legacy of Higginson's "ownership" over the meaning of sacred singing by black soldiers occludes our understanding of the nation's past and present. The songs or "Psalms" of the nation's first black regiment, a "gospel army" of black singing soldiers, is paradoxically embedded in the nation's sense of racial progress while at the same time the practices of black culture that emerged out of racial bondage are often reduced to mere sentiments of celebration. As W. E. B. Du Bois writes about the recurrent misunderstanding of the functions of black music, "A great song arose, the loveliest thing born this side of the seas. It was a new song. Those white Southerners who heard it and never understood. . . . those white Northerners who listened without ears. Yet it lived and grew; it always grew and swelled."[48] Higginson's phrase about a "mysterious race of grown-up children" distorts the complexity of the actions and ideas of the soldiers of the 1st South. Their "new song" of freedom ran "counterclockwise" to the nation's notion of progress, so that the sound of lament established a tri-part bridge between the past, present, and future. Songs of loss and lament secured the memory of the "many thousands gone." They forged a masculinity that was both individual and collective, public and private, and sorrowful and joyful, a masculinity not based on binary oppositions between youths and adults or men and women, but rather a constantly evolving equilibrium emerging from dialogue across places on a broad continuum.

---

46. Woods, *Development Arrested*.

47. Brueggemann, "The Costly Loss of Lament."

48. Du Bois, *Black Reconstruction*.

CHAPTER 4

Moon Rise

Songs of Loss, Lament, and Liberation in a Black Regiment

I know moon-rise, I know star-rise
Lay dis body down.
I walk in de moonlight, I walk in de starlight,
To lay dis body down.
I'll walk in de graveyard, I'll walk through de graveyard,
To lay dis body down.
I'll lie in de grave and stretch out my arms;
Lay dis body down.
I go to de judgment in de evenin' of de day,
When I lay dis body down;
And my soul and your soul will meet in de day
When I lay dis body down.
—SOUTH CAROLINA VOLUNTEERS, "I KNOW MOON RISE"

APPROXIMATELY 179,000 black soldiers served in the Union army during the Civil War. They made up roughly 10–12% of the Union forces. Out of this number, 40,000 died during the course of the war. Understandably death was a common theme in the musical repertoire of the 1st South Carolina Volunteers. While the members of the regiment were looking *ahead* toward freedom, they still had to reconcile themselves to their suffering, loss, and grief in the present. Their Gullah spirituality's belief system regarding death, space, and time led them to create what Karla Holloway calls the "altered universe of the black diaspora" in which "Western valuations of time and event (place and space)" were rearranged in accordance with the West African cosmology.[1] Using the songs of slavery as the foundation for their musical repertoire,

---

1. Mbiti, *Introduction to African Religion.*

the regiment created layers of temporalities that proclaimed a circular view
of death, one that recognized the terrors of slavery yet placed death within
the circle of human existence.[2] Crossings of rivers and incantations of water
in the regiment's musical repertoire conjured up the deity of the crossroads,
known as *Ellegua* in Cuban Santeria, *Papa Legba* in Haitian Vodou, and *Exu*
in Brazilian Candomblé.

Freedom was not merely a matter of "technical emancipation" for the regiment.[3] Although they recognized the power of the law and its urgency for
their material reality, they did not seek solely to become individual rights
bearing subjects of the law or atomized self-interested market subjects. Their
vision for freedom traversed time and space. It included the *many thousands
gone,* and the living dead who were lost physically within the violence of slavery. Music helped accomplish what simple legal emancipation could not do: to
construct a vision of black humanity and freedom that both transformed and
transcended the law and the market. Inside their Black Communal Conservatory, the members of the 1st South Carolina Volunteers engaged in performative practices that explored multiple meanings of death, loss, and longing.
Through rituals and music they engaged in what historian Drew Gilpin Faust
describes as the "work of death."[4] Soldiers went to war because they agreed
with Frederick Douglass when he exclaimed "Better even die as free than live
as slaves."[5] Yet facing death raised questions about the meaning of life.

Death was inherent in the institution of slavery. It hovered over the slaves'
entire existence. The social death of slavery subjected its subjects to physical torture and psychic terror.[6] Slaves lived at the whim of their owners; they
could be killed with impunity at any time. Yet slavery did not obliterate the
transcendent understandings of death that enslaved Africans brought with
them to the New World. They deployed meditations on death as a way of
resisting the essentialisms of bondage.[7] West African retentions in Gullah
spirituality enabled the soldiers in the 1st South Carolina Volunteers to redefine *ars moriendi,* the soldier's art of dying with honor. As soldiers they were
given official military funeral rites, but as African people fighting for freedom
in America they transformed these ceremonies through distinctive modes
of music, eulogizing, and the final positioning of the body according to the
Gullah belief system. Gullah spirituality recognized a life force informing all

2. Holloway, "Beloved: A Spiritual."
3. Baldwin, *The Fire Next Time.*
4. Faust, *This Republic of Suffering.*
5. Douglass, "Men of Color to Arms!"
6. Patterson, *Slavery as Social Death.*
7. Gilroy, *The Black Atlantic.*

currents of existence. The social identities, political vocabularies, and freedom epistemologies that emerged out of African American narratives of exile bear witness to intimacy with death and cultural engagement with it.[8]

Courageous attempts to come to grips with suffering, loss, and death connected African Americans to the past, to the land, and to their heritage in ways that interrupted the mythologies of American progress and exceptionalism. Unlike Anglo Americans who sought progress primarily by surpassing their ancestors, African Americans carried their ancestors with them into the present and future.[9] Influenced by their Gullah spiritual heritage, the soldiers of the regiment incorporated ancestors into their temporal and spatial thinking. "I Know Moon Rise," the lyrical epigraph that opens this chapter, reflects a common African myth concerning the origins of death. As documented by Hans Abrahamsson in his ethnographic study of African mythology, in the myth entitled "The Message That Failed," the moon is the central element that affirms an individual's life-after-death, "If anyone dies, he dies once and for all, but if the moon wanes (becomes dark), it shall reappear as the new moon. . . . Go and tell men that if they die, they shall rise again, but if the moon disappears, he shall not show himself again in the sky."[10]

∼

The BaKongo believed that the four moments of the sun (in which the moon and stars play key roles) corresponded with the cycle of life: sunrise = birth, ascendancy = maturity, sunset = death, and midnight = rebirth in the other world.[11] This circular motion corresponds with the counterclockwise direction of the ring shout. In slave religious narratives, an emphasis on "travel" reflects episodic visions in the slave's conversion experience.[12] The experiences of trance and spirit possession were part of the slave's "spiritual journey," a form of "trabelin'" that was intrinsic to Baptist theology yet also compatible with West African cosmology. Slave religion drew on an African idea that Mechal Sobel describes as the "little me in the big me. . . . The 'me' in this equation was regarded as the 'spirit,' the 'true me' that had existed before life and would continue after death. The goal in Africa was for this 'me' to go home to spirit."[13] The lyrics of "I Know Moon Rise" expressed a nocturnal vision of death, rest,

8. Glaude Jr., *Exodus!*.

9. Noble, *Death of a Nation*.

10. Abrahamsson, *The Origin of Death*, 12.

11. Thompson, *Flash of the Spirit*.

12. Sobel, *Trabelin' On*.

13. Ibid., 109.

and reunion. The song captures a sense of travel through an African cosmological sense of time, space, and context. The song captures the flow of the
two later dimensions of life's circle. The grave is the place to "lay dis body
down," and the "moon" and "stars" represent midnight as the nocturnal setting for rebirth in the afterlife. In the Sea Islands death was thought to entail a
necessary sacrifice. Yet there were few apprehensions about dying. The phrase
"lay dis body down" suggests a Gullah-informed fearlessness and a willingness to die a staged and choreographed death. As such, the choreo-music of
"I Know Moon Rise" does not focus on a lifeless body, but rather, the song
depicts a transcendent body on the walk "through the graveyard" that finds
the soldier facing his death and making up his dying bed under the stars.[14] Lt.
Col. Charles T. Trowbridge, first commanding officer of the 1st South Carolina
Volunteers, recalled hearing "I Know Moon Rise" sung frequently at funer-
als that were held at night. He described the song as "one of the most solemn
and characteristic of the customs of the negroes."[15] It cannot be ascertained
exactly what Col. Trowbridge meant in describing the song as "characteristic
of the customs of the negroes," but his comment resonates with the wonder
expressed by many white abolitionist observers struck by the cultural practices
and beliefs of African Americans concerning death.

In the Gullah soldiers' *ars moriendi,* the solemnity of the graveyard provided the preferred visual background. "I Know Moon Rise" describes an
ever-changing light that reflects the visual aesthetics of the Sea Islands, the
cradle of Gullah spirituality. The light of the sun, moon, and stars was central
to their entire worldview, but it held special relevance for thinking symbolically about death and dying. The change in atmospheric lighting symbolizes
the transition from life on earth to death to the spirit realm. This combination
of cosmology and mythology helped soldiers recognize and respond to their
grief, suffering, and loss, but it also promoted remembrance of the "many
thousands gone," those lost to slavery. They looked forward to reunion with
one another in the life beyond slavery and the war, expressed in the hope
that "my soul and your soul will meet in de day when I lay dis body down."
This is the most affectionate of all the songs documented by Higginson. This
short phrase sums up the oft-overlooked deep and sensuous humanity of
the regiment. Its affectionate side is made invisible when exclusive emphasis
on its valor occludes evidence of its humanity. Homosocial bonds of affec-

14. This song is documented in the historic collection, Allen, Ware, and Garrison, *Slave
Songs.* Out of the 136 songs included in the collection, this song received more interpretative
commentary than any of the others. This is likely due to the way the song stages a somber stroll
through the graveyard under the starlight.

15. Allen, Ware, and Garrison, *Slave Songs,* 19.

tion between the members of the regiment were significant and pronounced as evidenced in the song "Hold Your Light," with its cosmic signification of Canaan's shore. The soldier's expressed the bonds of camaraderie through the traditional homosocial framework of the military, but the aural episteme of song connected them to the cosmic vision of freedom. They were "one more valiant soldier" fighting on behalf of the broader pursuit of black freedom on earth but in memory of those "passed on." The combination of death, ancestral heritage, and transcendence not only rearticulated an alternate sense of collective masculinity, but this alternate expression also connects to the discussion of black divergent masculinities staged in the previous chapter. In terms of the study of black masculinity, "I Know Moon Rise" is hidden in plain view and its legibility is aural—made possible through a listening hermeneutics. The moon in the song below signifies the use of "light" as a means of recognition.

> Hold your light, Brudder Robert
> Hold your light,
> Hold your light on Canaan's shore

In describing Canaan's significance as a symbol of death, Albert Raboteau explains,

> most frequently Death was, in the spirits, the River Jordan, the last river to cross before reaching Canaan, the promised home for which the weary travelers had toiled so long. In Heaven, or the New Jerusalem, parents, relatives, and friends would meet again—a devout hope for slaves who had seen parents, sisters, brothers, and children sold away with no chance of reunion in this world.[16]

Similarly, Milton Sernett locates Canaan as a metaphor for the northern region of the United States.[17] Another rendering of Canaan in this way appears in Frederick Douglass's *My Bondage and My Freedom* in 1855:

> Mr. Freeland did not suspect that all was not right with us. It *did* seem that he watched us more narrowly, after the planned escape had been conceived

---

16. Raboteau, *Slave Religion*, 262.

17. Sernett, *Bound for the Promised Land.* James Cone's crucial text, *A Black Theology of Liberation*, pushes the political aspects of this configuration of land and religion. In chapter 7, "Church, World, and Eschatology in Black Theology," Cone argues that the question asked in black liberation theology has been something more immediate, "We want to know why cannot Harlem become Jerusalem and Chicago the Promised land."

and discussed amongst us. . . . We were, at times, remarkably buoyant, singing hymns and making joyous exclamations, almost as triumphant in their
tone as if we had reached a land of freedom and safety. A Keen observer
might have detected in our repeated singing of

> O Canaan, sweet Canaan,
> I am bound for the land of Canaan

was something more than a hope of reaching heaven. We meant to reach the
north—and north was our Canaan[18]

The U.S. North served as a symbolic destination of freedom in the "spirituals," but there are two words in the regiment's version of "Hold Your Light"
that suggest an additional meaning. The words "light" and "shore" support
the cosmic vision of freedom as part of the crossing from the earthly life
into a death where one resides in the land of spirit and ancestors. Like Robert Farris Thompson's description of the Kongo cosmogram, "as singing and
drawing points of contact between worlds," the references to Canaan in this
song describe a dialogue between worlds.[19] There are, of course, biblical references in these lyrics, but, as Vincent Wimbush explains, the African American engagement with the Bible does not begin with the ultimate meaning of
the text itself, "but about the whole quest for meaning."[20] The familiar black
embrace of the Old Testament's Exodus narrative underwrote many of the earliest documented spirituals. Yet while traditional biblical interpretation would
read the Exodus narrative as a story about the deliverance granted as a reward
of the children of Israel for their patience, the slave's relationship to the nation,
to bondage, and to God in the New World mandated a "spiritual militancy" in
which deliverance is sought more actively. It has to be conjured, not just called
for. In "My Army Cross Over" the 1st South "gospel army" imagines the regiment in *real time* crossing over. In these lyrics, Pharaoh's army is drowned by
forces seen and unseen:

> My army cross over,
> My army cross over,
> O, Pharaoh's army drownded!
> My army cross over.
> We'll cross de mighty river

---

18. Douglass, *My Bondage and My Freedom,* 278.
19. Thompson, *Flash of the Spirit,* 110.
20. Wimbush, *African Americans and the Bible,* 9.

My army cross over
We'll cross de river Jordan,
My army cross over;
We'll cross de mighty Myo,
My army cross over
O Pharaoh's army drownded!
My army cross over.

The Exodus narrative from the Old Testament was appropriated by enslaved Africans who saw their plight reflected in the children of Israel's enslavement in Egypt.[21] The image of Moses leading Israel out of bondage gained momentum during the Civil War for obvious reasons. Eventually the war offered slaves the legal opportunity to participate in the Union army. It brought to the fore a national debate over slavery that was concerned with the "legal" status of slaves, creating the potential for their recognition not only as citizens, but more importantly as persons. Slave theology posited that the God who magically parted the waters for the children of Israel would empower enslaved Africans to "cross over" into Canaan, a land of legal and spatial freedom.[22] Building on slave theology, slave *eschatology* summoned God for the ultimate Holy War to end enslavement. "My Army Cross Over" celebrates the exodus of African Americans as an enslaved people "crossing over" into freedom, a journey that would be made possible by the triumph of the "gospel army," God's righteous army, over that of Pharaoh in the battle against slavery.

This triumph would require acts of heroism and sacrifice that promised to lead to a common acceptance of the soldiers' humanity. In recent years, scholarly books, museum exhibits and popular films have delivered much-deserved and long-overdue acknowledgements of black soldiers' brave and decisive contributions to the Union victory. But military heroism is only one lens through which to view the history of the black regiments. The soldiers' singing offers a more complete display of their human sentiments, including their feelings about death and their longing for brotherhood, freedom, and reunion. Through singing, soldiers drew from the musical repertoire of slavery to further their transition from "objects to subjects." Yet as we have seen from Higginson and his colleagues, nineteenth-century listeners often misheard songs attempting to move blacks from nature into history as natural expressions of a people who deserved sympathy but not justice. As Jon Cruz observes, the surge of black singing during the Civil War attracted the inter-

21. Glaude, *Exodus*; Callahan, *The Talking Book*.
22. Cone, *A Black Theology of Liberation*.

est of northern intellectuals and abolitionists. However, "in the eyes of the most radical abolitionists, blacks were being transformed (ethnosympathetically) from chattel objects to subjects."[23] The paradoxical problem of the white sympathizer's notion of black subjectivity was an inability to imagine a black humanity that was equal. The regiment was quite likely aware that Higginson was listening, and yet they were not singing *to* him but *for* the cosmic edification of their own community: past, present, and future. In the context of their cosmology, the regiment asked to be remembered for their labor as soldiers on behalf of their community.

> O do, Lord, remember me!
> O do, Lord, remember me!
> Do, Lord, remember me, until de year roll round!
> Do, Lord, remember me!

> If you want to die like Jesus died,
> Lay in de grave,
> You would fold your arms and close your eyes
> And die wid a free good will.[24]

"Remember Me" is a signification on Luke 23:42 where the thief hanging next to Jesus asks him; "Remember me when thou comest into thy kingdom." However, the symbolism of the cross and death for Sea Island black soldiers also allows for a deeper consideration viewed through the lens of Gullah spirituality. The singer takes on the role of this other crucified man, but it is significant that the soldiers' version does not explicitly use the term "thief" to describe him. The regiment does not inhabit an apologetic stance. The crucified man in the song, like the soldiers, seeks to be recognized through a relationship with others. Higginson notes that "Lord, Remember Me" was popular during the Christmas season and that the phrase "de year roll round" was sung frequently. Gullah culture honored Christmas as a critical moment in the Christian calendar, but the phrase, "de year roll round" testifies to their placing of Christmas in a cyclical structure of time. The circular structure of time as the "year roll round" corresponds with the circular shape of the ring, but it also captures a counterclockwise sense of time. This means that when the "year roll round," it is a time to "remember" how the circle may have been broken because members of the community have transitioned into the land

---

23. Cruz, *Culture on the Margins*, 68.
24. "Lord, Remember Me."

of the ancestors. Heard in this way the soldiers express a deeply human desire not to be forgotten, but to be remembered when the "year roll round." There singing insists that their deaths—and their lives—have meaning, if not for the dominant society, then for each other.

The lyrics in the second stanza of the song provide choreographic instructions on staging a death according to the ways that spirituals say that Jesus was "laid in the tomb." The regiment's inclusion of Jesus inside their specific military context confirms the ways Jesus took on thematic prominence in spirituals during the Civil War.[25] But the song also finds the soldiers identifying with a Jesus who willingly died for the cause of justice. For the soldiers, this shared sense of identity means that one should physically and metaphorically "lay in de grave . . . fold your arms and close your eyes." This meticulously staged moment of death was different from the traditional *ars moriendi* because whereas white soldiers were able to stage their deaths using letters, Bibles, and other memorabilia, the 1st South used the resources available to them: their cosmology and their music. The regiment took up the religious themes of ships, angels, and even Jesus and used music to tailor these themes to their particular circumstance.

Dis de good ole ship o' Zion,
Dis de good ole ship o' Zion,
Dis de good ole ship o' Zion,
And she's makin' for de Promise Land.
She hab angels for de sailors, (*Thrice*)
And she's makin' for de Promise Land.
And how you know dey's angels? (*Thrice*)
And she's makin' for de Promise Land
Good Lord, shall I be one? (*Thrice*)

She's a-sailin' away cold Jordan, Jordan, Jordan
And she's makin' for de Promise Land.
King Jesus is de captain, captain, captain,
And she's makin' for de Promise Land.[26]

The soldiers' music was created out of a cosmology that expressed a communal epistemology. People, figures, places, events, and even objects were constructed as instruments of healing. As such, some of the musical selec-

---

25. Callahan, *Exodus,* 66.
26. "The Ship of Zion."

tions reflect a combined syncretism of heroic figures, mythic events, and large transportable objects. An event that inspired this kind of thinking took place on May 13, 1862, six months before the 1st South Carolina Volunteers were officially mustered into the Union army. A twenty-three-year-old slave named Robert Small seized and commandeered a Confederate steamer called the *Planter*. Small's capture of the *Planter* conjured it from its existence as a vessel of slave labor into a ship of Zion. The *Planter* was a 300-ton side-wheel steamer. It stretched 147 feet long extended forty-five feet in beam. It was built to navigate easily the inland waterways of the Sea Islands. With the capacity to transport fourteen hundred bales of cotton, the *Planter* offered a combination of speed, navigational flexibility, and a carrying capacity that appealed to the confederate navy. The ship was officially recorded in the U.S. Ship Registry in October of 1860 by John Ferguson, who leased it to the Confederate navy at the outbreak of the war. For crew member Smalls, this leasing agreement changed the political dynamics of his enslavement. His labor and enslavement were now being used to further defeat his own people. It is not clear how long Smalls planned his capture of the ship, but Smalls and his fellow enslaved crewmembers held a meeting on a Sunday afternoon in April 1862 in a horse stable on East Bay Street in Charleston. This small number of slaves carried out the plan for the ship's takeover. According to Andrew Billingsley, their number included "Smalls' family of liberation," a community of kinship that consisted of "nuclear, extended, and augmented family members" who had in common their "yearning to breathe free."[27]

At approximately 3:00 AM on May 13, 1862, Smalls and his crew executed their plan; they hoisted up the South Carolina State and Confederate flags and fired up the ship's engines. With Smalls as captain, they sailed the vessel past Fort Sumter, into Union-controlled territory and onto the shores of Port Royal at about 10:00 PM that night. With the commandeering of the *Planter,* Smalls and his crew authored a new chapter in the long history of African American revolt and resistance. Through the processes of parallel construction deeply engrained in Afro-diasporic culture, they recognized that a ship serving the cause of slavery could be turned into a maritime vessel for their emancipation. They joined a long lineage of seaborne insurrectionists. The potential for mutiny aboard slave ships posed a constant threat to the success of the trade. In response, slave owners created what Marcus Rediker calls a "war machine" through which Africans' violent responses to enslavement were contained by techniques of terror and violence.[28] Yet attempts to seize

27. Billingsley, *Yearning to Breathe Free,* 51.
28. Rediker, *The Slave Ship,* 9.

slave ships and redirect them back to the shores of Africa took place again and again in the history of the trade. In addition to well-documented slave ship revolts such as the one on the *Amistad,* other "ghost stories" like the myth of the Igbo landing in the New World were narratives that combined aspects of myth, resistance, and freedom. The legend of the Igbo landing is also known as "The Myth of the Flying Africans." In the spring of 1803 a small cargo of Igbo were unloaded on St. Simons Island on the coast of Georgia. The Igbo, renowned for their fierce rebellions, seized the ship. The white shipmen jumped overboard and drowned. The legend holds that the Igbo landed the ship and collectively transformed themselves into buzzards and flew back to Africa. Legendary stories like the Igbo landing were particularly appealing to residents of the Sea Island communities because of the ways the islands were surrounded by waterways.

As an event that took place in the dawn of the Civil War, Robert Small's seizure of the *Planter* enriched the lore and legend of slave-ship insurrections. It helped solidify, publicize, and dramatize the interconnections between death, water, escape, and freedom in black culture. The victory of Robert Smalls was mythic in scale because it transformed a slave vessel into a ship anointed with a different destination in mind: Zion. Another critical figure in this grand narrative is Jesus, who was the captain of any Zion ship. As another spiritual sung by the First South states, with Jesus serving as captain "no man can hinder" the liberation struggle.

Like the seizure of the *Planter,* several slave revolts happened at night in order to take advantage of the reduced surveillance of movement during that time. Some revolts were planned at night to be in accordance with the signs of the cosmos. For example, the most legendary insurrectionist, Nat Turner, believed that on the night that he had the vision that inspired his revolt, a solar eclipse appeared, which he read as a sign to plan the exact date to execute the attack against his community's enslavement. The power of cosmological signs was integrated even further into the music of the regiment via folklore that incorporated African mythologies. The connections of flight and freedom were passed down to future generations of African Americans, such as Virginia Hamilton's "The People Could Fly." In addition, freedom and flight was embodied in the popular forms of black dance like the "Buzzard Lope." The regiment's identification as a "gospel army" enabled song lyrics that claimed their status as humans created in the image of God. Proclaiming "I really believe I'm a child of God" declared their personhood over and against the ways they had been regarded as property.

Come, my brudder, if you never did pray,

I hope you may pray to-night
For I really believe I'm a child of God
As I walk in de heavenly road[29]

On the occasion of officiating at his first funeral for members of the regiment, Higginson not only describes its official military ritual aspects, but he records the aspects of nature surrounding the burial:

> A dense mist came up, with a moon behind it, and we had only the light of pine-splinters, as the procession wound along beneath the mighty, moss-hung branches of the ancient grove. The groups around the grace, the dark faces, the red. . . . The men sang one of their own wild chants. Two crickets sang also. . . . Three volleys were fired above the grave. Just before the coffins were lowered an old man whispered to me that I must have their positions altered—the heads must be towards the west; so it was done—though they are in a place so veiled in woods that either rising or setting sun will find it hard to spy them.[30]

As colonel of the regiment, Higginson's first and foremost responsibility was military procedure. His own abolitionist agenda would likely have steered him toward procuring a proper soldier's burial for a member of the nation's first black regiment. The details in Higginson's description, coming from an astute but apologetic student of black culture, confirm a determination on the soldiers' part that aspects of their faith and culture be fused into military burial rites. The old man who instructed Higginson that "the heads must be towards the west" exemplifies the intergenerational context of the regiment discussed in chapter two. Cultural practices and beliefs were shared and passed on from the elder soldiers to the younger ones. The burial instructions demonstrate how the regiment inserted Gullah spirituality into the official rites of the military, seeking to secure their fallen comrade's safe passageway into the afterlife. In accordance with Gullah spirituality, this also entailed a preference for a burial site near water. In their extensive study of African American cemeteries, Robert H. Wright and Wilbur B. Hughes III document the prominence of black cemeteries near waterways in the Sea Islands: "Most of the cemeteries in this region are located beside a river or marsh."[31] As Gullahs considered the final resting place to be a door between worlds, the waterways would have

29. "The Heavenly Road."
30. Higginson, *Army Life*, 34.
31. Wright and Hughes III, *Lay Down Body,* 41.

been an ideal host or escort into the next world.[32] The second funeral account recorded by Higginson affirms the critical relationship between water, scenery, and burial site selection. The moment described by Higginson captures the improvised nature of singing in the regiment. On this burial occasion it was likely that the "Jordan" might have been a fitting invocation.

> These sentences I noted down, as best I could. . . . We had chosen a pictur-
> esque burial-place above the river, near the old church and beside a little
> nameless cemetery, used by generations of slaves. It was a regular military
> funeral, the coffin being draped with the American flag, the escort march-
> ing behind, and three volleys fired over the grave. During the services there
> was singing, the chaplain deaconing out the hymn in their favorite way. This
> ended, he announced his text—"This poor man cried, and the Lord heard
> him, and delivered him out of all his trouble." Instantly, to my great amaze-
> ment, the cracked voice of the chorister was uplifted, intoning the text, as if
> it were the first verse of another hymn.

> O, Jordan bank was a great old bank
> Dere ain't but one more river to cross.
> We have some valiant soldier here
> Dere ain't but one more river to cross
> O, Jordan stream will never run dry
> Dere ain't but one more river to cross
> Dere's a hill on my leff, and he catch on my right,
> Dere ain't but one more river to cross[33]

Singing about the River Jordan served many simultaneous symbolic purposes. The Jordan River is the site of Jesus' baptism by John the Baptist. The ritual of water immersion is sacred to the river cults in West African spirituality. As a large body of water, the River Jordan referenced the Middle Passage and the need to remember the "many thousands gone." The river also represented the waterways important in escapes from slavery and journeys to freedom. The river was a necessary part of "crossing over" from one location to the next. Wading in the water left no scent for bloodhounds to follow. Small boats enabled faster flight. Crossing the Ohio River meant leaving slave territory.

---

32. See Washington, "Gullah Attitudes toward Life and Death."
33. "One More River."

References to waterways, such as the Jordan River, served a strategic function in redeploying the geographical and theo-political landscape of the Bible to express the urgency of the Civil War. The war became understood as the last river to cross before reaching Canaan.[34] The Africanization of Christianity appropriated references to the Jordan River as a critical site of ritual, transformation, and national identity. The Jordan *also* provided an opportunity to mythologize water as a means of escape, life, death, reunion, crossing, and freedom; when applied symbolically it built a bridge of water between the living and the ancestors. The Jordan symbolized the necessary crossing point at the moment of death. Yet this notion of death would have perceived the Jordan not as a final ending, but as a part of the cycle of life that crossed one over into the land of the ancestors. This view of death did not compete with Christianity. Resonating with the way in which Jesus's resurrection robbed death of its sting, West African cosmology prefigured death into the circle of existence.

The Black Atlantic canon of music contains numerous songs that speak to the Jordan River as a necessary crossing for political freedom. In addition to this political freedom and its imagined "end" of slavery, the river *also* served as a locus of "rememory," wherein the waterways, creeks, and rivers serve as a reminder of the Atlantic, that watery grave of numberless, nameless, and disremembered souls.[35] In African American history, the ocean, rivers, and creeks have been traumatic sites of loss, but they also signify a means of escape to freedom. Because black sacred singing expressed the desire for "orientation, in the ultimate sense," the river became an ideal metaphor capturing the flow of life.[36] Black sacred singing reflected the forced reality of exile in black life. Yet by conjuring the routes of passage to slavery into routes of passage out of it, song lyrics made symbolic yet pragmatic use of the river as a trope signifying depth, breath, memory, motion, push, and pull.

It was at the water, at the river, or on the shore of the ocean in holding pens where Africans conjured a collective will to struggle. The Middle Passage, an "unspeakable" terror, could indeed be rendered expressible through

---

34. Rachel Havrelock's *River Jordan: The Mythology of a Dividing Line* is an excellent study of the intersections between mythmaking, collective memory, national identities and boundaries, and religion. Although Havrelock's discussion is appropriately focused on ethnic/religious/political histories of Israel, Palestine, and their surrounding regions, the symbolic intersections explored in her book bear an uncanny resemblance to the symbolic strategies expressed in African American culture. Since African Americans did not share the same history as Jews with the region and the biblical text, I have elected not to stage a full and detailed exploration of their similarities. But one of the key aspects of their shared regard for the Jordan is this: just as the U.S. southern region was a plantation regime in which the Kingdom of Cotton had to be overturned militarily, the northern region of the nation was (re)imagined as their Canaan.

35. Morrison, *Beloved*.

36. Long, *Signfications*, 7.

music in ways that might have been impossible using only language. The currents of a river evoke what Anissa Janine Wardi calls "currents of memory." She observes, "The African American expressive tradition positions bodies of water as being haunted by the bodies of those who lost their lives in the currents."[37] Not only did the music carry the echo of those lost to the Middle Passage, the "sixty million and more," but also musically, the river reverberated with the sounds of resistance, suffering, trauma, and survival. Recasting the Jordan River as a vehicle for collective memory was a *choice* on the part of transatlantic Africans, a *choice* to confront the Middle Passage as an "ultimate" atrocity. Choosing to cross the river despite its dangers is also a choice to be healed, robbing the river's memory of its drowning potential. Transatlantic Africans have used the river as a metaphor constantly, so much so that historian of black life Vincent Harding writes, "we are indeed the river."[38] "Deep River," "Swing Low Sweet Chariot," and "Jordan River" were all popular slave spirituals in the eighteenth and nineteenth centuries. In the cultural performances of the regiment, "One More River to Cross" and "My Army Cross Over" express the same sentiments and deploy many of the same metaphors as these spirituals. References to the Jordan River assert the necessity of crossing over, of seeing oneself inside a continuum that includes the past and the present and the dead and the living while working toward freedom.

The trope of linking death to crossing bodies of water recurred again and again in Civil War sacred singing, Its powerful presence in the Black Communal Conservatories of the nineteenth century helped shape subsequent black production of works of expressive culture well into the twentieth. For example, it appears prominently and repeatedly in literary works by twentieth-century black authors. Henry Dumas's "Ark of Dry Bones" draws on the biblical narrative of dry bones to comment on black life, death, water, the Middle Passage, ancestors, and slave ships. The tone of the story, published in 1974, evokes the middle to late nineteenth or early twentieth century. Dumas writes,

He walked on pass me and loped on down to the river bank. This here old place was called Deadman's Landin because they found a dead man there one time. His body was so rotted and ate up by fish and craw dads . . . just a dead man.

Bones. I saw bones. They were stacked all the way to the top of the ship. I looked around. The underside of the whole ark was nothing but a great bone-house. I looked and saw crews of black men handlin in them bones.[39]

37. Wardi, "Currents of Memory."
38. Harding, *There Is a River,* xix.
39. Dumas, "Ark of Bones."

This short excerpt does not do justice to the rich complexity of Dumas's narrative, but the centrality of the river in this passage demonstrates how it functioned as a continuing critical trope in black expressive culture. The dead body found at Deadman's Landing, "so rotted and ate up by fish and craw dads," calls up the image of sharks circling tightly packed slave ships that fed on the flesh of Africans tossed overboard into the sea. The water will never return to its pre-slavery status. Transatlantic Africans are presented as what Dumas calls "river people," the only humans who "know how to talk to the river when it's mad." Dumas deploys a haunting image of the ark as a slave ship, referring of course to Noah's ark in the Bible. In this retelling, however, the ark is not a ship of refuge and safety, but instead it is a floating dungeon of despair and death.

James Baldwin's short story "Sonny's Blues," published in 1957, employs tropes of healing, memory, and freedom that hark back to the spirituals of the nineteenth century. Baldwin's narrative resonates with the spiritual lyric "take me to the water," as the character Sonny embodies the trepidation but necessity of wading in deep water:

> His [Sonny's] face was troubled, he was working hard, but he wasn't with it. And I had the feeling that, in a way, everyone on the bandstand was waiting for him, both waiting for him and pushing him along. . . . He [Creole] wanted Sonny to leave the shoreline and strike out for the deep water. He was Sonny's witness that deep water and drowning were not the same thing—he had been there, and he wanted Sonny to know. He was waiting for Sonny to do the things on the keys that would let him know that Sonny was in the water. . . . The musician has to fill it, this instrument, with the breath of life, his own.

This scene presents musical performance as a morally inflected ritual where the relationships between the individual and the collective get worked out. Baldwin describes playing music as concerned with much more than hitting the right notes. He shows that there is a depth of playing (and living) that is only possible when one leaves the safety of the "shoreline." As an art form that *requires* risks, jazz serves as a Black Communal Conservatory and a site of moral instruction about moving from oppression to resistance to freedom. Striking out for the deep water in this story serves as a metaphor for what Baldwin, in *Giovanni's Room,* calls saying "yes to life."

"Sonny's Blues" reads like a literary version of the "spiritual" "Wade in the Water," in which the venturing into deep waters requires one to "wade," to push and pull through the water's currents. The deeper the water, the deeper the risks of drowning. Yet this is not a purely personal concern. For Baldwin Sonny, "blues" are *our* blues, they belong to the collective. Sonny's depth of artistry matters to the collective ensemble as a whole. The ensemble cannot wade in the deep water until Sonny does. A linked fate creates the burden of mutual accountability. Fannie Lou Hamer sang this song in her civil rights organizing campaigns during the late 1950s and 1960s.

In these literary examples, the river is not to be feared but rather embraced. The river must be crossed over. What awaits on the other side could be literal geographic freedom or a metaphorical freedom where death reunites one with the ancestors. The mass slaughter in combat during the Civil War gave a new urgency to questions about death and life for African Americans. Drawing on their traditions, some viewed crossing over in terms of the Haitian Vodou cosmology of the "crossroads." In this tradition, *Papa Legba* is the Orisha standing at the crossroads, mediating between divinity and humanity. The soldiers applied this mediating role in which an Orisha stands at the crossroads "between worlds" to Jesus. The lyrics "Jesus a-waitin' go in de wilderness . . . to wait upon the Lord" signifies the convergence of crossing and conversion.[40] Higginson described "Go in the Wilderness" as a marching song with "spring and lilt." Just as Jesus conquered Satan, so too did the 1st South aspire to conquer slavery.

References to water, transformation, and freedom appear prominently in Toni Morrison's *Beloved,* published in 1987. The character Sethe attempts to "cross over" the frozen Ohio River "in a caravan of Negroes."[41] She is not alone, but part of a caravan that places her inside a broad communal history of slaves traversing the river as part of the underground railroad. Crossing the deep and frozen Ohio River simulates the crossing of the Jordan River. It marks the distance between bondage and freedom. Moreover, Sethe is transporting her children to freedom. Her journey might end her life, but the "crossing" is necessary because it rebukes the shared suffering of the past and provides the possibility for a shared future. Sharon Holland identifies a treacherous creek in this novel as a "liminal space" occupied by Sethe and her daughters. It serves as a "symbol of their collective discourse suspended in time. As a tributary of the river, from whence the bakulu emerge, the creek is the extension of their threefold relationship."[42] This suspension of "time" was their only option because the temporal confines of slavery could never be life giving for them. The alternate universe of transatlantic Africans was indeed a matter of a historical past, but it was also their most viable option of survival

---

40. Higginson, *Army Life,* 163.
41. Morrison, *Beloved.*
42. Holland, *Raising the Dead,* 63.

for the future. This alternate temporality is exemplary of the Gullah world-view of music and ritual. Ritualistically, the ring shout honored the ancestors, and the music served as an oral history, a record of the memory of important events, communities, and figures. The exiled community in *Beloved* holds in common with the Gullah community the centrality of the ring shout and the sense of "oneness" that it enables.

The historical record of the actions of Margaret Garner, on whose life Toni Morrison's *Beloved* is based, has become the most well-known account of a black female slave's escape. But Garner was not the only one. Waterways were necessary and unavoidable crossing points in a slave's pursuit of freedom, and those seeking freedom refused to be conquered by potential danger. In narrating the story of Fanny Wright, Higginson relates,

> Fanny was a modest little mulatto woman, a soldier's wife, and a company laundress. She had escaped from the mainland in a boat with that child and another. Her baby was shot dead in her arms, and she reached our lines with one child safe on earth and the other in heaven.[43]

The communal nature of the regiment produced songs that expressed the ethics of care among the members. The baby's passing was marked by the following song:

> De little baby gone home,
> De little baby gone home,
> De little baby gone along,
> For to climb up Jacob's ladder.
> And I wish I'd been dar,
> I wish I'd been dar,
> I wish I'd been dar, my lord,
> For to climb up Jacob's ladder.[44]

Death was a prominent theme in the musical repertoire of the South Carolina Volunteers. But it is important to note that the scope of the soldiers' concern with death was not limited to the members of the regiment. They were a "Gullah" regiment with the desire and determination to reckon with the realities of death, space, and time. Their participation in the war and their collective musical compositions thus took part in a *communal epistemology*. The

---

43. Higginson, *Army Life*, 192.
44. "The Baby Gone Home."

deceased "baby" memorialized in the above selection was being placed within the "altered universe of the black diaspora" where not only would the baby be free from slavery, but, like Fanny Wright's baby, would be reunited with loved ones. Not only does water represent the shared space of diasporic rupture and memory, but also a critical crossroads for enslaved Africans in America.

This alternate cosmology reveals deep cultural currents of African American history, but it also deepens our understanding of the potential limits of a freedom defined solely by the law. Themes of communal love and collective suffering in the songs of black singing soldiers helped them negotiate the realities of death and the demands of the struggle for freedom. Rather than fear death the regiment considered it a "river to cross," a sentiment expressed by W. E. B. Du Bois, "Of death the Negro showed little fear, but talked of it familiarly and even fondly as simply a crossing of the waters . . ."[45] Through their music they expressed a cosmic vision of freedom at one of the most critical junctures in African American history. This juncture represented a "crossroads," one in which practices of African American culture would secure the presence of ancestors, histories, and spirits into the next phase of African American life. In the broader currents of American media and scholarship it is often the case that this story of resilience, resistance, ancestors, and especially death is "not a story to pass on," and yet it must be passed on.

---

45. Du Bois, "Of the Sorrow Songs," 273.

CHAPTER 5

❦

Military "Glory" or Racial Horror

THE FILM adaptation of Toni Morrison's *Beloved*, directed by Jonathan Demme, contains a moving scene of a ring shout depicting the exiled community of African Americans gathering in what Morrison calls "the clearing." Although the novel and film are not about the Civil War experience of black regiments, in this scene a discerning viewer might have an image of the regiment "flash up in a moment of danger," to borrow the familiar phrase from Walter Benjamin. Unlike any other scene in this adaptation, the musicality of Morrison's prose is captured through the *song, dance, drum, and* the rhythm of the *sermon* preached by Baby Suggs who functions as liturgical priestess, presiding over the entire ritual. The *singing* consists of a simple three-note chant structured on a minor scale that ascends and descends in a plaintive folk-like manner. An independent treble melody carried by a lyrical descant of children's voices floats above the scale. The men *dance*, shuffling their feet and arms stretched up and out. But the men also use their voices to represent the drum with a "huh." The children's laughter combined with the women's weeping signifies joy and lament, a "both/and" worldview at the heart of black music, which the nineteenth-century diarists and apprentice musicologists could never grasp. The ring shout depicted here harks back to the brush-harbors of slavery. But what makes this moment stand out from all the others in the film is how the scene successfully "conjures" the profound power of the ring shout in African American life. This scene contains a certain honesty and fidelity, both to Morrison's prose but also to the ritual itself. To date, I could not locate the evidence that would support whether Morrison directly used Higginson's account of the ring shout for inspiration, but the historical record of the 1st South in the ring shout bears uncanny resemblance to the scene as depicted in both the novel and the film.

While the context for the scene in the film is not a military camp, both the regiment and the characters in *Beloved* engage in the ring shout through a collective will to conjure. Similar to the lyrics in the regiment's songs, Baby Suggs's sermon does not reinscribe the master's Christian theology. Instead, it reminds the gathering of a divinity that is only present when they learn to "love" their flesh, for as Baby Suggs intones, "yonder they do not love your flesh." The men dance in this scene, performing dances that were likely passed down from the 1st South and its related Black Communal Conservatories. The scene is a "visual performance" of conjure, which attests to the enduring power of ritual and culture in the "cosmic vision of freedom" in black struggle.

IN THE historical record, the 1st South Carolina Volunteers was the first black regiment to be officially mustered into the Union army. In popular memory, however, the 54th Massachusetts regiment is considered the quintessential black fighting unit of the Civil War because it has been memorialized in several paintings, engravings, even stone monuments and a major Hollywood film. The Irish-born sculptor Augustus Saint-Gaudens created several monuments to Civil War heroes, but his most well-known work is his tribute to the white commander of the 54th, the *Robert Gould Shaw Memorial,* which appropriately stands on Boston Common. This public monument depicts a mounted Colonel Shaw leading his soldiers into battle. It was the sight of this monument while strolling through the commons one day in Boston that led producer Freddie Fields and screenwriter Kevin Jarre to think "perhaps there is a movie here." A few years later, they collaborated on the 1989 Hollywood blockbuster film *Glory,* which provides a cinematic complement to the memorial legacy of the 54th Massachusetts Regiment.[1]

Glory is based on a brief chapter in the history of the first black regiment raised in the North. Directed by Edward Zwick, the motion picture featured some well-known and up-and-coming names in Hollywood, including Matthew Broderick (as Colonel Robert Shaw, son of a prominent abolitionist family), Morgan Freeman (as Sgt. Major John Rawlins), and Denzel Washington

---

1. Blatt, "*Glory,*" 217.

(as the rebellious character Tripp). *Glory* depicts a number of events in the memoir written by Colonel Shaw, the commander of the regiment. The film narrates the forming of the unit, some challenges and military successes, and, finally, its valiant but unsuccessful attack on Fort Wagner.[2] A closing sequence praises the 54th for its sacrifice—the regiment lost nearly half its men in the battle—and credits their bravery with encouraging the Union army to recruit more black soldiers.

Every cultural product belongs to its specific contexts of production, distribution and reception. *Glory* took part in the trends of its era as much as any other film. Following the Blaxploitation era of the 1960s and 1970s, the 1980s witnessed a "New Black Wave" of directors that included Spike Lee and John Singleton, who created films with urban African American themes. In the same decade, black actors Louis Gossett Jr., Whoopi Goldberg, and Denzel Washington received Oscar awards after decades of neglect of black talent on the part of the American film industry.[3] Though it may seem as if the Hollywood establishment had finally opened its arms to black representation in isolation from the larger social and political climate, this is not the case. This film emerged out of and in response to a surge of Civil War sentimentalism and nostalgia that emerged during the 1980s. Gary W. Gallagher describes the surge in books and popular symbolism of the Civil War as part of the public's turn "toward the use of military strength as a tool of national policy" during the presidential administrations of Ronald Reagan and George Herbert Walker Bush.[4] Gallagher cites the 125th anniversary commemorations of the Civil War in 1986, a celebratory review of James M. McPherson's book *Battle Cry of Freedom* that appeared in the *New York Times* on February 14, 1988, and the release of Ken Burn's documentary on the Civil War in 1990 as part of this process. In an attempt to erase the enduring antipathy toward war provoked by the Vietnam conflict of the 1960s and 1970s, Reagan, Bush, and their allies in scholarship, journalism, and commercial culture sought to create a redemptive militarism, one that could, in the words of George Bush celebrating his invasion of Panama, help the nation "kick the Vietnam Syndrome once and for all."[5] In ways that conform perfectly to what Jodi Melamed refers to as the manipulation of anti-racism as an apparatus of empire and a discourse that always guarantees white salvation, *Glory* was celebrated as a "discovery" of

---

2. This battle, also known as the Second Battle of Fort Wagner, took place on July 18, 1763, near Charleston, South Carolina.

3. Halle Berry did not receive her first Academy Award until 2001.

4. Gallagher, *Causes Won, Lost, and Forgotten,* 4–5.

5. See Herring, *"America and Vietnam: The Unending War."*

black history, a victory for America, and a triumph for African Americans.[6] But by perpetuating the romantic-heroic iconization of the 54th Mass., *Glory* actually enabled a hegemony of representation that obscured the actual histories of the 136 United States Colored Regiments that fought in the war.

Celebrated for its retrieval of a lost chapter in American history, *Glory* reveals itself as what Walter Benjamin calls the "history of the victor." The film is a hymn to white benevolence and national virtue. It presents military masculinity under white tutelage as the cure for the ills of the black community. The small snippets of black culture present in the film appear as little more than local color, decontextualized sights, and sounds of the sort that Colonel Thomas Higginson found titillating in his memoir. Themes such as freedom, religion, violence, and masculinity are not at all complicated, contextualized, or contested in the film. Instead these categories are colonized as the basis for a narrative of national progress. *Glory* presents a story of black men who fought bravely in the Civil War and even endured racial violence in the military in order to prove black people fit for freedom and worthy of citizenship. From this perspective, black regimentation made it safe for the nation to grant legal freedom. The film constructs black masculinity as seen only through the violent and paternalistic view of white manhood. It portrays black religion and music as expressions of an unchanging essentialist black essence with no political intent or outcomes. In one of the final scenes leading up to the film's conclusion, the regiment is portrayed in a campfire meeting praying, singing, and sermonizing as they prepare to fight the Battle of Fort Wagner. Yet in most scenes, white male abolitionists represent the liberal state's democracy and its necessary use of force and violence as a means to cajole and coerce formerly enslaved subjects to fight for the flag.

Colonels Thomas Wentworth Higginson and Robert Shaw and, of course, President Lincoln himself have become iconic images of white masculine liberalism from the Civil War. These three figures function as recurring symbols of white American liberal masculinity. Like Higginson, Shaw was born into a Boston-based family of Unitarian abolitionists and intellectuals. He attended Harvard only a few years after Higginson had graduated before moving on to his professional career in the ministry and his activism as an abolitionist. Shaw was already a member of the 7th New York Militia in 1862 when his father offered him command of a new state-sponsored black regiment. Shaw accepted with reluctance, and in March 1863 the Governor of Massachusetts, John A. Andrew, authorized the founding of the 54th Massachusetts. As the

---

6. Melamed, *Represent and Destroy.*

film depicts in great detail, Shaw's tenure with the famed regiment was brief, ending with his death in the unit's unsuccessful attack on Fort Wagner.

Just as Higginson was a product of the abolitionist culture in Boston, so too was the 54th Massachusetts Regiment. It was funded and founded by the abolitionist families of the state, prominent among them, the Shaw family. White abolitionists such as Wendell Phillips worked with Frederick Douglass to recruit soldiers. Douglass's two sons, Charles L. Douglass and Louis F. Douglass, both served in it. In preparation for his military assignment, Shaw met with Higginson to discuss his uncertainty about the military capabilities of black soldiers. In Higginson's essay, "The Black Troops: Intensely Human," he writes,

> When I rode out to meet him, on his arrival with his northern Colored regiment, [he] seriously asked me whether I felt perfectly sure that the Negroes would stand in fire in line of battle, and suggested at worst, it would at least be possible to drive them forward by having a line of white soldiers advance in their rear, so that they would be between two fires.[7]

Although *Glory* is based on the memoir by Shaw about his service with the 54th Massachusetts Regiment, its script exhibits remarkable similarities to Higginson's memoir about the 1st South Carolina Volunteers. This is not entirely unexpected, given that the same Boston abolitionist tradition produced both Higginson and Shaw. Although Shaw was a career military man and Higginson a minister who took up the anti-slavery cause as part of his religious ideology, both men self-consciously embodied a nineteenth-century white liberal masculinity. They were given posts of command in order to represent the kind of manhood that the Army thought should be mastered by black male slaves. Higginson and Shaw also embody an ideal of benevolent masculine racial liberalism for fellow whites. They represented ways of advocating for the anti-slavery cause while simultaneously retaining racial difference to safeguard the hierarchy of white manhood. Just as Higginson's memoir of his time with the 1st South served to construct a version of black masculinity in the white imagination, so the film portrayal of Colonel Shaw in *Glory* performs a similar task.

With Colonel Shaw at its helm, the 54th Massachusetts Regiment made a significant military statement with its role in the storied attack on Fort Wagner. Speaking in memory of the regiment's valor, Massachusetts Governor

---

7. Higginson, "*The Black Troops: Intensely Human,*" *Atlantic Monthly,* May 1904, quoted in Meyer, *The Magnificent Activist,* 186.

John A. Andrew commented, "I know not where, in all of human history, to any given thousand men in arms there has been committed a work at once so proud, so precious, so full of hope and *glory* [emphasis mine]."[8] President Lincoln noted the regiment's fortitude as a key component in securing the Union's ultimate victory. Yet when Union officials attempted to reclaim Colonel Shaw's body, Confederate commander Brigadier General Johnson Hagood sent a message to Shaw's father informing him that "We buried him with his niggers."[9]

Higginson referred to Shaw as a "young hero," a notable compliment given his negative views of other white masculine abolitionist figures. Higginson's reliance on the conventions of a literary text to construct black masculinity may have led him intentionally to omit any acts of violence committed against the soldiers by white offers, *Glory*, on the other hand, portrays Shaw as both sympathizer to the anti-slavery cause and simultaneously a perpetrator of slavery's violence. In one of the most memorable scenes in *Glory*, the soldier Tripp receives a flogging as punishment for running away to find shoes, an amenity that was withheld from black soldiers. In this scene, Tripp is referred to as "the prisoner," thereby invoking the fugitive slave language of human property. As Tripp is marched to the flogging post, the musical accompaniment consists of a single snare drum being played by a small non-uniformed black boy. Once Tripp arrives at the "whipping post," the regiment's Colonel Shaw orders Sergeant Major Mulcahy (played by John Finn) to "commence . . . proceed." While being flogged Tripp presents a black manhood that is largely unaffected by pain: he cries a single tear. Thus Tripp's flogging is restaged as a means to valorize black military masculinity. The camera moves in on the defiant eyes of Tripp, who flings the shirt off his back. The sound and choreography of this moment is a setup for whipping itself. But the scene is haunted by the specters of racial horror: Tripp's back bears the hard evidence of that which even Frederick Douglass's vision of the black soldier in uniform could never conceal. For not only do the scars of slavery lie underneath any exterior sign of progress, but *Glory* presents a rather vexing scenario in which violence against black bodies is regretfully necessary to the nation's idea of progress.

The makers of *Glory* did not stage the whipping of Tripp out of fidelity to the historical record. As historian Joseph T. Glatthaar has explained, the scene is completely inaccurate. The use of the whip against soldiers by military officers was outlawed in 1861. Tripp was not a deserter, only a soldier absent without leave, an offense that would have led to a hearing at which he might

---

8. Emilio, *A Brave Black Regiment*.
9. Burchard, *One Gallant Rush*, 143.

have had his pay docked or been sentenced to a brief period of confinement.[10] Yet the scene appears to placate white audiences, to soothe their irrational anxieties about out-of-control black violence, and to establish white control as the necessary precondition of concessions made to blacks.

The preexistent scars seen on Tripp's body did exist, however, not only on this fictional character, but in real life on the body of another black soldier known simply as "Gordon." Photographs of Gordon were taken by the studio of McPherson and Oliver in Baton Rouge in 1863.[11] The image of Gordon's whip-scarred back (known as the "Scourged Back") was reproduced by a well-established family business run by the McAllister family, whose area of specialty included the reproduction of commercial photographs. It was circulated as an instrument of propaganda in the U.S. and England during the Civil War. Three images of Gordon appeared in *Harper's Weekly* dated July 4, 1863. The first image, *Gordon as He Entered Our Lines,* depicts Gordon seated and barefoot, wearing tattered clothing and looking directly into the eye of the camera. The second image, *Gordon under Medical Inspection,* is the image that was commercialized in the service of abolitionist propaganda. When viewed in the context of the film *Glory,* the final image, *Gordon in His Uniform as a U.S. Soldier,* reads as a testimony on the nature of race and violence on the U.S. psyche. The title of the final image in this photographic trilogy is strangely phrased "in *his* uniform." The uniform, the "scourged back," the anonymity of being called by only his first name by an abolitionist movement presumably invested in black freedom, and the spectacular display of his back as a visual commodity all attest to the unhealed scars of race, violence, and nationhood in the U.S. in the 1860s. As Cassandra Jackson comments, "contemporary representations of the wounded black male body suggest that the meaning of the wound is not fixed."[12] The casual treatment of this image by anti-slavery campaigners corresponds neatly with the celebration of Tripp's flogging in *Glory,* some 125 years later. The Civil War is remembered as the defining moment in which the suffering and pain of black people's enslavement in the U.S. was terminated, not by their own actions, but by the intervention of stern white men. The circulation of these images in the 1863 photograph and the 1989 film tells a different story, however, testifying to the ways in which the unresolved nature and legacy of the Civil War has been a continuation of slavery's torture.

The reenacted flogging in *Glory* is a depiction of the idea that discipline and punishment were crucial to the manufacturing of manhood for blacks. The specters of such racialized violence have become standard features of Hol-

10. Blatt, "*Glory,*" 223.

11. See Collins, *Shadow and Substance.*

12. Jackson, *Violence,* 5.

lywood films that deal with the topics of race and the Civil War. The camera repeatedly finds the whip-scarred backs of black male bodies. In *Glory*, Tripp's back bears the lurid scars of the lash—even as he is yet to be flogged. In *Lincoln*, the photo-plate of *The Scourged Back* is presented as a fetish held dearly by President Lincoln's young son Tadd. Taken together, the scars on the back of Tripp and Gordon (*The Scourged Back*) are essential to the "visual economy" of these films and to the national imagination about gender and race. The construction, production, and distribution of images creates inscribed and implied meanings for the viewership they court.[13] The use of *The Scourged Back* in *Lincoln* and the staging of Tripp's flogging in *Glory* are presented as a kind of black masculine achievement: the transition from slave to soldier is simultaneously a cause for celebration and grief. Slavery's techniques of torture are vindicated because they help produce soldiers. The bodies of these black soldiers are also "scenes of subjection," images that promote pleasure for whites by rendering blacks as abject. Saidiyah Hartman explains that these images trace their origins back to the slave coffle—a public parade of chained black humans for the amusement of whites. Legal emancipation altered, but did not erase, the ideological function of the humiliated black body and its role in fusing white spectatorship to white citizenship. Hartman argues that "the entanglements of slavery and freedom trouble facile notions of progress that endeavor to erect absolute distinctions between bondage and liberty."[14] Inasmuch as these films are presented as "historical," the casual treatment of violence against black bodies presumes that the restaging of these images is necessary for the sake of realism. Yet Gordon's and Tripp's whip-scarred backs comprise only a part of a larger narrative of national progress in which the signs of racialized violence are not to be viewed as signs of the hard trials and tribulations of a people, but rather as signs of the triumph of the nation and its vindication because it allegedly decided that this violence is obsolete. Notions of freedom, liberty, and progress—notions that are presumed to be inherent to the profile of America—*must* be sustained; they must be reinvented and reoriented over time. Hence the labor of films like *Glory* and *Lincoln* is to make use of spectacular images of violence against black bodies in order to displace the routine racialized violence intrinsic to the society itself. These films contrive to represent racialized violence as a heroic trope explaining the agonistic construction of black masculinity and its role in the progress of the nation. But as Elaine Scarry reminds us, "The body is not simply an element in a scene of confirmation; it is the confirmation."[15] What does the nexus of

13. Poole, *Vision, Race, and Modernity*, 7.
14. Hartman, *Scenes of Subjection*, 172.
15. Scarry, *The Body in Pain*.

race, violence, and masculinity as presented in these films confess about the *progress* of America in this particular hour?

Glory and *Lincoln* may be presented as artifacts of American and African American history, but they are also carefully crafted contributors to the construction of black and white masculinity in the present. To add to this seemingly racial dialectic, the use of racialized violence perpetrated by white American masculine heroes is both an admission of the punishing force of violence against blacks and its disavowal and erasure. Colonel Robert Shaw and Abraham Lincoln both symbolize the mythical liberal profile of the empire. These two figures help retell and reinforce the empire's relationship to race. In this instance the image of *The Scourged Back* is recirculated for the sake of teaching history in popular culture. Nevertheless this recirculation is an example of what Maurice Wallace theorizes as a "spectragraphia," an "illusory cultural vision" in which we are invited to view a black masculine body being flogged as a testimony to *his* strength and capacity to endure violence and pain for the sake of black manhood.[16] This scope of vision stubbornly refuses to see the nation as perpetrator, preferring to lionize the endurance of such violence as an achievement for black manhood and the black race. Shaw represents the nation's relationship to the construction of black masculinity and of blackness itself. Elaine Scarry's questioning statement raises the rather peculiar racial paradox of racial violence and America: "How is it that one person can be in the presence of another person in pain and not know it—not know it to the point where he himself inflicts it, and goes on inflicting it?"[17] Immediately following Denzel Washington's acceptance of an Oscar award for his performance of Tripp, media commentators on morning talk shows looped this very scene as the determining factor that earned Washington his reward. Although the film was lauded as an American historical artifact, the suffering, pain, and violence enacted on the black soldier's body was subsumed into Washington's achievement as an actor—and even his winning was considered to be a "win" for the nation and the African American community.

Tripp's flogging was one the most memorable scenes in *Glory,* but its contrast with another less celebrated scene is noteworthy. The campfire scene borrowed much of its dialogue from Higginson, but it does not portray a ring shout. Instead, in *Glory* Tripp closes the campfire scene with the declaration: "We Men Ain't We?" Compared to the 1st South Carolina Volunteers' repertoire, this scene appears conveniently simplistic. The 54th sings a repetitive

16. Wallace, *Constructing the Black Masculine,* 30.
17. Scarry, *The Body in Pain,* 12.

chorus of "oh my lord, lord, lord, lord, lord, oh my lord," accompanied by a harmonica and tambourine. The soldier who has been teased by his fellow soldiers for being inarticulate offers the following prayer:

> Tomorrow, we go into battle, so Lordy, let me fight with the Rifle in one hand and the good book in the other, that if I should die at the mercy of the rifle, die on water or on land, I may know that you blessed Jesus almighty are with me, and I have no fear.

The above narrative bears a striking resemblance a prayer transcribed by Higginson in the Gullah dialect,

> Let me lib wid de musket in one hand an' de Bible in de oder, dat if I die at de muzzle ob de musket, die in de water, die on de land, I may know I hab de bressed Jesus in my hand, an' hab no fear.

The differences between these two prayers are small but important in terms of how religion is used in the film. Whereas the prayer recited in *Glory* appears just before the regiment's battle at Antietam, the prayer from the 1st South is embedded in the ongoing culture of the regiment. After describing the soldiers' ring shout in full detail, Higginson concludes that in addition to the ring shout itself, the soldiers gather "night after night, while in other parts of the camp the soberest prayers and exhortations are proceeding sedately."[18] In contrast the portrayal of religion in *Glory* isolates it from the political culture of the regiment. This portrait is enabled by the *sonic politics* of the film's soundtrack. Aside from snippets performed by the Boys Choir of Harlem, the soundtrack consists of lush orchestral arrangements reminiscent of European classical composers such as Richard Wagner and Robert Schumann. These choices reflect the general body of work by the film's composer, James Horner, who has created large orchestral scores for other films such as *Braveheart, Avatar,* and *Titanic.* However, the labor performed by these sounds is a political one in that the densely arranged orchestra silences the singing voices of the soldiers, despite the pervasive singing of black soldiers in a regiment such as the 1st South and other black regiments. The conjurational power of the historical ring shout was informed by the use of chant and drum. Civil war films, however, make use of orchestral horns and strings in a way that denies the political power of black culture. The politics of race and representation in Hollywood films are not void of sound but are invested in a sonic politics

---

18. Higginson, *Army Life,* 20.

that determines how black humanity cannot simply seen but also rendered aurally. As discussed in chapter 3, while it is the tradition of scholarship to attend to song lyrics the key to their interpretation, at the core of the soldier's experience with those lyrics was an "aural epistemology" that requires a listening hermeneutics. The ways in which sound is deployed or not constitute a form of sonic politics that can render a people's culture silent or it can bestow on them a sense of agency. The campfire scene is used in a way that deracinates black religion from its African soil. As Charise Cheney comments on this scene in *Glory*, "In a style assumed to be familiar to the slave quarters of the antebellum South, these soldiers break out into an improvised melody (as black folk in movies are prone to do) and begin to conjure God."[19] The film's staging of the 54th Mass. seated and huddled coincides with the perception of black religion as passive, but the cultural record of the 1st South testifies to an intentional and combined use of music and religion in the ring shout that, in its connection to the West African circle dance, was a combination of song, story, drum, and dance.

The campfire scene in *Glory* is a crucial moment in a film that proposes to valorize black masculinity and the nation's progress. This scene crafts a version of black religion that denies the soldiers the powerful agency that *their* culture provides them. The campfire scene is perfectly contained and uncomplicated because to present black Civil War soldiers in any other light would not serve the master narrative of benevolent racial progress. In this instance the campfire scene reinforces the function of *Glory* as a "history of the victor." On the night before the soldiers will lay down their lives in the name of freedom, they assemble for a collective moment of prayer. As the scene closes Tripp is prodded to offer remarks but is too overcome with emotion to speak succinctly. But what he *does* say captures the essence of the film's preoccupation with black masculinity: "Ain't much a matter what happen tomorrow, 'cause we men, ain't we?" Despite the poetic resonance of Tripp's dialogue, the musical masculinity constructed by the 1st South proposes that *what happens tomorrow will indeed matter.* Unlike *Glory*, the black alternate universe heard in the songs of the 1st South did not settle for mastering the master's masculinity. The 1st South proclaimed itself to be the "gospel army" of the Civil War, and as such their cosmic vision of freedom enabled a black alternate universe in which the past and present would inform the future. In this altered temporality, masculinity and manhood alone was not enough. Slavery and all its techniques of torture had to be no more. And such was heard in the regiment's song of lamentation and celebration:

---

19. Cheney, "We Men Ain't We?," 38.

No more auction block for me,
No more, no more
No more auction block for me,
Many thousands gone

No more drivers' lash for me
No more, no more
No more drivers' lash for me
Many thousands gone

The cinematic portrayal of the 54th Massachusetts regiment and the historic record of the 1st South suggest that they both have in common a capacity for collective conjuring of religion through music. However, whereas the music in *Glory* lends itself toward a black religiosity void of any political and/or cosmological significance, the music of the 1st South offers a "counter-narrative" to the film's more popular version. It is important to note that the song "Many Thousands Gone" was not only sung by the 1st South. In practice, when a group of slaves were found singing this song they were arrested for fear that they were planning a rebellion. The lyric "no more" in this selection is a musical precursor to the "Freedom Now" phrase articulated in the twentieth-century Civil Rights struggle. Phrases such as "no more auction block for me," "Freedom Now," and Frederick Douglass's statement "power concedes nothing without a demand, it never did and it never will" are all part of the salient repertoire of black political philosophy. The absence of this political stance in *Glory* attests that such political agency is a revolutionary element in the black freedom struggle that is not made for movies. As Gil Scott-Heron observed, "The revolution will not be televised." As *Glory* retrieves a historical narrative for the sake of representation, this act of revisionism results in a "history of the victor" in which black culture has to be depoliticized in order for the nation's narrative of progress to be preserved. The "victor" in this equation is by no means an abstract collective; in film, the victor is embodied in figures such as Shaw and even Abraham Lincoln.

In ways similar to those in which Higginson epitomized the nineteenth-century white male anti-slavery intelligentsia, Colonel Robert Shaw symbolized the future of white male American wealth, militarism, and liberalism. *Glory* presents the racial paradox that despite Shaw's anti-slavery beliefs it was under his official command that the rebellious soldier Tripp was flogged before his fellow soldiers. The whip-scarred back of an enlisted slave named "Gordon" was conjured on Tripp's back in *Glory* and again for the second time in *Lincoln*. Of course, Abraham Lincoln is not missing from American popular history. But with the election of the nation's first black president, Barrack Obama, Lincoln's legacy has taken on new heights of popularity. In addition to Lincoln and President Obama's shared connection to the state of Illinois, there was also Obama's use of Lincoln's Bible during his inauguration ceremony of 2009. The attachment to Mr. Lincoln by the nation's first black president resurrected contentious sentiments about the political "feelings" held by Mr. Lincoln with respect to race and slavery. *Lincoln,* acted memorably by method-actor Daniel Day-Lewis, does not portray Abraham Lincoln as an emotionally sympathetic progressive on the subject of race. The film instead captures the day-to-day maneuvering of one of America's most legendary political heroes. While the film does not present Lincoln as having committed acts of violence, it is noteworthy that the *Scourged Back* image of Gordon is a critical trope in the film.

The film sets up a later appearance of the *Scourged Back* early in the narrative when, during a late-night walk through the White House, President Lincoln enters the bedroom of his youngest son, Tad Lincoln, who has fallen asleep with his hands clasped onto two photographic plates. One of these is a "before and after" image of *Drummer Jackson,* which was widely circulated during the war. The other plate bears the image of two young slave boys who, like the "before" image of *Drummer Jackson,* were dressed in tattered clothes but were literally holding their clothing together with their hands, looking into the camera with blank expressions. The President looks at both images with bemusement, and since there is no dialogue in the scene the viewer is left to wonder if his bemusement is concerned with Tad's fixation on these images or whether he is confounded by the narratives the images suggest. Tad's fascination with the images of slaves is followed up later when he discovers the plate for the *Scourged Back.* The young Tad examines the plate and asks his older brother, "Why do some slaves cost more than others?" Lincoln orders the young Tad to "put them back in the box you scoundrel." But Tad persists, asking the president's butler Mr. Slade (played by Stephen Henderson), "When you were a slave did they beat you?" Mr. Slade responds promptly, "I was born a free man. Nobody beat me except I beat them right back. Mrs. Keckley was a slave. Ask her if she was beaten." Mr. Lincoln shakes his head disapprovingly, "Tad—." But Mrs. Keckley, the black female domestic (played by Gloria Reuben), explains, "I was beaten with a fire shovel when I was younger than you."

Gordon's *Scourged Back* was rewritten on Tripp's back in *Glory* in order to reconstruct an image of black masculinity as innately tough, even in the face of and on behalf of violence perpetrated by the nation. The use of the *Scourged Back* in *Lincoln* does not aim so much to (re)construct black masculinity as to provide a more honest confession regarding the pain of African Americans as othered denizens. Just as *Glory* stages a flogging on behalf of heroic white masculinity and courageous black masculinity, *Lincoln* bears out the truth of race and masculinity through the casual nature in which violence is framed in the film. *Glory* proposes masculinity to be the ultimate achievement in the nation's racial/gendered relations, whereas *Lincoln* affirms the mythic status of white American masculinity. It is not coincidental that both films use Gordon's *Scourged Back* as a trope of violence because this image fittingly represents the "unhealed wounds" of slavery. Yet the ongoing circulation of this image exposes even the contemporary fascination with the nexus of race, violence, and masculinity. This fascination may serve to further exalt the stronghold of white supremacy on popular American history, but it will not make known the deeper and broader notions of black freedom animated through culture. As it pertains to the Civil War, the cultural activities in music and religion as seen in the 1st South gave shape both to the cosmic vision of black freedom dreams and to their engaged forms of struggle. It is this vision of freedom that inspired even the regiment's construction of masculinity, which thereby makes valuable their self-declaration: "One More Valiant Soldier."

This form of soldiering embraced the U.S. definitions of a soldier, but through their singing they transcended such confines and created a regiment of black singing soldiers. This form of soldiering broke the doctrinal rules of religious identity and theology to combine an Afro-American mix of spiritual militancy and authorized themselves the "Gospel Army" of the Civil War, in which they sang the gospel of black freedom. They seized military masculinity as a path toward U.S. freedom and manhood, but they also went beyond this to create a musical masculinity that embraced all dimensions of the human condition. The regiment gathered nightly in their counterclockwise circle of song, dance, drum, and story as a way of summoning the gods' presence to imagine a "cosmic vision of freedom."

It was there, in the circle, that the soldiers had permission to sing of freedom before it had "officially" come to them. In the circle they could dance their way toward an alternate masculinity and manhood. The circle was the place where new rhythms were played on old drums. All of what happened in the circle was "both" a means by which to sustain themselves "and" it was also a message to the America that had exploited them.

My Army Cross Over

My army cross over
My army cross over
O, Pharaoh's army drownded!
My army cross over

—1st South Carolina Volunteers

IN 1865, two years after the 1863 Emancipation Proclamation, a group of African Americans gathered at Zion Church in Charleston, South Carolina, to deliberate on their "intellectual, moral, industrial, civic, and political condition."[1] Known as the "Colored State Convention" of Charleston, the close proximity of time and distance here is significant, as Charleston is only a few miles east of the military camp of the 1st South. The need to organize confirms that which Higginson noted with regard to the history of black revolts, "the blacks prefer organization."[2] Even as the 1st South would sing "my army cross over" while "Pharaoh's army drownded," a new social technology of race and terror was resurrected through legal and unfree practices of black codes, lynching, sharecropping, and convict leasing. Lincoln's emancipation turned out to be a "technical emancipation" that not only compromised black people's freedom, but its withholding of resources and lack of preparation undermined the entire meaning of freedom for the nation. The cultural practices of the 1st South created a bridge between the black freedom dreams of slavery and the

---

1. "Address of the Colored State Convention to the People of the State of South Carolina." State Convention of the Colored People of South Carolina. *Proceedings of the Colored People's Convention of the State of South Carolina.* Zion Church, Charleston, November, 1865 (Charleston: South Carolina Leader Office, 1865), 23.

2. Higginson, *Army Life,* 194.

post emancipation era—and beyond. These practices retained the "both/and" realities of black life in America, and the specters of these practices are still with us today.

As it pertains to the cultural practices of the regiment, several changes in the rhythms and harmonies of black culture took place in the decades following the Civil War. The "collective will to conjure" seen in the regiment became an enterprise maintained by individual professional conjurers and specialists, an enterprise that thrived alongside the new black church of freedom. The Holiness movement in America expanded in general during this era. The Black Holiness movement, however, went beyond the doctrines of perfectionism and made the song, dance, and drum the basis for its liturgy. The Holiness Church and its sister institution, the "Sanctified Church," set the stage for the gospel blues in the twentieth century. Gospel music in the early twentieth century expressed Christian theology and as an offspring of the blues, gospel *also* told the story of "reality and change" of black life in America.[3] Similar to the ways Higginson acted as an ethnographer of black music and culture, a different set of figures emerged in the founding of historically black colleges and universities (HBCUs). A set of white male music instructors helped to discipline the ring shout out of the music that would come to define the very character of HBCUs. While they would not have the final word on "how" to arrange spirituals, the role played by these instructors in the transition between white choral directors and black choral directors at HBCUs is worth examining. Several songs from the catalogue of the 1st South continued into the modern arranged spirituals of HBCUs and beyond. Dorothy Love-Coates and the Gospel Harmonettes sustained the sentiments in songs such as "O'er the Crossing" and "One More River to Cross" in modern gospel songs such as "Jordan River" and "Get Away Jordan." "Cry Holy" is expressed in the Staple Singers' "Holy Unto the Lord," and "The Ship of Zion" and "Many Thousands Gone" retained their titles. Inasmuch as the black choral tradition associated with HBCUs helped to "preserve" spirituals, they are only but one aspect of a black "performance genealogy" that can be traced back to the regiment.

RACE, CULTURE, AND THE
CONUNDRUMS OF AMERICAN FREEDOM

In his farewell address of February 9, 1866 Lieutenant-Colonel Trowbridge offered the following remarks to the United States Colored Troops, formerly known as the 1st South Carolina Volunteers:

---

3. Woods, *Development Arrested*, 29.

The flag of our fathers, restored to its rightful significance, now floats over
every foot of our territory, from Maine to California, and beholds only freedmen! The prejudices which formerly existed against you are will nigh rooted
out. Soldiers, you have done your duty, and acquitted yourselves like men,
who, actuated by such ennobling motives, could not fail; and as the result of
your fidelity and obedience, you have won your freedom. And O, how great
the reward!

The terminology of Col. Trowbridge's speech on such an occasion speaks volumes in terms of how the vocabularies of nation, power, and freedom retain
the inequities of race. Terms such as "acquitted" and "obedience" retained the
racial paradox of the American empire: all men are *created* equal but black
people had to win their freedom. In the days following the election of the
nation's first black president, a prominent black gospel singer, Rev. Shirley
Caesar, expressed a similar sentiment when she proclaimed, "God has vindicated the black folk."[4] Both the comments of Trowbridge and those of the
evangelist Caesar reveal the strange notion that despite the ways blackness
and black bondage have been central to the nation's profile of wealth and
democracy, blackness requires "vindication." This assertion runs counter to
the practices of black culture in the regiment, in which their "cosmic vision
of freedom" did not seek to "vindicate black folk," but instead their nightly
engagement with the ring shout sought to expand the notion of freedom
beyond the parameters of legal bondage and affirm black life through a counterclockwise ritual of song, dance, drum, and narrative. Emancipation would
not be the end of cultural practices cultivated in slavery, as they would follow
black people even though technically they were slaves no more.

The debates over how to save the Union did not include a serious contemplation as to how the nation would support a newly freed population of
formerly enslaved Africans. Winning the war or defeating the South took
priority over the making of a new and equal society created through "abolition democracy."[5] As had been the case since their arrival in America, black
people's vision of freedom would require African Americans to invent new
modes and means of struggle and culture that held the nation accountable for
equal protection and the rights of the ballot. But they were also challenged to
create a culture that affirmed black humanity in an anti-black society. They
understood this to be the spiritual labor that the law could not do. Similar to
the ways the ring shout served as a vital resource whereby enslaved Africans
created a culture of sustenance and resistance, once again, African Ameri-

---

4. Breed, "Churches across America."
5. Du Bois, *Black Reconstruction*.

cans turned to the counterclockwise song, dance, drum, and story to (re)create expressions of religion, to write new songs of freedom, and to make new forms of gender. Thus they created their own conservatories of performance arts.

WILL THE CIRCLE BE UNBROKEN: HEALERS, CONJURERS, AND SPIRITUAL MILITANCY

After the battle of Antietam in September 1862, President Lincoln warned the Confederates that unless they surrendered he would decree the slaves in Confederate territories "forever free." On the night before this decree was to be issued, slaves gathered in churches across the South to mark the end of the slavery and the beginning of freedom. Known as "Watch Night," the slave's religion was being improvised in such a way that blended their expectations of legal freedom with collective thanksgiving, remembrance, and determination. More specific to this original context of watch-night is how this service assured them that they would hear the news of emancipation as a collective, and how, in accordance with their "cosmic vision for freedom," watch-night called the names of those who had passed on during the previous year, thereby keeping them within the circle of the community. In black church communities and beyond "watch-night" services are held annually in the late night hours on December 31. This service is an example of how the slaves' religion blended the Christian calendar and the transition from slavery to legal freedom and how this combination of religion and culture influenced American religious culture more broadly.

While they are not synonymous, the religious history of African Americans and the religious history of America are correspondents of each other. One example is the Black Holiness movement in the late nineteenth century. The Holiness movement was borne out of strain of American Methodism that began as early as the 1840s. Holiness theology preached "perfectionism," that one could live free from sin through a second work of grace. Liturgically, however, the Holiness movement's "camp meeting" fervor held special appeal for African Americans because of the ways the movement made space for them to reclaim an "old-time" religion, borne out of the "ring shouts" like those of the regiment. Yvonne Chireau offers an excellent description of the ways African Americans shaped the Holiness movement to meet their own needs:

African American Holiness churchgoers revived the spirited practices of the slave church, including inspired preaching and song, its shouts, ecstatic devotionals, and visionary experiences. In their pursuit of folk primitivism, blacks in the Holiness movement rekindled the embers and traditions of a religious culture that belonged to the past, which had been abandoned by many mainstream African American Protestant churches.[6]

The ring shout had enabled a sense of "oneness" for the 1st South. But here, in the post-emancipation era, it represented the folk practices of a slave culture that countered the aesthetic definitions of respectable racialized citizenship. However, the vast rural populations of newly freed African Americans were persistent in their commitments to making sure the circle would not be broken, while in contrast prominent black religious leaders such as the AME Bishop Daniel Alexander Payne discouraged these practices. In his memoir Payne recalls:

> About this time I attended a "bush meeting," where I went to please the pastor whose circuit I was visiting. After the sermon they formed a ring, and with coats off[,] sung, clapped their hands and stamped their feet in a most ridiculous and heathenish way. I requested the pastor to go and stop their dancing. At his request they stopped their dancing and clapping of hands, but remained singing and rocking their bodies to and fro. This they did for about fifteen minutes. I then went, and taking their leader by the arm[,] requested him to desist and to sit down and sing in a rational manner. . . . To the most thoughtful and intelligent I usually succeeded in making the "Band" disgusting; but by the ignorant masses, as in the case mentioned, it was regarded as the essence of religion.[7]

The *collective will to conjure* at work in the regiment's nightly engagement with the ring shout was resurrected here in this example of an AME Church. While Bishop Payne saw the ring shout as a symptom of "ignorance," other black religious movements, such as the Black Holiness movement, made it the basis of their worship. This movement reflects the regiment's collective will to conjure even as simultaneously, other forms of individualized conjure emerged in African American communities. The will to mix sacred texts with charms and herbs thrived among individual conjurers during the later decades of the nineteenth century as a small population of literate African American sacred specialists incorporated the Bible into their private practices. As Yvonne Chireau comments, "Lore and images from the Christian Bible

---

6. Chireau, *Black Magic,* 108.

7. Payne, *Recollections of Seventy Years,* 253.

also provided fertile territory from which African American specialists could acquire conjuring materials."[8] Having achieved the technical meanings of freedom in America, they nonetheless often did not have access to institutional forms of health care. Practitioners of "black magic," conjurers, herbalists, and root workers provided a service that traditional social institutions did not: conjurers in various forms stimulated a belief in the invisible and supernatural forces of existence.

Figures such as David Walker and Frederick Douglass had always used writing to stage vehement critiques of the hypocrisy of American Christianity. Their writing corresponds with the *spiritual militancy* in the regiment's music. Both of these practices demonstrate the ways black people have used the religious discourse of the empire to expose its own contradictions. This is a tradition of spiritual militancy in black culture that has been used consistently to inspire confrontation and movement. In the twentieth century, examples of spiritual militancy can be seen in the sermonizing of Malcolm X and Rev. Dr. Martin Luther King Jr. Malcolm X's "The Ballot or the Bullet" makes clear that the religious affiliations of a few African American leaders could not displace the overall political agenda of the many.

Though Dr. King is often over-read but insufficiently understood by being portrayed as simplistically non-violent, the prophetic political and economic vision he advanced condemned the nation and its values. His combination of vocal timbre, southern dialect, and his fiery impatience with American injustice is cadenced in notable examples such as his 1968 "Mountain Top" speech in Memphis, Tennessee, where he *commanded*, "Let justice roll down like waters and righteousness like a mighty stream."[9] Here, King takes a passage from the Bible (Amos 5:24), and endowed with the power of *ashe* King invokes the "flood" as a necessary cleansing for American injustice. King's poetics here do not encourage a passive waiting, but rather an active combination of water and movement that harks back to those themes in the regiment. Waterway poetics are a significant trope in the black freedom movement as they conjure the spirit for empowerment at the crossroads. Here rhetoric was used as a "Jihad of words" against "American institutional racism," to borrow a phrase from Steven Barboza, who describes the spoken word affect of Malcolm X as "talking back at white America," a form and style of speech that functioned as a "potent intellectual tool for spiritual and political consciousness raising."[10] The holy war waged against the injustice of American society and its stubborn racism was fought by a number of these spiritual militants across time.

8. Chireau, *Black Magic*, 25.
9. King Jr., *I've Been to the Mountaintop*.
10. Barboza, *American Jihad*, 18.

Of course, the prayer of Dutty Boukman in Haiti and those from the soldiers in the 1st South were correspondent with the sentiments in David Walker's *Appeal* and Frederick Douglass' distinction between the Christ of Christianity and the Christianity of the slaveholding nation. The performativity of their words is *intended* to both bring comfort to the afflicted and to afflict those who are comfortable with injustice.

The history of black religion has produced a tradition of freedom soldiers who conjured the spirit of freedom through their stylization of the spoken word. Figures such as Malcolm X and Dr. King were burdened with the task of inspiring a peaceful people toward freedom in a society that had engaged in centuries of racial violence while proposing to lead the world in democracy. Too little attention is paid to the smaller activist collectives such as "The Deacons for Defense and Justice," a self-armed protection squad of black men in Jonesboro and Bogalusa, Louisiana. Though their naming process is elusive, Lance Hill's history of the Deacons puts forth a few explanations. One is that the group's name was a *play* on the church deacons who bore the responsibility of taking care of the church. Another explanation suggests that the term "deacon" would conceal their identity as a collective armed for self-defense.[11] That the group signified on the church is of concern here because the members of the Deacons were indeed active in their various churches and fraternal orders. In this instance the Deacons' armed endeavor aimed at protecting the black community as a kind of spiritual labor, a spiritual militancy whose purpose was to wage war on racial terror.

David Walker, Dutty Boukman, Malcolm X, Ella Baker, James Baldwin, Dr. King Jr., Fannie Lou Hamer, and the Deacons for Defense all waged a spiritual warfare that demanded freedom on what Sonia Sanchez terms "this battlefield called life."[12] The duet between Sanchez's poem and "Sweet Honey in the Rock," by the legendary Black folk female group of the same name, was beautifully complemented by the ensemble's rendition of the old congregational song "I'm Going to Stay on the Battlefield."[13] This rendition calls forth the role of music in the spiritual militancy of the black freedom struggle. The singing of "I'm Going to Stay on the Battlefield" bears the echo of the 1st South when they sang,

Ride in, kind Saviour!
No man can hinder me

---

11. Hill, *The Deacons for Defense*, 46.
12. Sanchez, *For Sweet Honey in the Rock*, 148.
13. Sweet Honey in the Rock, *Sacred Ground*.

Songs such as this were at the core of the musical repertoire in the founding of historically black colleges and universities (HBCUs). The repertoire's transition from slavery, to the regiment, and further into the institutions of higher learning speaks volumes as to how the American public "learns" to hear—or not hear—black music.

THE SONGS OF BLACK FOLK:
BLACK COMMUNAL CONSERVATORIES

The "Port Royal Experiment" served as a model of racial reform that was replicated in the founding of HBCUs in the nineteenth century. The founding curricula of these institutions focused on agriculture, science, classical studies, and mechanic arts, but the musical memory of the ring shout followed the students. The few examples put forth here reveal how Black Communal Conservatories established in slavery were disrupted by black institutions and white instructors who sought to preserve black culture. This disruption was later addressed by the first generations of classically trained black music educators who created modern versions of teaching and learning musical styles. Their arrangements of spirituals reflected the modern *Africanisms* of other black modernists such as Scott Joplin. Black colleges and universities played a critical role in how post-emancipation black musicians were trained. Some musicians, however, went beyond their individual institutions and extended into the churches where many of them worked. They formed and led barbershop and community-based male vocal quartets and created music programs in public schools. Similar to the plight of black music during slavery, the popularity of black music in the late nineteenth and early twentieth century was often heard through essentialist ears with no regard to the epistemological aspects of this music; let alone its relationship to the racial politics of society.

One outgrowth of the HBCUs, Black Communal Conservatories, was the emergence of communal-based forms of teaching and learning of black music traditions across schools, churches, and small and independent sites for musical training. These conservatories consisted of networks of teachers and students that were official in the sense that the teachers were anointed and appointed by the black community, but they were also unofficial in the ways that the epistemic perception of black music was considered epistemologically inferior to European forms of music knowledge.

WHILE THE compromised project of black freedom presented several conundrums in terms of responses and strategies, there was a general consensus among black colleges and universities that "spirituals" *had* to be central to campus life. Founded while slavery was still legal in the United States, Wilberforce University was established by the African Methodist Episcopal Church in Ohio in 1856. Following the tumultuous times of the Civil War the school closed its doors in 1862 and reopened in March 1863 with Bishop Daniel A. Payne as its president.[14] The earlier discussion of Payne's disdain for the ring shout was elaborated further in his memoir when he described their songs as "cornfield ditties." He further stated that, "to indulge in such songs from eight to ten and half-past ten at night was the chief employment of these Bands."[15] Archival evidence concerning Payne's feeling about music at Wilberforce is scarce, but his comments about the ring shout suggest that he would not have welcomed it.

At Fisk University, founded only two years after the 1863 Emancipation Proclamation, one of the original members of the Jubilee Singers, named Ella Sheppard, told the group's first director, a white man named George White, that "the slave songs were never used by us then in public. . . . They were sacred to our parents, who used them in their religious worship and *shouted* over them [emphasis mine]."[16] Over time White, who was only moderately trained as a musician, was able to collect over one hundred songs from Sheppard, an accomplished pianist who made transcriptions of them. While she cooperated with her teacher, she remained hesitant about singing the songs of her ancestors in public. She recalled, "sitting upon the floor (there were but a few chairs)" rehearsing "softly, learning from each other the songs of our fathers. We did not dream of ever using them in public."[17] The concern for singing this music in public has political importance as black religious singing during slavery had been encoded with messages of revolt and escape. Some songs, like those of the 1st South make explicit their intentions of freedom. Higginson recalled that one song, "We'll Soon Be Free," had such an effect. He wrote that those singing the song "had been put in jail in Georgetown, S. C . . . [because] we'll soon be free was too dangerous an assertion."[18] Still, the singing of black music in "private" was not only a matter of explicit political intention, but it also distinguishes between what was sacred in private and what became a public performance. This musical transition at Fisk is a progression that corresponded with the progressions at other black colleges and universities of turning an internal community resource into a directed external performance.

14. Payne, *Recollections*, 152.
15. Ibid., 255.
16. Ward, *Dark Midnight*, 110.
17. Ibid., 110.
18. Higginson, *Army Life*, 168.

Similar to Fisk, the Hampton Normal and Agricultural Institute was founded soon after the end of the Civil War. Samuel Chapman Armstrong, a high-ranking military officer during the Civil War and a dedicated worker in the Freedmen's Bureau, established the school in 1868. One of the earliest histories of Hampton (re)captures the language of the Port Royal Experiment; "this experiment of negro education is too serious a matter to be treated with the severest honesty."[19] Hampton followed the example of Fisk University by organizing a group of students singing spirituals to tour the country to raise funds for the school. Thomas Fenner, a professor from the New England Conservatory of Music, arrived at Hampton in June 1872. Fenner was a trained musician with the skills to create musical notation. Despite this he echoed the limitations of transcription expressed by Higginson. In the preface to his published collection of "cabin and plantation songs" in 1874 Fenner wrote:

> Half its effectiveness, in its home, depends upon accompaniments, which can be carried away only in memory. The inspiration of numbers; the overpowering chorus, covering defects; the swaying of the body; the rhythmical stamping of the feet; and all the wild enthusiasm of the negro camp meeting—these obviously cannot be transported to the boards of a public performance.[20]

Fenner hears an "affect" as a "defect," a way of hearing that doesn't allow black music its own epistemological legitimacy so it has to be corrected. The "swaying of the body, the rhythmical stamping of the feet, . . . the wild enthusiasm of the negro camp meeting" that harks back to Higginson's description of the ring shout, it too must be corrected. Though it is not clear from Fenner's description if the students were actually performing the songs in a ring shout, this hypothesis is not unlikely. What is clear, however, is that while Fenner produces an important archive through his collection of black music, his is a record that confesses a contradiction between black institutions and black cultural practices: it reveals how the ring shout was disciplined out of the students' musical memory while it was simultaneously being preserved (as if the music had been preserved thus far merely by accident). It is highly probable that some of the students in Fenner's chorus would have privately recreated their own ring shout, as an early biographer of Hampton attests, "with four exceptions, all the rest of the company have lived in slavery."[21]

19. Armstrong and Ludlow, *Hampton and Its Students*, 9.
20. Ibid., 172.
21. Ibid., 129.

When Booker T. Washington, a graduate of Hampton, founded the Tuskegee Institute in Alabama, he insisted that "spirituals" be sung at every weekly chapel service. The first choir director hired by Washington, Robert H. Hamilton, served Tuskegee from 1887 to 1895. After graduating from Hampton in 1877, Hamilton made it his mission to teach vocal music to the entire school, "especially keeping up the plantation songs."[22] Like Fenner and White at their respective institutions, Hamilton created arrangements of spirituals based on European choral standards, which reflected what he learned at Hampton, as well as reflecting Washington's vision of race and respectability. Ultimately, the dislocation of the ring shout from black singing at black institutions is a political displacement that aims to discipline black music from its embodied context. And yet, the fact that the songs born in the context of the West African ring shout were initially domesticated by white men who sought to de-Africanize them is not the end of the story.

A graduate of Fisk, John Wesley Work II, returned to the university as the school was experiencing a decline in interest of the spiritual. According to Joe Richardson's concise *History of Fisk University 1865–1946*, John W. Work II was hired to teach Latin, but his passionate work as a collector of folk spirituals led to his restoration of "folk music at Fisk. The publication of *Folk Songs of the American Negro* in 1907 by John and Frederick Work (his brother) and *The Folk Songs of the American Negro* by John in 1915 stimulated a new study of folk music in America."[23] John Work II's own compositions and arrangements of spirituals aimed to resurrect the feeling of the ring shout into choral arrangements. Work II's particular use of rhythmic punctuation emphasized the dance quality of the ring shout spirituals. The esteemed musicologist of black music Samuel F. Floyd describes John W. Work II's "Dancing in the Sun" as having a "clear, crisp melody, dance-like accompaniment," a description that adequately corresponds to several of Work's spirituals. John Work II is an inaugural figure in the black musical tradition of musician and scholar. His example was continued in the work of his son, John Work III.

A trained musician at the Julliard school, a collector of black folklore, a composer whose music was inspired by the Negro folk tradition of music, John Work III epitomized the aesthetic philosophy of the "New Negro" artist at the dawn of the twentieth century. He was chair of the music department at Fisk during the first three decades of the twentieth century and composed for and conducted the Jubilee Singers during his tenure at the university. He set to music Arna Bontemps's "Golgotha Is a Mountain," which was performed by

---

22. *The Southern Workman and Hampton School Record*, 24, no. 4 (April 1895): 55.
23. Richardson, *A History*, 150.

the Fisk choir in 1949 and he is one of the silent black heroes who worked with the folklorist Alan Lomax.[24] John Work III was one of several black musicians/ scholars/teachers who was trained both by the formal academy of Western music in America but he was also trained by the Black Communal Conservatories of black communities. While he did not stage actual performances of the ring shout, his passion for black folk music is reflected in the African rhythms, syncopation, chant, and close harmonies of his arrangements. This marks an important shift from white arrangers to trained black musicians like Work III.

Nathaniel Dett became Hampton's first black director of music in 1913. At the famed Oberlin Conservatory Dett was a student prodigy who was influenced by the Czech composer Antonin Dvorak, claiming that Dvorak's music reminded him of the music of his grandmother.[25] Dett was inspired in this context to use spirituals to frame his symphonic work and of course, he used folk melodies and rhythms to frame his choral arrangements of spirituals. Like Work's, Dett's arrangements are starkly different from his predecessors.

Joining John Work II and III along with Nathaniel Dett was William Dawson, considered the "Dean of African American Choral Composers." Born in Anniston, Alabama, Dawson was trained in classical music at an early age, studying at the Chicago Musical College and later at the American Conservatory of Music. Before he arrived at Tuskegee he made his mark as a public school teacher in Kansas City, MO. The "Dawson spirituals," as they are called, are known for their rhythmic complexity, which Dawson took great lengths to notate on the musical score.[26] All three of these examples reveal the "both/ and" epistemology of Black Communal Conservatories in the transition from the nineteenth into the twentieth century. There was an attempt to move the folk spiritual into black institutions, and, even under the guise of preserving it, white choral directors sought to arrange it for white audiences. The first generations of black musicians to take up the baton of black choral singing at these institutions combined their classical training with the ring shout aesthetics that had been disavowed by their white predecessors. This is significant as it corresponds with the African story in America: these musicians were looking back to the past as a resource by which to invent something new. This new invention looked back toward old *Africanisms* and even this effort held investments in the performance of musical mastery, a mastery that often aimed to legitimize the spiritual as a musical form.

---

24. Ibid., 146. Also see Gordon and Nemerov, *Lost Delta Found.*
25. See Southern, *The Music of Black Americans.*
26. Ibid.

The arranged spirituals of Work (II and III), Dett, and Dawson were not "purely" folk nor were they completely modern in the classical sense, but they were a hybrid that enabled new ensembles and new modes of musical arranging. In their folk melodies and syncopated rhythms even these new forms offered a musical critique on American music, one that Antonin Dvorak described in the following way:

> In the negro melodies of America I discover all that is needed for a great and noble school of music. They are pathetic, tender, passionate, melancholy, solemn, religious, bold, merry, gay or what you will. It is music that suits itself to any mood or any purpose. There is nothing in the whole age of composition that cannot be supplied with themes from this source.[27]

Dvorak's phrase "noble school of music" is an excellent way to think of how the first generation of black classically trained musicians not only taught at their institutions of higher learning, but they also helped to establish a network of black music education in black communities across musical genres.

The black choral tradition of arranged spirituals sketched here is not to ignore the ways the spiritual influenced additional forms of expression beyond the classical genre. For touring purposes of fundraising, male quartets were established at Fisk, Tuskegee, and Hampton, which resurrected the gendered nature of singing spirituals seen in the 1st South. The first Jubilee Quartet was organized at Fisk in 1871. Initially, the "jubilee spirituals" of these quartets were closer to their larger mix-voiced counterparts, but this would eventually change when the quartet phenomenon took off in the broader black community. As Kip Lornell comments regarding the shift in jubilee groups,

> The Fisk University Jubilee Singers broke ground for other "jubilee" groups, most of which were associate with colleges and Universities; by the 1890's, however, many were professional groups that may have come up through the academic ranks but that now performed on the professional stage.[28]

The proliferation of black masculinities in the form of "race men" in the late nineteenth and early twentieth centuries tends to obscure the role of culture and specifically music in the making of black manhood. A distinction is to be made here regarding the construction of masculinity with respect to that of the 1st South: whereas the regiment used the tactics and language

---

27. Beckerman, *Dovrak and His World,* 138.
28. Lornell, *Happy in the Service of the Lord,* 5.

of the military to articulate an explicit masculinity, male vocal quartets used close harmonies, their uniform style of dress, and their grooming trends to construct a masculine identity.

Musically, the esteemed scholar of black culture and music James Weldon Johnson reflected at length on the popularity of these quartets at the beginning of the twentieth century,

> Pick up four colored boys or young men anywhere and the chances are ninety out of a hundred that you have a quartet. Let one of them sing the melody and the others will naturally find the parts. Indeed it may be said that all male Negro youth of the United States is divided into quartets. In the days when such a thing as a white barber was unknown in the South, every barber shop had its quartet, and the men spent their leisure time playing on the guitar—not banjo, mind you—and "harmonizing." I have witnessed some of these explorations in the field of harmony and the scenes of hilarity and backslapping when a new and peculiarly rich chord was discovered. There would be demands for repetitions, and cries of "Hold it!" until it was firmly mastered. And well it was, for some of these chords were so new and strange for voices that, like Sullivan's *Lost Chord,* they would never have been found again except for the celebrity with which they were recaptured. In this way was born the famous but much abused barber shop chord.

The history of black barbershops and barbershop quartets is not unlike the contradictory but "both/and" history of music in the black institutions discussed here. In his cultural history of black barbershops Quincy T. Mills argues, "historians must move beyond the blacks-made-money-too thesis and explore the challenges and tensions that capitalism played in visions of individual and racial progress within black communities."[29] Similar to the ways black music was both adjusted for white audiences and yet preserved for the sake of black culture, black barbershop quartets were a bridge between these two institutions, the barbershop and the educational institution. Black barbershops were quite often rehearsal spaces for developing black barbershop quartets. Johnson's comments require no elaboration in terms of music, except to say that these experimental harmonies were the seeds for jazz, as is confirmed in Lynn Abbott's article on African Americans and the origins of Barbershop harmony.[30] In addition to this, the popularity of black barbershops and Jubilee quartets paved the way for the development of gospel quartets at the begin-

---

29. Mills, *Cutting Along the Color Lines,* 4.
30. Abbott, "Play the Barbershop Chord."

ning of the twentieth century.[31] Inspired by the Black Communal Conservatories of school-based instruction and community singing, black gospel quartets experimented with blues, jazz, and gospel. But as Black Communal Conservatories are also a matter of epistemology, vocal experts trained and taught gospel quartets "how" to perform their music as part of a tradition. This is thoroughly explained in the appropriately titled volume *To Do This, You Must Know How: Music Pedagogy in the Black Gospel Quartet Tradition,* where Lynn Abbott and Doug Seroff present a thorough case for the epistemological history of black gospel quartets and their place in Black Communal Conservatories in the early twentieth century.

> The variety and abundance of black vocal music training available early in the twentieth century suggests a bold socio-cultural experiment. There were countless initiatives, often conceived as personal commitments, conducted on both national and local levels by music educators of both races.[32]

Gospel quartets in the early twentieth century enjoyed popularity throughout the southern U.S, and they used the sounds of labor to tweak the style of jubilee singing. Early gospel quartets took advantage of syncopated rhythms to accentuate the harmony and melody, and their uniformed presentation of clothing and grooming extended the notion of a black musical masculinity even further. The influence of these early quartets has played a critical role in the development of black male singing in America and beyond. Gospel quartets were the prelude to the modern gospel movement of Thomas A. Dorsey and Mahalia Jackson. The Chicago School of Gospel, and its accompanying quartet tradition, has produced some of the most important "voices" in American music, such as the Sunset Four Jubilee Quartette, the Pace Jubilee Singers, The Soul Stirrers (featuring Same Cooke and later Lou Rawls), and the Gospel Chimes, which featured Reverend James Cleveland. However, musical forms of black masculinity have not been manufactured in isolation from women. Julia Mae Kennedy, a legendary music educator at Industrial High School in Birmingham, Alabama, was herself a premier soloist and vocal teacher whose tutelage helped to produce top-notch male quartets. She led the school to great heights in high school choral music. Notably Kennedy landed at the First Church of Deliverance in Chicago, Illinois, in 1931 where Rev. Clarence H. Cobbs was pastor. First Church of Deliverance is one of the most important black churches in the history of modern gospel music. Kennedy's arrangement

---

31. See Abbott, "Play the Barbershop Chord."
32. Abbott and Seroff, *To Do This, You Must Know How,* 5.

of Malotte's "Lord's Prayer" continues to be sung by church choirs throughout the nation. Moreover First Church was a primary classroom for gospel composers such as Thomas A. Dorsey and Roberta Martin, both of whom taught their compositions to the choir in order to gauge their performance quality. The Chicago School of Gospel established its own communal conservatory around the First Church of Deliverance, and it should come as no surprise that this church was the first to popularize the Hammond organ in gospel music.

For sure, the often forgotten black barbershop quartets forged a pathway for vocal male ensembles that were gospel quartets at the beginning of the twentieth century, later do-wop ensembles, and then Motown male groups of the mid-twentieth century. The spread of the quartet movement demonstrates the fertile quality of black culture and its capacity for musical (re)invention. Such cultural fertility often results in the restaging of old forms under new names and new stages that obscure their historical origins.

SPECTERS OF THE 1ST SOUTH

Discussing music and other forms of expressive culture as a powerful but distorted mirror of black history, James Baldwin wrote:

> It is only in his music, which Americans are able to admire because a protective sentimentality limits their understanding of it, that the Negro in America has been able to tell his story. It is a story which otherwise has yet to be told and which no American is prepared to hear. As is the inevitable result of things unsaid, we find ourselves until today oppressed with a dangerous and reverberating silence; and the story is told, compulsively, in symbols and signs, in hieroglyphics. . . . The ways in which the Negro has affected the American psychology are betrayed in our popular culture and in our morality.[33]

Some of the complexity of culture as a historical sign and symbol is illuminated by the sacred singing of black Civil War soldiers and its enduring relevance. On January 1, 1866 in Charleston, South Carolina, a parade commemorating the Emancipation Proclamation featured a procession of black dignitaries, clergy, and personalities from throughout the region. On hand to lend their military magic were members of the 1st South accompanied by a

---

33. Baldwin, "Many Thousands Gone," 19.

small drum corps. In the years that followed, this kind of assembly manifested itself in the elaborate parades of special days in the African American community, the half-time entertainment at HBCU football games and homecomings, the step shows of black sororities and fraternities, and the highly stylized march and drill team ensembles that are part of the "genealogies of performance" in black history that conjure up the aesthetics of the ring shout.[34] The enduring theatricality of black music, dance, and militarism conjure the specters of the 1st South. For example, Higginson's description of drummer boys in the 1st South could pertain to even the most contemporary parade in an African American community: "The little drum-corps kept in advance . . . their drums slung on their backs, and the drum-sticks perhaps balanced on their heads."[35] With the exception of George Lewis's *A Power Stronger Than Itself: The AACM and American Experimental Music,* the study of black drum and bugle corps has received little attention. In his generative discussion of a black drum corps, however, Lewis describes how these musical institutions provided black youth with a refuge from street life as well giving them an alternative to racial segregation.[36]

The specter of these "drummer boys" is alive in the street performances of "bucket boys" in Chicago, Illinois. As I exit the Dan Ryan Freeway at Garfield Street a group of four to five young black men improvise on plastic buckets, alternating between military march drills and African polyrhythms. The synchronized beats and the tricks they perform with their drumsticks do not simply "flash-up" memories of the 1st South drummer boys. The ghosts in these rhythms "conjure" the haunting histories of race, musical performance, and American democracy. The "bucket-boys" expose the economic needs that produced these performances: they serve as a musical reminder of what Dr. King called the "cancelled check" of emancipation.

According to Higginson the regiment improvised around the "route step," which during military training "is an abandonment of all military strictness. . . . They are not required to keep step." And yet, the regiment improvised by keeping step "anyhow" and inventing new movement and new music. This creative choreography of military march and "step" lives on in the performances of "step shows" by black fraternities, where both uniformity and individual creativity coexist.

Though the rearticulated performances of the ring shout may *appear* as mere holograms in the current popular moment, when viewed historically these performances offer critical wisdom for the continued project of the black

---

34. Roach, *Cities of the Dead,* 25.

35. Higginson, *Army Life,* 102.

36. Lewis, *A Power Stronger Than Itself,* 243.

freedom struggle as well as the abstract aims of American democracy. The ring shout provided black soldiers with the space to construct *their* version of masculinity through music. Composed at one of the most important crossroads in American and African American history, the songs of black singing soldiers have reverberated across time. Theirs is a reverberating echo in which the spiritual, moral, and civic wisdom of the African's history in America is encoded into the rhythm, melody, and dance of the music. The nation's first black regiment, the 1st South Carolina Volunteers, represents not only the racial paradox of America, but it *also* embodies its potential. On January 1, 1863, when they gathered beneath "Emancipation Oak" in Beaufort, South Carolina, on the same exact land that was previously known as the "Smith Plantation," they lifted their voices to sing "My Country 'tis of Thee." Awaiting them on the other side of slavery's legal abolition was the stark reality that the country they had hoped would be theirs betrayed them. But rather than "hang up their harps" they set out to salvage their cosmic vision of freedom in the churches and religious practices created in slavery. They continued to established Black Communal Conservatories and transformed even the most inferior public schools into halls of black erudition, athleticism, and artistic creativity.

The cosmic vision of freedom of the 1st South Carolina Volunteers is a story to pass on, it is a sample of the "both/and" story of America and African American culture. Performances of black culture continue to haunt the social landscape of America. During the inauguration of the nation's first African American president in January 2009, the "queen of soul," Aretha Franklin, sang "My Country 'tis of Thee." For sure, an unquestionable product of the black church Aretha Franklin embodies the rich pedigree of Black Communal Conservatories. Franklin's soulful rendition of the patriotic song connected the dots between blackness, culture, and progress, but was also a moment of conjure. For on January 1, 1863, many miles away from where Franklin stood to sing, the African American community in the Georgia Sea Islands along with the 1st South Carolina Volunteers raised that same song. Franklin's version made the echo of *their* hopes for a nation where "Black Lives Matter" would be heard again. While it is convenient to hear Franklin's soulfulness through the "protective sentimentality" that Baldwin describes, when such performances are understood as a musical conjuration, this comprehension raises the necessary social/historical/political and even spiritual intersections that are still urgent for black freedom here and now.

BIBLIOGRAPHY

Abbott, Lynn. "Play the Barbershop Chord: A Case for the African American Origin of Barbershop Harmony." *American Music* 10, no. 3 (1992): 289–325.

Abbott, Lynn, and Doug Seroff. *To Do This, You Must Know How: Music Pedagogy in the Black Gospel Quartet Tradition.* Jackson, MI: University of Mississippi Press, 2013.

Abrahamsson, Hans. *The Origin of Death: Studies in African Mythology.* Chicago: University of Chicago Press, 1951.

"An Account of the Negro Insurrection in South Carolina, 1739." In *The Colonial Records of the State of Georgia.* Ed. Allen D. Candler et al., 232–36. Vol. 33, part 2. Atlanta: Byrd, 1913.

Albanese, Catherine L. *America Religions and Religion.* Belmont, CA: Wadsworth Publishing, 1999.

Allen, William Francis, Charles Pickard Ware, and Lucy McKim Garrison. *Slave Songs of the United States.* 1861. Reprint. Bedford, MA: Applewood Books, 2009.

Anderson, Victor. *Beyond Ontological Blackness: An Essay on African American Religious and Cultural Criticism.* New York: Continuum, 1999.

Anzaldua, Floria E. *Borderlands/La Frontera: The New Mestiza.* San Francisco: Aunt Lute Books, 1987.

Armstrong, M. F., and Helen W. Ludlow. *Hampton and Its Students. By Two of Its Teachers. With Fifty Cabin and Plantation Songs.* New York: Putnam's Sons, 1874.

Asante, Molefi. *The Afrocentric Idea: Revised and Expanded.* Philadelphia: Temple University Press, 1998.

Austin, Allan D. *African Muslims in Antebellum America: Transatlantic Stories and Spiritual Struggles.* New York: Routledge, 1997.

Awad, Marwa, and Edward E. Curtis, IV. "Autobiography." In *Encyclopedia of Muslim-American History.* Vol. 1. Ed. Edward E. Curtis, IV, 72–75. New York: Facts on File, 2010.

Badger, Reid. *A Life in Ragtime: A Biography of James Reese.* Oxford: Oxford University Press, 1995.

Bagwell, James E. *Rice Gold: James Hamilton Couper and Plantation Life on the Georgia Coast.* Macon, GA: Mercer University Press, 2000.

Bakhtin, Mikhail. *Toward a Philosophy of the Act.* Trans. Vadim Liapunov. Ed. Vadim Liapunov and Michael Holquist. Austin: University of Texas Press, 1993.

Baldwin, James. *The Fire Next Time*. New York: Dial Press, 1962.

———. "Many Thousands Gone." In *Baldwin: Collected Essays*. Ed. Toni Morrison, 19–34. New York: Penguin, 1998.

Banfield, William C. *Cultural Codes: Makings of a Black Music Philosophy. An Interpretive History from Spirituals to Hip Hop*. Toronto: Scarecrow Press, 2010.

Barboza, Steven. *American Jihad: Islam after Malcolm X*. New York: Doubleday, 1994.

Barrett, Leonard E. *Soul-Force: African Heritage in* Afro-American *Religion*. Garden City, NY: Anchor Press, 1974.

Barthes, Roland. *Image, Music, Text*. Trans. Stephen Heath. New York: Hill and Wang, 1977.

Basler, Roy P., ed. *The Collected Works of Abraham Lincoln*. Vol 5. New Brunswick, NJ: Rutgers University Press, 1955.

Beckerman, Michael. *Dovrak and His World*. Princeton: Princeton University Press, 1993.

Bell, Catherine. *Ritual Theory, Ritual Practice*. New York: Oxford University Press, 1992.

Benjamin, Walter. *Illuminations: Essays and Reflections*. New York: Shocken, 1969.

Bernier, Celeste-Marie. *African American Visual Arts: From Slavery to the Present*. Chapel Hill: University of North Carolina Press, 2008.

Bielskis, Andrius. "Power, History and Genealogy: Freidrich Nietzsche and Michel Foucault." *Problemos* (Lithuania) 79 (2009): 73–84.

Billingsley, Andrew. *Yearning to Breathe Free: Robert Smalls of South Carolina and His Families*. Columbia: University of South Carolina Press, 2007.

Blatt, Martin. "*Glory*: Hollywood History, Popular Culture, and the Fifty-Fourth Massachusetts Regiment." In *Hope and Glory: Essays on the Legacy of the 54th Massachusetts Regiment*. Ed. Martin Blatt, Thomas H. Brown, and Donald Yacovone, 215–35. Amherst, MA: University of Massachusetts Press, 2001.

Blight, David W. "The Shaw Memorial in the Landscape of Civil War Memory." *Hope and Glory: Essays on the Legacy of the 54th Massachusetts Regiment*. Ed. Martin Blatt, Thomas H. Brown, and Donald Yacovone, 79–93. Amherst, MA: University of Massachusetts Press, 2001.

Bohlman, Phillip V., Edith Blumhofer, and Maria Chow, eds. *Music in American Religious Experience*. New York: Oxford University Press, 2006.

Bradford, Sarah. *Scenes in the Life of Harriet Tubman*. Auburn, NY: W. J. Moses, 1869.

Breed, Allen G. "Churches across America Reflect on Obama Election." *USA Today*, November 9, 2008, http://usatoday30.usatoday.com/news/nation/2008–11–09–4125943569_x.htm.

Brody, Jennifer Devere. *Impossible Purities: Blackness, Femininity, and Victorian Culture*. Durham, NC: Duke University Press, 1998.

Brueggemann, Walter. "The Costly Loss of Lament." In *The Psalms: The Life of Faith*. Ed. Patrick D. Miller, 98–111. Minneapolis: Fortress, 1995.

Buff, Rachel. *Immigration and the Political Economy of Home: West Indian Brooklyn and American Indian Minneapolis, 1945–1992*. Berkeley: University of California Press, 2001.

Burchard, Peter. *One Gallant Rush: Robert Gould Shaw and His Brave Black Regiment*. New York: St. Martin's Press, 1989.

Cacho, Lisa Marie. *Social Death: Racialized Rightlessness and the Criminalization of the Unprotected*. New York: New York University Press, 2012.

Callahan, Allen D. *The Talking Book: African Americans and the Bible*. New Haven, CT: Yale University Press, 2006.

Camp, Stephanie. *Closer to Freedom: Enslaved Women and Everyday Resistance in the Plantation South*. Chapel Hill: University of North Carolina Press, 2004.

de Certeau, Michel. *The Practice of Everyday Life*. Trans. Steven Rendall. Berkeley: University of California Press, 1984.

Chauncey, George. *Gay New York: Gender, Urban Culture, and the Making of the Gay Male World, 1890–1940*. New York: Basic Books, 1994.

Cheney, Charise. "We Men Ain't We? Mas(k)ulinity and the Gendered Politics of Black Nationalism." In *Brothers Gonna Work It Out: Sexual Politics in the Golden Age of Rap Nationalism*, 27–62. New York: New York University Press, 2005.

Chireau, Yvonne. *Black Magic: Religion in the African American Conjuring Tradition*. Berkeley: University of California Press, 2003.

Coddington, Ronald. *African American Faces of the Civil War*. Baltimore: Johns Hopkins University Press, 2012.

Collins, Kathleen. *Shadow and Substance: Essays on the History of Photography*. Bloomfield Hills, MI: Amorphous Institute Press, 1990.

Cone, James. *A Black Theology of Liberation*. 1970. Reprint. Maryknoll, NY: Orbis Books, 2010.

Cooke, Phillip St. Geo. "Cavalry Tactics or Regulations for The Instruction, Formations, and Movements of The Cavalry of the Army and Volunteers of the United States." 1862. Reprint. Mechanicsburg, PA: Stackpole Books, 2004.

Covey, Herbert. *African American Slave Medicine: Herbal and Non-Herbal Treatments*. New York: Lexington Books, 2007.

Creel, Margaret Washington. *A Peculiar People: Slave Religion and Community-Culture Among the Gullahs*. New York: New York University Press, 1989.

Creelman, James. "The Real Value of Negro Melodies." *New York Herald,* May 21, 1893.

Crenshaw, Kimberle. "Race, Reform and Retrenchment: Transformation and Legitimation in Anti-discrimination Law." In *Critical Race Theory: The Key Writings That Formed the Movement*. Ed. Kimberle Crenshaw, Neil Gotanda, Gary Peller, and Kendall Thomas, 103–26. New York: The New Press, 1995.

Cross, Wilbur. *Gullah Culture in America*. Winston-Salem: J. F. Blair Publishers, 2012.

Cruz, Jon. *Culture on the Margins: The Black Spiritual and the Rise of American Cultural Interpretation*. Princeton, NJ: Princeton University Press, 1999.

Cummings, Naomi. *The Sonic Self: Musical Subjectivity and Signification*. Bloomington: Indiana University Press, 2000.

Curtis, Edward E., IV. *Encyclopedia of Muslim-American History*. 2 vols. New York: Facts on File, 2010.

Davis, Angela. *Women, Race and Class*. New York: Vintage, 1981.

De Nyew Testament. New York: American Bible Society, 2005.

Diouf, Sylviane A. *Servants of Allah: African Muslims Enslaved in the Americas*. New York: New York University Press, 1998.

Donaldson, Alfred L. *A History of the Adirondacks*. Vol. 2. New York: The Century Company, 1921.

Douglass, Frederick. "Men Of Color, To Arms!" In *Life and Writings of Frederick Douglass*. Vol. 3, *The Civil War*. Ed. Philip S. Foner. New York: International Publishers, 1952.

———. *My Bondage and My Freedom*. New York: Miller, Orton & Mulligan, 1855.

———. *Narrative of The Life of Frederick Douglass, an American Slave*. Reprinted with original introduction by William Lloyd Garrison. 1845. Mineola, NY: Dover, 1995.

Du Bois, W. E. B. *Black Reconstruction in America, 1860–1880*. New York: Free Press, 1992.

———. "Of the Sorrow Songs." In *id., The Souls of Black Folk*. 1903. Reprint. New York: Penguin, 1982.

Dubois, Laurent. *Avengers of the New World: The Story of the Haitian Revolution*. Cambridge, MA: Belknap of Harvard University Press, 2005.

Dumas, Henry. "Ark of Bones." *Ancestral House: The Black Short Story in the Americas and Europe*. Ed. Charles H. Rowell. Boulder: Harper Collins, 1995.

Durkheim, Emile. *The Elementary Forms of Religious Life*. Oxford: Oxford University Press, 2001.

Edelstein, Tilden J. *Strange Enthusiasm: A Life of Thomas Wentworth Higginson*. New Haven, CT: Yale University Press, 1968.

El Hamel, Chouki. "Constructing a Diasporic Identity: Tracing the Origins of the Gnawa Spiritual Group in Morocco." *Journal of African History* 49, no. 2 (2008): 241–60.

Emilio, Luis. *A Brave Black Regiment: The History of the Fifty-Fourth Regiment of Massachusetts Volunteer Infantry 1863–1865*. New York: Da Capo Press, 1995.

Epstein, Dena J. *Sinful Tunes and Spirituals: Black Folk Music to the Civil War*. Urbana, IL: University of Illinois Press, 1977.

Faust, Drew Gilpin. *This Republic of Suffering: Death and the American Civil War*. New York: Alfred A. Knopf, 2008.

Federal Writers Project. "Sam Mitchell: Ex-Slave, Age 87." In *Slave Narratives: A Folk History of Slavery in the United States*, 200–202. Vol. 14, part 3. n.p.: Federal Writers Project, 1936–1938.

———. *Slave Narratives: A Folk History of Slavery in the United States*. Vol. 14, *South Carolina Narratives*, part 3. Washington, DC: Library of Congress, 1941.

Ferguson, Roderick. *Aberrations in Black: Toward a Queer of Color Critique*. Minneapolis: University of Minnesota Press, 2004.

Fields, Barbara, and Karen Fields. *Racecraft: The Soul of Inequality in American Life*. New York: Verso, 2012.

Fitzhugh, George. *Cannibals All: Slaves without Masters*. Cambridge, MA: Belknap Press, 1996.

Frazier, E. Franklin. *The Negro Family in the United States*. Chicago: University of Chicago Press, 1939.

Freire, Paulo. *Pedagogy of the Oppressed*. New York: Continuum, 2009.

Gallagher, Gary W. *Causes Won, Lost, and Forgotten: How Hollywood and Popular Art Shape What We Know About the Civil War*. Chapel Hill: University of North Carolina Press, 2008.

Gilroy, Paul. *The Black Atlantic: Modernity and Double Consciousness*. Cambridge, MA: Harvard University Press, 1993.

Giovanni, Nikki. *On My Journey Now: Looking at African American History Through Spirituals*. Somerville, MA: Candelwick, 2009.

Glaude, Eddie S., Jr. *Exodus! Religion, Race and Nation in Early Nineteenth Century Black America*. Chicago: University of Chicago Press, 2000.

Glory. Dir. Edward Zwick. Culver City, CA: Sony Pictures, 1989. DVD.

Gomez, Michael A. *Exchanging Our Country Marks: The Transformation of African Identities in the Colonial and Antebellum South*. Chapel Hill: University of Chapel Hill Press, 1998.

Gordon, Avery. *Ghostly Matters: Haunting and the Sociological Imagination*. Minneapolis: University of Minnesota Press, 1997.

Gordon, Robert, and Bruce Nemerov, eds. *Lost Delta Found: Rediscovering the Fisk University-Library of Congress Coahoma Country Study, 1941–1942*. Nashville: Vanderbilt University Press, 2005.

Haraway, Donna J. *Simians, Cyborgs, and Women: The Reinvention of Nature*. New York: Routledge, 1991.

Harding, Rachel. "É a Senzala: Slavery, Women, and Embodied Knowledge in Afro-Brazilian Candomblé." In *Women and Religion in the African Diaspora: Knowledge, Power, and Performance*. Ed. R. Marie Griffith and Barbara Savage, 3–18. Baltimore: John Hopkins University Press, 2006.

Harding, Vincent. *There Is a River: The Black Struggle for Freedom in America*. San Diego: Harcourt Brace, 1981.

Hartman, Saidiya V. *Scenes of Subjection: Terror, Slavery, and Self-Making in Nineteenth-Century America*. New York: Oxford University Press, 1997.

Havrelock, Rachel. *River Jordan: The Mythology of a Dividing Line*. Chicago: University of Chicago Press, 2011.

Herring, George. "America and Vietnam: The Unending War." *Foreign Affairs*, Winter 1991–92. http://www.foreignaffairs.com/articles/47440/george-c-herring/america-and-vietnam-the-unending-war.

Herskovits, Melville J. *The Myth of the Negro Past*. Boston: Beacon Press, 1958.

Higginson, Mary Thacher. *Thomas Wentworth Higginson: The Story of His Life*. Boston: Houghton Mifflin Company, 1914.

Higginson, Thomas Wentworth. *Army Life in a Black Regiment*. 1870. Reprint. New York: Penguin Books, 1997.

———. "The Black Troops: 'Intensely Human.'" In *The Magnificent Activist: The Writings of Thomas Wentworth Higginson*. Ed. Howard N. Meyer, 178–89. New York: Da Capo Press, 2000.

———. *Cheerful Yesterdays*. Boston: Houghton, Mifflin and Company, 1898.

———. "Literature as Art." *Atlantic Monthly*, December 1867, 745–55.

———. "To Louisa Storrow Higginson, November 9, 1862." In *The Complete Civil War Journal and Selected Letters of Thomas Wentworth Higginson*. Ed. Christopher Looby, 243. Chicago: University of Chicago Press, 2000.

Hill, Lance. *The Deacons for Defense: Armed Resistance and the Civil Rights Movement*. Chapel Hill: University of North Carolina Press, 2004.

Holland, Sharon. *The Erotic Life of Racism*. Durham, NC: Duke University Press, 2012.

———. *Raising the Dead: Readings of Death and Black Subjectivity*. Durham, NC: Duke University Press, 2000.

Holloway, Karla. "*Beloved*: A Spiritual." *Callaloo* 13, no. 3 (1990): 516–25.

Horton, James Oliver. "Defending the Manhood of the Race: The Crisis of Citizenship in Black Boston at Mid-Century." *Hope and Glory: Essays on the Legacy of the 54th Massachusetts Regi-*

ment. Ed. Martin Blatt, Thomas H. Brown, and Donald Yacovone, 7–20. Amherst: University of Massachusetts Press, 2001.

Humphreys, Margaret. *Intensely Human: The Health of the Black Soldier in the American Civil War*. Baltimore: John Hopkins University Press, 2008.

Hunwick, John. *The Religious Practices of Black Slaves in the Mediterranean Islamic World*. Ed. Paul. E. Lovejoy. Princeton, NJ: Markus Wiener Publishers, 2004.

Hurgronje, C. Snouck. *Mohammedanism: Lectures on Its Origin, Its Religious and Political Developments*. New York: Putnam's, 1916.

Jackson, Cassandra. *Violence, Visual Culture, and the Black Male Body*. New York: Routledge, 2011.

Johnson, James Weldon. *The Book of American Negro Spirituals*. New York: Viking Press, 1925.

Jones, Jacqueline. *Labor of Love, Labor of Sorrow: Black Women, Work, and the Family, from Slavery to the Present*. New York: Perseus Books, 1985.

Jones, Sir Williams. "On the Musical Modes of the Hindus." In *Hindu Music from Various Authors*. Ed. Sourindro Mohum Tagore, 123–60. Cambridge: Cambridge University Press, 2013.

Joyner, Charles. *Down by the Riverside: A South Carolina Slave Community*. Champaign: University of Illinois Press, 1985.

Juengst, Daniel P., ed. *Sapelo Papers: Researches in the History and Prehistory of Sapelo Island, Georgia*. West Georgia College Studies in the Social Sciences 19. Carrollton: West Georgia College, 1980.

Kapchan, Deborah. *Traveling Spirit Masters: Moroccan Gnawa Trance and Music in the Global Marketplace*. Middletown, CT: Wesleyan University Press, 2007.

Keeler, Harriet L. *Our Native Trees: And How to Identify Them*. New York: Charles Scribner's Sons, 1908.

Kelley, Robin. *Race Rebels: Culture, Politics and the Black Working Class*. New York: The Free Press, 1994.

Kim, Claire Jean. *Bitter Fruit: The Politics of Black–Korean Conflict*. New Haven, CT: Yale University Press, 2003.

King, Rev. Dr. Martin Luther, Jr. "I've Been to the Mountaintop." Address delivered at Mason Temple Church of God in Christ, Memphis, TN, April 3, 1968.

King, Suzie. *A Black Woman's Civil War Memoirs: Reminiscences of My Life in Camp with the 33rd U.S. Colored Troops 1St South Carolina Volunteers*. Boston: printed by author, 1902.

Kinnamon, Kenneth, and Michel Fabre, eds. *Conversations with Richard Wright*. Jackson: University of Mississippi Press, 1993.

Larson, Kate Clifford. *Bound for the Promised Land: Harriet Tubman, Portrait of an American Hero*. New York: Ballantine Books, 2004.

Levine, Lawrence W. *Black Culture and Black Consciousness*. New York: Oxford University Press, 1977.

Lewis, George E. *A Power Stronger Than Itself: The AACM and American Experimental Music*. Chicago: University of Chicago, 2008.

Lincoln. Dir. Steven Spielberg. Glendale, CA: DreamWorks, 2012. DVD.

Lipsitz, George. *Footsteps in the Dark*. Minneapolis: University of Minnesota Press, 2007.

Littlefield, Daniel C. "Blacks, John Brown, and a Theory of Manhood." In *His Soul Goes Marching On: Responses to John Brown and the Harpers Ferry Raid*. Ed. Paul Finkelman, 67–97. Charlottesville, VA: University Press of Virginia, 1995.

Litwack, Leon F. *Been in the Storm So Long: The Aftermath of Slavery*. New York: First Vintage Books, 1980.

Long, Charles. "Perspectives for a Study of African-American Religion." In *African American Religion: Interpretive Essays in History and Culture*. Ed. Timothy E. Fulop and Albert J. Raboteau, 21–36. New York: Routledge, 1997.

———. *Significations: Signs, Symbols, and Images in the Interpretation of Religion*. Aurora, CO: Fortress Press, 1986.

Looby, Christopher. "'As Thoroughly Black as the Most Faithful Philanthropist Could Desire': Erotics of Race in Higginson's *Army Life in a Black Regiment*. In *Race and the Subject of Masculinities*. Ed. Harry Stecopoulos and Michael Uebel, 71–115. Durham, NC: Duke University Press, 1997.

———. *Civil War Journal and Selected Letters of Thomas Wentworth Higginson*. Chicago: University of Chicago Press, 2000.

Lord, Francis. *Uniforms of the Civil War*. Mineola, NY: Dover Publications, 1970.

Lornell, Kip. *Happy in the Service of the Lord: African-American Sacred Vocal Harmony Quartets in Memphis*. Knoxville: University of Tennessee Press, 1995.

Lovell, John, Jr. *Black Song: The Forge and the Flame: The Story of How the Afro-American Spiritual Was Hammered Out*. New York: MacMillan Publishing, 1972.

Marks, Morton. "Performance Rules and Ritual Structures in Afro-American Music." PhD diss., University of California, Berkeley, 1972.

———. "Uncovering Ritual Structures in Afro-American Music." In *Religious Movements in Contemporary America*. Ed. Irving I. Zaretsky and Mark P. Leone, 61–134. Princeton, NJ: Princeton University Press, 1974.

Mbiti, John. *Introduction to African Religion*. 2nd ed. Oxford: Heinemann Educational Books, 1991.

McClary, Susan. *Feminine Endings: Music, Gender, and Sexuality*. Minneapolis, MN: University of Minnesota Press, 1991.

McGee, Isaiah R. "The Historical Development of Prominent Professional Black Choirs in the United States." PhD diss., Florida State University, 2007.

McPherson, James. *Marching Toward Freedom: Blacks in the Civil War 1861–1865*. 1965. Reprint. New York: Facts on File, 1994.

———. *The Negro's Civil War: How American Negroes Fled and Acted during the Civil War for the Union*. Urbana: University of Illinois Press, 1982.

Melamed, Jodi. *Represent and Destroy: Rationalizing Violence in the New Racial Capitalism*. Minneapolis: University of Minnesota Press, 2011.

Meyer, Howard N. *Colonel of the Black Regiment: The Life of Thomas Wentworth Higginson*. New York: W. W. Norton & Company, 1967.

Miller, James E. *Walt Whitman*. New York: Twayne Publishers, 1962.

Mills, Quincy T. *Cutting along the Color Lines: Black Barbers and Barber Shops in America*. Philadelphia: University of Pennsylvania Press, 2013.

Mohr, Clarence L. *On the Threshold of Freedom: Masters and Slaves in Civil War Georgia*. Athens: University of Georgia Press, 1986.

Morrison, Toni. *Beloved*. New York: Random House, 1987.

———. "Home." In *The House That Race Built*. Ed. Wahneema Lubiano, 3–12. New York: Vintage, 1998.

Moten, Fred. *In the Break: The Aesthetics of the Black Radical Tradition*. Minneapolis: University of Minnesota Press, 2003.

Mowitt, John. *Percussion: Drumming, Beating, Striking*. Durham, NC: Duke University Press, 2002.

Mullin, Gerald W. *Flight and Slave Resistance in Eighteenth-Century Virginia*. London: Oxford University Press, 1975.

Mulvey, Laura. "Visual Pleasure and Narrative Cinema." *Screen* 16, no. 3 (1975): 3–16.

Muñoz, José Esteban. *Disidentifications: Queers of Color and the Performance of Politics*. Minneapolis: University of Minnesota Press, 1999.

Murphy, Joseph M. *Working the Spirit: Ceremonies of the African Diaspora*. Boston: Beacon Press, 1994.

Nelson, Robert K., and Kenneth M. Price. "Debating Manliness: Thomas Wentworth Higginson, William Sloane Kennedy, and the Question of Whitman." *American Literature* 73, no. 3 (September 2001): 497–524.

Ngũgĩ wa Thing'o. "Notes towards a Performance Theory of Orature." *Performance Research* 12, no. 3 (2007): 4–7.

Noble, David W. *Death of a Nation*. Minneapolis: University of Minnesota, 2002.

Nott, Josiah Clark, and George Robins Gliddon. *Types of Mankind*. 1871. Reprint. Bristol, England: Thoemes Press, 2002.

Oates, Stephen B. *To Purge This Land with Blood: A Biography of John Brown*. New York: Harper & Row, 1970.

Parsons, Elsie Clews. *Folk-Lore of the Sea Islands, South Carolina*. Cambridge, MA: American Folklore Society, 1923.

Patterson, Orlando. *Slavery as Social Death: A Comparative Study*. Cambridge, MA: Harvard University Press, 1985.

Payne, Daniel Alexander. *Recollections of Seventy Years*. New York: Arno Press, 1968.

Pinckney, Roger. *Blue Roots: African American Folk Magic of the Gullah People*. St. Paul: Llewellyn Publications, 1998.

Pitts, Walter F. *Old Ship of Zion: The Afro-Baptist Ritual in the African Diaspora*. New York: Oxford University Press, 1993.

Pollitzer, William S. *The Gullah People and Their African Heritage*. Athens, GA: University of Georgia Press, 1999.

Poole, Deborah. *Vision, Race, and Modernity: A Visual Economy of the Andean Image World*. Princeton, NJ: Princeton University Press, 1997.

Porterfield, Amanda. "Shamanism: A Psychosocial Definition." *Journal of the American Academy of Religion* 55 (1987): 721–39.

Pratt, Mary Louise. *Imperial Eyes: Travel Writing and Transculturation*. New York: Routledge, 1992.

Raboteau, Albert J. *Slave Religion: The Invisible Institution in the Antebellum South*. Oxford: Oxford University Press, 1978.

Rawick, George P. *From Sundown to Sunup: The Making of the Black Community*. Westport: Greenwood Press, 1972.

Records of the Adjutant General's Office, Book Records of Volunteer Union Organizations, 33 United States Colored Infantry, Regimental Descriptive Book E112–115 PI-17. National Archives, RG 94. Vol. 1.

Reddy, Chandan. *A Freedom with Violence.* Durham, NC: Duke University Press, 2011.

———. "Time for Rights? Loving, Gay Marriage and the Limits of Legal Justice." *Fordham Law Review* 76, no. 6 (2008): 2849–72.

Rediker, Marcus. *The Slave Ship.* London: Viking, 2007.

Report on the Proceedings of a Meeting Held at Concert Hall, Philadelphia, on Tuesday Evening, November 3, 1863, to Take into Consideration the Condition of the Freed People of the South. Philadelphia: Merrihew & Thompason, 1863.

Richardson, Joe M. *A History of Fisk University 1865–1946.* Tuscaloosa, AL: University of Alabama Press, 1980.

Roach, Joseph. *Cities of the Dead: Circum-Atlantic Performance.* New York: Columbia University Press, 1996.

Robinson, Cedric. *Forgeries of Memory and Meaning: Blacks and the Regimes of Race in American Theater and Film before World War II.* Chapel Hill, NC: University of North Carolina Press, 2007.

Rose, Willie Lee. *Rehearsal for Reconstruction: The Port Royal Experiment.* New York: Vintage Books, 1964.

Rowland, Lawrence, Alexander Moore, and George Rogers. *The History of Beaufort County South Carolina.* Vol. 1, 1514–1861. Columbia, SC: University of South Carolina Press, 1996.

Said, Edward. *Orientalism.* New York: Random House, 1979.

Saillant, John. "The Black Body Erotic and the Republican Body Politic, 1790–1820." In *Sentimental Men: Masculinity and the Politics of Affect in American Culture,* 403–28. Berkeley: University of California Press, 1999.

Sanchez, Sonia. "For Sweet Honey in the Rock." In *Shake Loose My Skin: New and Selected Poems by Sonia Sanchez,* 148–50. New York: Beacon Press, 1999.

Savannah Unit of the Georgia Writer's Project (WPA). *Drums and Shadows.* Athens, GA: University of Georgia Press, 1940.

Scarry, Elaine. *The Body in Pain: The Making and Unmaking of the World.* New York: Oxford University Press, 1985.

Scott, James C. *Domination and the Arts of Resistance: Hidden Transcripts.* New Haven, CT: Yale University Press, 1990.

Sedgwick, Eve. *Between Men: English Literature and Male Homosocial Desire.* New York: Columbia Press, 1985.

Sernett, Milton C. *Bound for the Promised Land: African Americans and the Great Migration.* Durham, NC: Duke University Press, 1997.

Sexton, Jared. "The Social Life of Social Death: On Afro-Pessimism and Black Optimism." *InTensions Journal* 5 (Fall/Winter 2011): 1–47.

Shah, Nayan. *Contagious Divides.* Berkeley: University of California Press, 2000.

Small, Christopher. *Music of the Common Tongue: Survival and Celebration in African American Music.* Hanover, NH: Wesleyan University Press / University Press of New England, 1998.

Smith, Jonathan Z. *To Take Place: Toward Theory in Ritual.* Chicago: University of Chicago Press, 1987.

Smith, Theophus. "The Spirituality of Afro-American Traditions." In *Christian Spirituality: Post-Reformation and Modern*. Ed. Louis Dupré and Don E. Saliers, 372–414. New York: Cross Roads, 1989.

———. *Conjuring Culture: Biblical Formations of Black America*. New York: Oxford University Press, 1995.

Sobel, Mechal. *Trabelin' On: The Slave Journey to an Afro-Baptist Faith*. Westport, CT: Greenwood Press, 1979.

Southern, Eileen. *The Music of Black Americans: A History*. New York: W. W. Norton & Company, 1997.

Strathern, Marilyn. *Partial Connections*. Walnut Creek, CA: Alta Mira Press, 2004.

Stuckey, Sterling. *Slave Culture: Nationalist Theory and the Foundations of Black America*. New York: Oxford University Press, 2013.

Sweet Honey in the Rock. *Sacred Ground*. Earthbeat Records, 1995, compact disc.

Takaki, Ron. *Iron Cages: Race and Culture in 19th-Century America*. New York: Oxford University Press, 1979.

Taylor, Suzie King. *A Black Woman's Civil War Memoirs*. Boston: Library of Congress, 1902.

Taylor, Verta. "Social Movement Continuity: The Women's Movement in Abeyance." *American Sociological Review* 54 (1989): 761–75.

Thompson, Katrina D. *Ring Shout, Wheel About: The Racial Politics of Music and Dance in North American Slavery*. Urbana: University of Illinois Press, 2014.

Thompson, Robert Farris. "Bighearted Power: Kongo Presence in the Art and Landscape of Black America." In *Keep Your Head to the Sky: Interpreting African American Home Ground*. Ed. Grey Gundaker, 37–64. Charlottesville: University of Virginia Press, 1998.

———. *Flash of the Spirit: African and Afro-American Art and Philosophy*. New York: Vintage, 1984.

Thornton, John K. "African Dimensions of the Stono Rebellion." *American Historical Review* 96, no. 4 (1991): 1101–13.

Thylefors, Markel. "'Our Government Is in Bwa Kayiman': A Vodou Ceremony in 1791 and Its Contemporary Significations." *Stockholm Review of Latin American Studies* 4 (March 2009): 73–84.

Towne, Laura M. *Letters and Diaries of Laura M. Towne Written From the Sea Islands, 1862–1884*. Ed. Rupert Sargent Holland. 1912. Reprint. New York, Negro Universities Press, 1969.

Turner, Lorenzo D. *Africanisms in the Gullah Dialect*. Chicago: University of Chicago Press, 1949.

Turner, Richard Brent. *Islam in the African-American Experience*. Bloomington: Indiana University Press, 1997.

Tushnet, Mark. "An Essay on Rights." *Texas Law Review* 62 (1984): 1363–1403.

Villoteau, Guillaume André, and E. F. Jomard. *Description de l'Égypte*. Trans. Maryvonne Mavrou-kakis. Paris: Imprimerie impériale, 1809.

Walker, David. *Appeal in Four Articles; Together with a Preamble, to the Coloured Citizens of the World, but in Particular, and Very Expressly, to Those of the United States of America*. 3rd edn. Boston: 1830.

Wallace, Maurice. *Constructing the Black Masculine: Identity and Ideality in African American Men's Literature and Culture, 1775–1995*. Durham, NC: Duke University Press, 2002.

Wallace, Maurice O., and Shawn Michelle Smith. *Pictures and Progress: Early Photography and the Making of African American Identity*. Durham, NC: Duke University Press, 2012.

Walton, Janet. "Women's Ritual Music." In *Music in American Religious Experience*. Ed. Philip V. Bohlman, Edith Blumhofer, Maria Chow, 255–70. Oxford: Oxford University Press, 2005.

Ward, Andrew. *Dark Midnight When I Rise: The Story of the Jubilee Singers Who Introduced the World to the Music of Black America*. New York: Farrar, Straus and Giroux, 2000.

Wardi, Anissa Janine. "Currents of Memory: Ancestral Waters in Henry Dumas's 'Ark of Bones' and August Wilson's *Gem of the Ocean*." *Interdisciplinary Studies in Literature and Environment* 16, no. 4 (2009): 727–42.

Washington, Margaret. "Community Regulation and Cultural Specialization in Gullah Folk Religion." In *African-American Christianity: Eight Historical Essays*. Ed. Paul Johnson. Oakland, CA: University of California Press, 1994.

———. "Gullah Attitudes toward Life and Death." In *Africanisms in American Culture*. Ed. Joseph E. Holloway, 152–86. Bloomington: Indiana University Press, 1990.

Weir, David. *American Orient: From the Colonial Era to the Twentieth Century*. Amherst: University of Massachusetts Press, 2011.

White, Deborah Gray. *Ar'n't I a Woman: Female Slaves in the Plantation South*. New York: W. W. Norton, 1985.

Wiegman, Robyn. *American Anatomies: Theorizing Race, Theorizing Gender*. Durham, NC: Duke University Press, 1995.

Wilderson, Frank B., III. *Red, White and Black: Cinema and the Structure of U. S. Antagonisms*. Durham, NC: Duke University Press, 2010.

Wiley, Bell Irvin. *Southern Negroes 1861–1865*. New York: Rinehart Publishers, 1938.

Williams, Raymond. *Marxism and Literature*. New York: Oxford University Press, 1977.

Wilmore, Gayraud S. *Black Religion and Black Radicalism*. New York: Anchor Press, 1973.

Wilson, Joseph T. *The Black Phalanx: Black Troops in the Union Army 1863–1865*. Published in Hartford, CT: American Pub. Co., 1890.

Wilson, Keith. *Campfires of Freedom: The Camp Life of Black Soldiers during the Civil War*. Kent, OH: Kent State University Press, 2002.

Wimbush, Vincent. *African Americans and the Bible: Sacred Texts and Social Texts*. New York: Continuum, 2001.

Wood, Peter H. *Black Majority: Negroes in Colonial South Carolina*. New York: Knopf, 1974.

Woods, Clyde. *Development Arrested: The Blues and Plantation Power in the Mississippi Delta*. New York: Verso Books, 1998.

Wright, Roberta Hughes, and Wilbur B. Hughes III. *Lay Down Body: Living History in African American Cemeteries*. New York: Visible Ink Press, 1996.

Zon, Bennett. "From 'Very Acute and Plausible' to 'Curiously Misinterpreted': Sir William Jones's 'On the Musical Modes of the Hindus,' 1792, and Its Reception in Later Musical Treatises." In *Romantic Representations of British India*. Ed. Michael J. Franklin, 197–219. London: Routledge, 2006.

INDEX OF SONGS

GENERAL INDEX